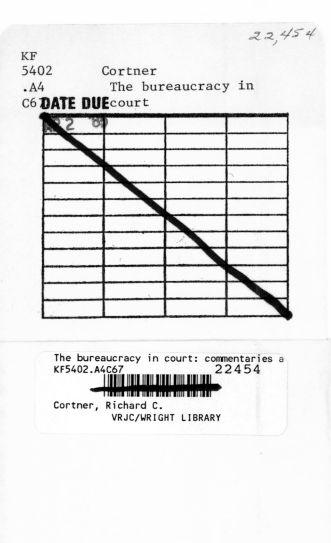

# THE BUREAUCRACY IN COURT

Kennikat Press
**National University Publications**
Multidisciplinary Studies in Law and Jurisprudence

*General Editor*
Honorable Rudolph J. Gerber
*Phoenix, Arizona*

*Acquisitions Editor*
Victor L. Streib
*Cleveland-Marshall College of Law*

Richard C. Cortner

# THE
# BUREAUCRACY
## IN
# COURT

## Commentaries
## and Case Studies
## in Administrative Law

National University Publications
KENNIKAT PRESS // 1982
Port Washington, N. Y. // London

Manufactured in the United States of America

Published by
Kennikat Press Corp.
Port Washington, N.Y. / London

Library of Congress Cataloging in Publication Data

Cortner, Richard C.
    The bureaucracy in court.

    (Multidisciplinary studies in law and
jurisprudence) (National University publications)
        Bibliography: p.
        Includes index.
        1. Administrative law—United States—Cases.
2. Judicial review of administrative acts—United
States—Cases. I. Title. II. Series.
KF5402.A4C67        342.73'06        81-18133
ISBN 0-8046-9299-8    347.3026        AACR2

# PREFACE

This book is designed for use as a supplemental text in courses in administrative law, the bureaucracy, public administration, and related undergraduate college courses. It is not intended to be a comprehensive survey of administrative law, but is rather intended to acquaint students with selective issues and doctrines of administrative law which have contemporary significance. Through the use of six in-depth case studies, the text also seeks to familiarize students with the functioning of the federal bureaucracy and the role of the federal courts in reviewing and checking the exercise of bureaucratic power. The principal topics of administrative law which are covered in the text include (1) the obstacles litigants encounter in attempting to obtain access to the federal courts for the purpose of challenging administrative actions; (2) the administrative exercise of judicial power and the role of the courts in reviewing administrative adjudications; (3) the exercise of legislative power by administrative agencies and the scope of judicial review of administratively promulgated rules and regulations; and (4) the relationship between administrative access to information and the constitutional right to privacy.

The heart of the exploration of these topics is six case studies of recent U.S. Supreme Court decisions in which important interpretations of administrative law have occurred. The case studies are designed, not only to acquaint students with a spectrum of administrative law doctrines, but also to demonstrate how the bureaucracy functions in a variety of contexts. The Supreme Court decisions which are the subjects of the case studies were therefore selected on the basis of their potential for student interest, their capacity to demonstrate the widest variety of bureaucratic functions, and the importance of the doctrines or rules of administrative law that they involved.

In exploring the obstacles litigants encounter in gaining access to the federal courts for the purpose of challenging administrative actions, *United States* v. *SCRAP,* 412 U.S. 669 (1973), and *Scheuer* v. *Rhodes,* 416 U.S. 232 (1974), were therefore selected as the subjects of case studies. The *SCRAP* case involved an important and interesting question of standing to sue, which is an important barrier to access to the federal courts. And the *SCRAP* case also involved the response of the oldest independent regulatory agency, the Interstate Commerce Commission, to the National Environmental Policy Act (NEPA), and illustrates the difficulties involved in modifying ingrained bureaucratic behavior even in response to a congressional mandate. The *SCRAP* case is explored in depth in the case study "Banzhaf's Bandits Strike Again: Standing and the SCRAP Case."

The *Scheuer* case, on the other hand, grew out of the tragic shooting of Kent State University students by the Ohio National Guard in May of 1970. The Kent State tragedy triggered a great deal of litigation concerning the doctrine of political questions, sovereign immunity, and, in the *Scheuer* case, official immunity, all being additional barriers to access to the courts. In the case study "Suing the Bastards: The Kent State Case," all the litigation spawned by the Kent State tragedy is surveyed in addition to the central issue of official immunity, which was raised in the *Scheuer* case.

The examination of the administrative exercise of judicial power through adjudication is also conducted via two case studies involving *Goldberg* v. *Kelly,* 397 U.S. 254 (1970), and *Richardson* v. *Perales,* 402 U.S. 389 (1971). The case study of the *Goldberg* case "Mr. Kelly and the Bureaucracy in the Big Apple: Due Process Comes to Welfare," explores the reaction of the welfare bureaucracy in New York to attacks from welfare rights groups and the litigation in the *Goldberg* case, which produced a significant decision by the Supreme Court eroding the right-privilege dichotomy in administrative law. In the case study "The Law, the Bureaucracy, and Mr. Perales's Back," administrative adjudication as practiced by the Social Security Administration is examined, and the scope of judicial review of administrative adjudications under the substantial evidence test is analyzed.

The case study concerning the exercise of legislative, rule-making powers by administrative agencies, "The Broadcasters and the Bureaucracy: The FCC and the *Red Lion* Case," analyzes the litigation in *Red Lion Broadcasting Co.* v. *Federal Communications Commission,* 395 U.S. 367 (1969). The method by which administrative policies are evolved through informal adjudication and under the informal rule-making procedures of the Administrative Procedure Act is illustrated in the case study of the *Red Lion* case. And the power of the Federal Communications

Commission over the broadcast media, made possible by the differential treatment of the broadcast media under the First Amendment, is analyzed.

Finally, the text addresses the problems posed for the constitutional right to privacy, as guaranteed by the Fourth Amendment and the Self-Incrimination Clause, by the needs of administrative agencies for information. And the validity of administrative searches by a relatively new agency, the Occupational Safety and Health Administration, is examined in the case study "Bill Barlow Can't We Please Come In? OSHA Searches and the Fourth Amendment." This case study of *Marshall* v. *Barlow's, Inc.,* 436 U.S. 307 (1978), highlights the different Fourth Amendment standards applicable to administrative searches in contrast to those required in the case of criminal searches.

The possession of enormous power by the bureaucracy is a fact of life in modern governments, and an understanding of the operations of the bureaucracy and how legal rules enforced by the courts relate to those operations is vital to an understanding of modern government. The subject matter of administrative law is nevertheless seriously neglected in the education of most students. In writing this text, I have been painfully aware that the mere mention of administrative law is sufficient to induce massive yawning among most audiences. And unfortunately this circumstance is not improved by most of the texts available for undergraduate courses which deal with issues of administrative law, since they too often seem designed to reduce their readers to a comatose condition. If this text succeeds in convincing at least some who read it that, while the subject matter of administrative law is frequently complex, it need not be uninteresting, and that administrative law deals with issues that lie at the heart of the governmental system, I shall count it a success.

For Peggy, Charles,
Nancy and Stephen

# CONTENTS

# THE BUREAUCRACY IN COURT

## ABOUT THE AUTHOR

Richard C. Cortner (Ph.D., University of Wisconsin) has been actively engaged in research and teaching in the field of public and administrative law for over twenty years. His experience is well documented by his eight published books since 1964. He is a professor of political science at the University of Arizona.

# INTRODUCTION

In exploring some aspects of administrative law in the chapters that follow, we shall be dealing with the flow of litigation involving administrative agencies and officials in the federal courts. It should prove useful, therefore, to examine briefly the structure of the federal court system and how litigation involving federal administrative agencies is conducted.

## THE STRUCTURE OF THE FEDERAL JUDICIAL SYSTEM

Article III of the Constitution, the judiciary article, provided for the U.S. Supreme Court, but it did not require the creation of lower federal courts, leaving instead the question of whether there should be lower federal courts to Congress. Congress, however, provided for lower federal courts in the Judiciary Act of 1789, and that fundamental decision affecting the structure of the federal judicial system has never been reversed. At the present time, therefore, there exist below the Supreme Court the U.S. district courts, which were created by the Judiciary Act of 1789, and the U.S. courts of appeals, which were provided for in the Circuit Courts of Appeals Act of 1891.

## THE U.S. DISTRICT COURTS

In the Judiciary Act of 1789, Congress provided for a U.S. district court in each of the thirteen states. As the country expanded and the amount of federal litigation increased, the number of U.S. district courts also increased, and there are now ninety-five U.S. district courts throughout the country. Each state has at least one district court, and many states are divided into two or more districts with a district court sitting in each district. The district courts are the trial courts within the federal judicial system, and the district judges thus preside over the trial of civil and criminal cases under the federal laws and Constitution.

As far as administrative law litigation is concerned, the U.S. district courts frequently decide in the first instance suits for injunctions and declaratory judgments filed by parties challenging actions or policies of the federal administrative agencies, and they also hear suits for damages filed against federal and state officials who violate federally protected rights. In some instances, in the statutes creating certain agencies, Congress has also provided that decisions or actions of the agencies are reviewable by the district courts. A denial of a claim for disability benefits by the Social Security Administration, for example, is reviewable in the first instance by a U.S. district court.

Most proceedings and trials in the district courts are presided over by a single U.S. district judge. Until 1976, however, Congress provided that some proceedings in the district courts had to be decided by a three-judge district court. Suits challenging federal and state statutes and seeking injunctions against the enforcement of such statutes, Congress thus provided, had to be decided by three-judge district courts. In addition, certain cases involving challenges to decisions of the Interstate Commerce Commission were also required by Congress to be decided by three-judge district courts. And the decisions of the three-judge courts were appealable directly to the Supreme Court by-passing the courts of appeals that normally review decisions of the district courts.

In 1976, however, Congress repealed most of the statutes requiring certain cases to be heard by three-judge district courts. Suits challenging state or federal statutes and seeking injunctions against their enforcement, for example, are now heard by a district court presided over by a single district judge, and the ICC decisions previously reviewed by three-judge district courts are now reviewed by the courts of appeals. Because this abolition of the three-judge district court requirement is relatively recent, we shall therefore encounter some cases involving three-judge district courts in the case studies to follow.

## THE U.S. COURTS OF APPEALS

With the congressional abolition of the requirement of three-judge district courts in most instances, along with the direct appeal of the judgments of the three-judge courts to the Supreme Court, the decisions of the district courts in almost all instances are now appealable to the U.S. courts of appeals. The courts of appeals were created by the Circuit Courts of Appeals Act of 1891, and there are presently eleven courts of appeals presiding over the eleven circuits into which the country is divided. A twelfth court of appeals sits in Washington, D.C., and hears the heavy volume of government litigation that is generated in the District of Columbia Circuit. The courts of appeals are multijudge courts, but they normally decide cases in panels of three judges. Only upon their agreement to hear a case *en banc* will all the judges of a court of appeals participate in the decision of a case. Regardless of the number of judges on a particular court of appeals, therefore, most appeals to the courts of appeals are decided by a panel of three judges.

In addition to hearing appeals from the decisions of the district courts, the courts of appeals are also the principal reviewers of decisions and actions of federal administrative agencies. Although Congress has provided for the review of some administrative actions by the district courts, it has more often lodged the power of judicial review of administrative actions in the courts of appeals. The courts of appeals are therefore the primary sources of decisions involving administrative law issues within the federal judicial system. And in this regard the U.S. Court of Appeals for the District of Columbia Circuit is an especially important source of decisions affecting administrative law issues, since the heaviest volume of government litigation is conducted in the District of Columbia Circuit.

## APPEALS TO THE SUPREME COURT

Cases that are appealed to the courts of appeals from the district courts, or administrative agency cases reviewed by the courts of appeals in the first instance, are in turn normally appealable to the U.S. Supreme Court. Since the 1920s, cases have been appealable to the Supreme Court primarily via either writs of appeal or via petitions for writs of certiorari, with the writ of certiorari being the method of appeal to the Court in the overwhelming majority of cases.

Under the Judiciary Act of 1925, Congress gave the Supreme Court almost complete discretionary power to choose which cases it will hear of those appealed to it. Whether a case reaches the Court via appeal or via certiorari, therefore, the Court applies the rule of four in determining which cases will be given a hearing. Under the rule of four, at least four of the nine justices must vote to hear a case on the merits before the Court will agree to hear the case. If a case does not command the votes of at least four of the justices, the case is denied a hearing, and the decision of the lower court in the case stands. As a result of the discretionary power the Court possesses to decide which cases it will hear and decide, approximately 90 percent of the cases appealed to the Court are denied review.

## THE CONDUCT OF GOVERNMENT LITIGATION

The conduct of litigation affecting federal administrative agencies in the federal courts has undergone several organizational changes since the establishment of the Republic. The office of Attorney General of the United States was created by the Judiciary Act of 1789, and under that act the attorney general was given the duty "to prosecute and conduct all suits in the Supreme Court in which the United States shall be concerned. . . ." The Office of U.S. Attorney General was nevertheless regarded in the early years as involving only a part-time job for its occupant, and in the pre-Civil War era it was not unusual for the federal government to retain private attorneys to represent it in litigation, including Supreme Court litigation. During this period, the responsibility for advising agencies and departments of the government on legal matters as well as the conduct of government litigation was also shared by lawyers scattered throughout the government, as agencies proliferated and hired their own lawyers to both advise them legally and represent them in court.

In the statute creating the Department of Justice in 1870, Congress sought to put an end to the scattering of legal services throughout the government by attempting to confer upon the Department of Justice a monopoly not only over the conduct of litigation on behalf of the government but also over the provision of legal advice and counseling services to all other governmental departments and agencies. In the Department of Justice Act the Congress also ended the practice of retaining private counsel to represent the government in the Supreme Court by creating the Office of U.S. Solicitor General and conferring upon the solicitor general the authority to represent the United States in Supreme Court litigation.

The congressional attempt to centralize all legal services in the Department of Justice nonetheless failed, since as new agencies were created after 1870 they were frequently authorized to hire their own legal counsel and to conduct litigation on their own. By the time of the New Deal in the 1930s, therefore, the scattering of the responsibility for legal services across the government bureaucracy, which the Department of Justice Act sought to end, had once again become the norm within the federal government.

Recognizing that the attempt to centralize all legal services in the Department of Justice had failed, President Franklin Roosevelt issued an executive order in 1933 reallocating the responsibility for legal services within the government. Unlike the act creating the Department of Justice, the president's executive order did not attempt again to confer a monopoly of all legal services upon the Department of Justice. Instead, the executive order distinguished between legal counseling and advice and the conduct of government litigation in court. The departments and agencies were allowed under the executive order to continue to employ attorneys to counsel and advise them on legal matters, but the executive order conferred the responsibility for the conduct of government litigation exclusively upon the Department of Justice. And this basic division of legal labor within the government has continued to the present.

The result of this division of legal services within the federal government is that, with some exceptions, federal administrative agencies are dependent upon the Justice Department for the defense of their actions and decisions in litigation in the courts. In litigation affecting the agencies in the lower federal courts, therefore, the agencies will be defended by a U.S. attorney or, more commonly, by attorneys from the Civil Division of the Department of Justice.

## THE U.S. SOLICITOR GENERAL

If a case to which the government is a party is appealed to the U.S. Supreme Court, the litigation on behalf of the government is conducted by the Office of the U.S. Solicitor General. The solicitor general is the third-ranking officer in the Department of Justice and controls the conduct of all government litigation before the Supreme Court. The solicitor general additionally has the power to decide which cases of those the government has lost in the lower federal courts will be appealed. If an administrative agency is dealt an adverse decision by a U.S. district court or a court of appeals, the agency must usually convince the solicitor general that the case is worthy of an appeal, or otherwise the litigation will end with the decision of the lower federal court. Finally, the solicitor general also has the authority to intervene as amicus curiae (friend of the court) on behalf of the United States in litigation in the Supreme Court to which the government is not a party.

Since the creation of his office in the Department of Justice Act in 1870, therefore, the U.S. solicitor general has become "the lawyer for the government" as far as Supreme Court litigation is concerned. And by his power to control what cases are appealed by the government, he not only plays a crucial role in determining what legal issues are pursued by the government in the appellate courts but also exercises significant power over the litigation of issues affecting federal administrative agencies. Because of the virtual monopoly over the conduct of litigation which has been conferred upon the Department of Justice attorneys and the solicitor general, the administrative agencies are therefore not the masters of their own fates when it comes to litigation in the federal courts.

In order to obtain access to the federal courts, therefore, administrative agencies must normally operate through the Department of Justice. Individuals challenging actions of the administrative agencies, on the other hand, encounter a formidable array of hurdles which must be successfully overcome before they may obtain access to the federal courts and judicial review of agency actions. It is to those obstacles to access to the courts faced by those seeking judicial review of administrative actions that we shall now turn.

# 1

## ACCESS TO THE COURTS
### Obstacles to Obtaining Judicial Review

A person desiring to challenge the action or policy of an administrative agency in the courts is confronted by a variety of obstacles that must be successfully overcome before judicial review may be obtained. Some of these obstacles affect the timing and sequence of judicial review. Others, deriving from the provision of Article III of the Constitution limiting federal judicial power to "cases" and "controversies," may result in a denial of judicial review altogether. In either case, the practical effect of these obstacles is to condition access of individuals to the courts—determining to whom, when, and under what circumstances judicial review of administrative action will be available.

### THE EXHAUSTION OF ADMINISTRATIVE REMEDIES

One such obstacle frequently encountered in administrative law litigation, the requirement that administrative remedies be exhausted, may significantly delay judicial review of administrative action. The exhaustion requirement means that if an issue is pending before an administrative agency, and there exist within the agency administrative remedies that may result in a settlement of the issue, these administrative remedies must be resorted to or exhausted before judicial review of the issue is sought in the courts. The exhaustion requirement is in part a matter of conserving the time and resources of the courts. If a remedy for a problem exists in an administrative agency before which it is pending, a resort to the administrative remedy may result in an administrative solution of the problem satisfactory to all concerned, and resort to the courts will be unnecessary. If, on the other hand, the available administrative remedies are ignored and the courts are called upon to settle the issue, the time and resources of the courts may be wasted on a problem that could have been settled in the administrative process. The effect of the insistence by the courts that administrative remedies be exhausted by a party before judicial review of administrative action is sought thus is not to cut off judicial review altogether, but rather the exhaustion requirement has the effect of delaying judicial review until the exhaustion of administrative remedies has occurred.

## THE DOCTRINE OF PRIMARY JURISDICTION

Another barrier to access to the courts which is sometimes encountered in administrative law litigation is the doctrine of primary jurisdiction. First enunciated by the Supreme Court in *Texas and Pacific Railway Co.* v. *Abilene Cotton Oil Co.* in 1907, the doctrine of primary jurisdiction generally holds that, when both a law court and an administrative agency have jurisdiction over a particular legal problem, the parties seeking a solution to the problem should first invoke the jurisdiction of the administrative agency and seek an administrative solution before resorting to the courts. In such situations, the administrative agency is said to have primary jurisdiction over the problem, and the agency's decision must first be sought before the problem is brought to a court.

The formulation of the doctrine of primary jurisdiction by the Court in the *Abilene Cotton Oil* case served the important function of fitting administrative agencies into the existing legal framework. As Congress increasingly created administrative agencies with jurisdiction over subject matters which also fell within the jurisdiction of the courts, the potential for conflicting policies to emerge from the agencies and the courts also increased. By formulating the doctrine of primary jurisdiction, the Supreme Court eliminated the possibility of much of this potential conflict by requiring that the jurisdiction of administrative agencies be given priority when both the courts and the agencies arguably had jurisdiction over the same subject matter. At the same time, the Court preserved for the courts the ultimate power of decision, since judicial review of agency decisions remained available after, but only after, the primary jurisdiction of the agencies was exercised.

The doctrine of primary jurisdiction thus does not close the doors of the courts as far as judicial review is concerned, but rather the doctrine affects the timing of judicial review. If the doctrine of primary jurisdiction is applied by a court in a particular case, the parties are simply instructed to invoke the jurisdiction of the appropriate administrative agency and seek a decision of the agency regarding the problem involved. The decision of the agency usually will remain subject to review by the courts after it is rendered.

## THE CASES AND CONTROVERSIES REQUIREMENT

In addition to the exhaustion of administrative remedies requirement and the doctrine of primary jurisdiction, further hurdles are imposed upon one seeking to obtain access to the federal courts by the provision of Article III of the Constitution limiting the power of the federal courts to cases and controversies arising under the Constitution, laws, or treaties of the United States. In the process of determining what a "case" or "controversy" is, the Supreme Court has developed the concept of "justiciability," holding that there must be a *justiciable* case or controversy pending before a federal court before its power may be exercised.

The concept of justiciability has in turn been defined to contain several elements. In order for there to be a justiciable case or controversy, the issues in the case must be ripe for decision by a court, the issues must not be moot, the question to be decided must not be a political question, the court must not be asked to render an advisory opinion, and the parties in the case must have standing to sue. All these elements of justiciability must be met before a federal court may exercise its judicial power under Article III of the Constitution. Unlike the doctrines of exhaustion of administrative remedies and primary jurisdiction, which affect the timing of but do not preclude judicial review, unless the various elements of justiciability are met in a case, the doors of the federal courts are simply closed to a party seeking judicial review. For, without a justiciable case or controversy, federal judicial power may not be validly exercised.

## THE PROHIBITION OF ADVISORY OPINIONS

One of the earliest restrictions recognized by the federal courts to be imposed by the cases and controversies requirement was the prohibition of advisory opinions. In 1793, the Supreme Court refused a request by Secretary of State Thomas Jefferson on behalf of President Washington that it advise the administration of its views regarding the legal issues raised by foreign policy problems. A request for advice, the Court concluded, did not present to the Court a case or controversy involving the adverse clash of legal interests between two parties, and therefore an advisory opinion was beyond the power of the federal courts to render under Article III. Similarly, the federal courts will not decide so-called friendly suits in which there is no real adverse clash of legal interests between the parties and in which both parties seek the same result. For the federal courts to decide such friendly suits would be equivalent to rendering advisory opinions in the absence of a real case or controversy, as required by Article III.

### RIPENESS

Closely akin to the prohibition of advisory opinions is the concept of ripeness, which requires that the issues in a case must be "ripe" for decision before a federal court will decide them. An unripe issue is generally an issue which has been prematurely raised by a party and which would require the courts to decide speculative, hypothetical, or theoretical matters. In order to be ripe for decision, therefore, the issues in a case must possess sufficient immediacy and concreteness for the parties to justify the exercise of power by the federal courts.

In *Roe* v. *Wade,* one of the 1973 Abortion Cases, the Supreme Court thus ruled that a married couple, who alleged that the wife might become pregnant in the future and then might want but would be unable to obtain an abortion under the Texas antiabortion statute, had raised unripe issues requiring the dismissal of their case. The wife might never become pregnant, the Court noted, and the federal courts were being asked to decide speculative or hypothetical issues that would not arise until the wife became pregnant and sought an abortion, contingencies that might never arise. The determination of whether issues in a case are ripe for decision, the Court has also indicated in recent decisions, involves the evaluation of the "fitness of the issues for judicial decision," as well as consideration of the "hardship to the parties of withholding court consideration." The ripeness requirement, as Justice Frankfurter once said, means that the "Court cannot be umpire to debates concerning harmless, empty shadows."

### MOOTNESS

If, during the course of litigation, the issues in a case have been settled, they are said to be moot, and under the cases and controversies requirement the federal courts will not pass upon or decide moot issues. A good recent example of mootness was presented in *DeFunis* v. *Odegaard,* decided by the Supreme Court in 1974. Marco DeFunis was refused admission to the University of Washington School of Law, while under an affirmative action program students who were members of minority groups were admitted to the law school although their academic records and law school admission test scores were lower than those of DeFunis. Charging that he had been discriminated against because of his race in violation of the Equal Protection Clause of the Fourteenth Amendment, DeFunis sought and secured an injunction from a Washington trial court ordering his admission to the law school. The Washington Supreme Court, however, reversed the decision of the trial court on appeal, although it left the trial court's injunction in effect. The result was that DeFunis was admitted to the law school and continued his legal education while an appeal of the case was taken to the U.S. Supreme Court.

When it reached the DeFunis litigation, the Supreme Court dismissed the case on the ground that the issues involved had become moot. The Court pointed out that DeFunis was by 1974 in his third year of law school and presumably would soon graduate. The issue of discrimination that DeFunis had alleged in his lawsuit had thus become moot because of the passage of time during the course of the litigation.

## THE DOCTRINE OF POLITICAL QUESTIONS

The Supreme Court indicated as early as *Marbury* v. *Madison* in 1803 that the federal courts should not decide questions that are "political" in nature. And in *Luther* v. *Borden* in 1849, the Court formulated the classic definition of political questions which were beyond the jurisdiction of the federal courts. Political questions, the Court indicated in the *Luther* case, are essentially questions that the Constitution has assigned for ultimate resolution by Congress or the president, or both, and are therefore questions that cannot be resolved by the federal courts.

In addition to the concept that certain questions have been left by the Constitution for ultimate resolution by Congress and/or the president, lurking behind the doctrine of political questions is the very practical judgment by the federal courts that certain issues cannot be effectively resolved by the exercise of judicial power. Evaluations of the appropriateness of particular questions for judicial resolution and the problems of implementing judicial decisions regarding particular issues must also be counted as elements leading the courts to label certain issues as political. For the federal courts to label an issue a political question, whatever the reasons therefor, results in the closing of the judicial process to the resolution of that issue and forces the issue to be resolved, if at all, outside the judicial process.

## STANDING TO SUE

A final element that must be satisfied under the cases and controversies requirement is that the parties in a case must have standing to sue. In order to have standing to sue, a person must generally possess a direct, personal, concrete interest in the outcome of a case. That is, in order to invoke the protection of the federal courts, a person must demonstrate that his personal legal interests will be, or have been, adversely affected or injured. As the Supreme Court has said, in order to have standing a person must have "such a personal stake in the outcome of the controversy as to assure that concrete adverseness which sharpens the presentation of issues upon which the court so largely depends for illumination of difficult constitutional questions." Unlike ripeness, mootness, and the doctrine of political questions, which relate to what types of issues may be decided by the courts, standing to sue determines who may and may not bring cases in the federal courts.

The requirement that one must allege a personal interest in the outcome of litigation in order to possess standing to sue generally requires a party to assert his own personal rights and not those of others. The Supreme Court has, however, made notable exceptions to this general rule prohibiting the assertion of rights of persons not parties to the litigation. In *Griswold* v. *Connecticut,* decided in 1965, for example, the Court upheld the argument that a Connecticut statute, prohibiting the use of contraceptives for the purpose of preventing conception, violated the right of married couples to privacy in their marriages, even though the parties in the *Griswold* case were not married couples. In the *Griswold* case, the Court thus allowed parties to assert the rights of persons not party to the litigation and made an exception to the general rule that in order to have standing one must assert one's own personal rights and not the rights of others.

One of the more important developments in recent years has been the Supreme Court's relaxation of the requirements governing standing to sue. This trend toward liberalization of the standing requirements may be seen in the Court's treatment of taxpayers' suits. In *Frothingham* v. *Mellon* decided in 1923, a federal taxpayer brought suit challenging a spending program authorized by Congress, but the Court held that the taxpayer lacked standing to maintain the suit. The taxpayer's personal interest in the expenditure of federal funds, the Court held, was "comparatively minute and indeterminable," and the effect of the challenged program on the taxpayer's future tax obligations was "remote, fluctuating, and uncertain." The taxpayer therefore lacked the requisite direct, personal stake in the litigation which was required before the taxpayer could have standing to sue in the case.

For over forty years, the *Frothingham* ruling meant that federal tax-payers lacked standing to maintain suits challenging federal spending programs based on their status as taxpayers. But in *Flast* v. *Cohen* in 1968, the Court significantly modified the *Frothingham* rule. A federal tax-payer, the Court ruled in *Flast,* would henceforth have standing, by asserting his status as a taxpayer, to challenge federal spending programs by invoking specific constitutional limitations upon the power of Congress to spend. There must, however, be a connection or nexus between the asserted status as a taxpayer, the Court held, and the challenged governmental program. A taxpayer thus had standing to attack a spending program, but not a program of a general governmental nature that only incidentally involved the spending of tax money. And, finally, the tax-payer must invoke a specific limitation on the congressional power to spend and not seek "to employ a federal court as a forum in which to air his generalized grievances about the conduct of government or the allocation of power in the Federal System," the Court concluded.

The liberalization of the standing requirement exemplified by the *Flast* case has also occurred in recent years in the field of administrative law litigation. In *Tennessee Power Co.* v. *TVA,* decided in 1939, the Supreme Court held that those attempting to challenge administrative action lacked standing "unless the right invaded is a legal right—one of property, one arising out of contract, one protected against tortious invasion, or one founded on a statute which confers a privilege." The *Tennessee Power Co.* case thus limited the kinds of personal interests upon which standing to challenge administrative action could be based to a rather narrow range of interests—essentially economic and property interests. The result of such a strict interpretation of standing was to considerably limit the numbers of those who could challenge administrative action as well as to limit narrowly the kinds of reasons that could be advanced as bases for such challenges.

In 1946, however, Congress enacted the Administrative Procedure Act (APA), and in Section 702 of the act provided for judicial review of administrative agency actions. Section 702 of the APA provides that a "person suffering legal wrong because of agency action, or adversely affected or aggrieved by agency action within the meaning of a relevant statute, is entitled to judicial review thereof." Section 702 of the APA thus became a commonly invoked basis upon which actions of administrative agencies were challenged, and in interpreting Section 702 the Supreme Court considerably relaxed the requirements of standing from what they appeared to be under the *Tennessee Power Co.* decision.

In *Data Processing Service* v. *Camp* and *Barlow* v. *Collins,* both decided in 1970, the Court noted that where "statutes are concerned, the trend is toward enlargement of the class of people who may protest administrative action," and it enunciated a liberalized, two-pronged test for standing. When parties seek standing to challenge administrative action on the basis of Section 702 of the APA, the Court said, the "first question is whether the plaintiff alleges that the challenged action has caused him injury in fact, economic or otherwise." And secondly, the Court held, is "the question whether the interest sought to be protected by the complainant is arguably within the zone of interests to be protected or regulated by the statute or constitutional guarantee in question." The interest asserted, the Court added, "may reflect 'aesthetic, conservational, and recreational' as well as economic values."

Under Section 702 of the APA, the Court thus held, a person need only allege an "injury in fact" and assert an interest falling within a "zone of interests" protected by a statute or provision of the Constitution in order to obtain standing to challenge administrative action. And, in contrast to the narrow range of economic and property interests mentioned in the *Tennessee Power Co.* case, the Court recognized that individuals had standing to challenge administrative action adversely affecting not only their economic interests but also their "aesthetic, conservational, or recreational" interests. The result of the *Data Processing* and *Barlow* v. *Collins* cases was thus to considerably broaden the range of interests that could be asserted against administrative actions, as well as to increase the number of persons who could have standing to assert those interests.

The *Data Processing* and *Barlow* cases were of course especially encouraging to environmental and conservation organizations, since the Court had explicitly held that administrative actions adversely affecting or injuring aesthetic, conservation, or recreational interests could be challenged under Section 702 of the APA. As a long-established environmental organization concerned with the preservation of the national parks, game refuges, and the quality of the natural environment generally, the Sierra Club soon sought to obtain a ruling from the Supreme Court recognizing that groups like the Sierra Club had standing to challenge governmental actions affecting the environment simply because of their well-established interest in environmental protection. When the Department of Interior and the Forest Service thus agreed to allow Disney interests to develop an elaborate resort and ski facility in the Mineral King Valley of the Sierra Nevadas in California, the Sierra Club filed suit challenging the legality of the action in a U.S. district court and seeking an injunction to stop the project, which the club felt would despoil a wilderness area.

Basing its suit on Section 702 of the APA, the Sierra Club alleged that for "many years the Sierra Club by its activities and conduct has exhibited a special interest in the conservation and the sound maintenance of the national parks, game refuges and forests of the country, regularly serving as a responsible representative of persons similarly interested. One of the principal purposes of the Sierra Club is to protect and conserve the natural resources of the Sierra Nevada Mountains. Its interests would be vitally affected by the acts [of the Department of Interior and the Forest Service] and [it] would be aggrieved by those acts. . . ." The Sierra Club thus did not allege that the building of the ski resort would result in an injury in fact to any specific person, including any of its members, but rather the club sought to establish standing for itself as an organization to bring suits directed at protecting the environment.

When the litigation involving the Mineral King Valley reached the Supreme Court in *Sierra Club* v. *Morton* in 1972, the Court dismissed the case on the ground that the Sierra Club lacked standing to maintain its suit. Pointing out that the *Data Processing* and *Barlow* cases had held that in order to have standing there must be an allegation of an injury in fact, the Court held that the injury in fact test "requires more than an injury to a cognizable interest. It requires that the party seeking review be himself among the injured." "The Sierra Club," the Court noted, "failed to allege that it or its members would be affected in any of their activities or pastimes by the Disney development. Nowhere in the pleadings or affadavits did the Club state that its members use Mineral King for any purpose, much less that they use it in any way that would be significantly affected by the proposed actions of the [Department of Interior and the Forest Service] ."

The Court conceded that it had liberalized the requirements for standing in recent years, but it pointed out that "broadening the categories of injury that may be alleged in support of standing is a different matter from abandoning the requirement that the party seeking review must himself have suffered an injury." A "mere 'interest in a problem,' " the Court concluded, "no matter how long-standing the interest and no matter how qualified the organization is in evaluating the problem, is not sufficient by itself to render the organization 'adversely affected' or 'aggrieved' within the meaning of [Section 702] of the APA."

As a result of the *Sierra Club* case, environmental organizations were denied standing to challenge governmental actions allegedly adversely affecting the environment solely on the basis of their long-standing interests in preserving the environment. Despite the liberalization of standing that had occurred, the Court was still insisting that there must be an allegation of an injury in fact to the interests of an individual or an organization before standing to sue would be recognized. How serious a setback to the liberalization of the requirement of standing the decision in the *Sierra Club* case represented became manifest in the case of *United States* v. *SCRAP*, decided by the Supreme Court in 1973. The *SCRAP* case thus became an important case involving the contemporary requirements of standing, and it also involved the application to the administrative process of a new statute protecting the environment—the National Environmental Policy Act of 1969 (NEPA). The SCRAP litigation also spotlighted a remarkable new group challenging administrative actions—Banzhaf's bandits. We shall now therefore turn to an in-depth examination of the *SCRAP* litigation.

**CASE STUDY**
## BANZHAF'S BANDITS STRIKE AGAIN
Standing and the *SCRAP* Case

John F. Banzhaf III received an undergraduate degree in engineering at MIT, but he opted for a career as a lawyer and entered the Columbia Law School in September of 1962. He made an impressive record at Columbia, serving on the *Columbia Law Review* and graduating magna cum laude in 1965. After having served as law clerk for Judge Spottsworth W. Robinson III of the United States District Court for the District of Columbia, Banzhaf joined a New York law firm specializing in patent law, but he soon made his first move in a series of legal activities that would gain him a national reputation as a legal gadfly.

A nonsmoker, Banzhaf was irritated by the frequency of cigarette commercials on television, and he consequently wrote CBS demanding equal time to answer the cigarette commercials appearing on that network. After a negative response from CBS, he then filed a formal complaint with the Federal Communications Commission on June 5, 1967, arguing that the issue of cigarette smoking was a controversial issue of public importance, and that under the FCC's fairness doctrine, the networks sould be required to make available free air time for antismoking messages. In a memorable decision, the FCC upheld Banzhaf's complaint and ordered the networks to make available "significant" free time for antismoking commercials, and the U.S. Court of Appeals for the District of Columbia Circuit upheld the FCC's action.

**THE RISE OF BANZHAF'S BANDITS**

It was only after he had launched his attack on cigarette commercials that Banzhaf discovered that one of the clients of the New York law firm that employed him was the Philip Morris Company. He therefore subsequently left the law firm and accepted an appointment as a law professor at George Washington University's National Law Center in Washington, D.C. As a professor, Banzhaf encouraged his students to identify unfair, unhealthful, or misleading practices being engaged in by industry and to file complaints against the practices with the appropriate regulatory agencies or the law courts.

Banzhaf's students were thus soon organizing themselves into groups with attention-attracting names and attacking a wide spectrum of problems in the agencies and courts. The Federal Trade Commission, for example, found that the Campbell Soup Company had engaged in misleading advertising by putting marbles in bowls of soup in its television ads to make it appear the soup contained more solids than was the case. Some of Banzhaf's students, organized as SOUP (Students Opposed to Unfair Practices), filed a complaint with the FTC arguing that the commission should not have merely ordered the soup company to cease such misleading advertising but should also have required the company to run ads correcting the previous deceptive advertising. The FTC ruled against SOUP, but did acknowledge that requiring companies to run corrective advertising might be appropriate in future cases in which misleading advertising was found to have occurred.

Similarly, TUBE (Termination of Unfair Broadcasting Excesses) filed a complaint with the Federal Communications Commission seeking to force the FCC to police television advertising, rather than leaving that question to the FTC. PUMP (Protesting Unfair Marketing Practices) protested to the FTC that gasoline stations should be required to post the octane ratings of gasoline on station pumps. SNOOP (Students Naturally Opposed to Outrageous Prying) urged the District of Columbia City Council to regulate credit agencies. CRASH (Citizens to Reduce Airline Smoking Hazards) petitioned the Federal Aviation Administration to require segregated seating on airlines for smokers and nonsmokers.

As a result of these and other actions, Banzhaf's students at the George Washington University's National Law Center were soon being called Banzhaf's bandits. The students reflected Banzhaf's belief that you "can often get best results by suing the hell out of people, using all the legal pressure points you can find. And if you're going to spend the rest of your life suing, you might as well sue the *bastards*." And Banzhaf's students also appeared to enjoy their experiences, since as one said, "By the second year, law students tend to get bored with classes. Professor Banzhaf triggers the urge to do something different and exciting."

Banzhaf and his bandits also won praise from FTC Commissioner Mary Gardiner Jones, who said that Banzhaf "has a philosophy of how a citizen fits into the government and is doing concrete, positive things to make the government respond. We surely need this kind of effort." Banzhaf's flamboyance and aggressiveness, however, alienated some of his colleagues on the George Washington University law faculty, and when he came up for tenure in the spring of 1971, the law faculty voted eighteen to thirteen to deny him tenure. Eight hundred students, on the other hand, signed petitions in protest, and the vote denying Banzhaf tenure was subsequently reversed.

## NEPA AND THE INTERSTATE COMMERCE COMMISSION

The enactment of the National Environmental Policy Act of 1969 by Congress imposed important new responsibilities upon federal agencies as far as their actions affected the environment. In NEPA, Congress declared the fullest possible protection of the human environment to be a national policy and, in furtherance of that goal, directed that:

to the fullest extent possible: (1) the policies, regulations, and public laws of the United States shall be interpreted and administered in accordance with the policies set forth in [NEPA], and (2) all agencies of the Federal Government shall—. . .
(C) include in every recommendation or report or proposals for legislation and other major Federal actions significantly affecting the quality of the human environment, a detailed statement by the responsible official on—
(i) the environmental impact of the proposed action,
(ii) any adverse environmental effects which cannot be avoided should the proposal be implemented,
(iii) alternatives to the proposed action,
(iv) the relationship between local short-term uses of man's environment and the maintenance and enhancement of long-term productivity, and
(v) any irreversible and irretrievable commitments of resources which would be involved in the proposed action should it be implemented.
Prior to making any detailed statement, the responsible Federal official shall consult with and obtain the comments of any Federal agency which has jurisdiction by law or special expertise with respect to any environmental impact involved. Copies of such statement and the comments and views of the appropriate Federal, State, and local agencies, which are authorized to develop and enforce environmental standards, shall be made available to the public. . .and shall accompany the proposal through existing agency review processes. . . .

Under NEPA, therefore, before taking any major actions "significantly affecting the quality of the human environment," federal agencies were required to rather elaborately consider the effects of their actions upon the environment and develop environmental impact statements (EIS) embracing the various elements required in NEPA. The degree to which the various federal agencies adapted to the new procedures required by NEPA, however, varied considerably, and, indeed, some agencies made only minimal efforts to meet the new responsibilities imposed upon them by the act.

The Interstate Commerce Commission, for example, proved to be one of the most recalcitrant of the agencies in meeting its NEPA responsibilities. The ICC was created by Congress under the Interstate Commerce Act of 1887, and it is the oldest of the independent regulatory commissions. It is thus sometimes called the grandfather of the federal independent regulatory commissions, since it served as the model for several subsequently created federal agencies. The ICC's jurisdiction includes the responsibility of regulating the rates charged by interstate railroads, trucking companies, and barge lines.

Under the provisions of NEPA, the "responsible official" was required to prepare an environmental impact statement meeting the act's requirements when an agency proposed to take major action "significantly affecting the quality of the human environment." Although the "responsible official" in the case of the ICC appeared to be the commission itself, the ICC decided that NEPA's requirement for an EIS would be met if the parties appearing in ICC proceedings were required to submit statements regarding the environmental impact of the commission's actions. Rather than itself assuming the responsibility for preparing EISs, as NEPA appeared to require, the ICC thus imposed that responsibility on the parties appearing in its proceedings. The commission additionally decided that the burden of proof that an adverse impact on the environment would result from its proposed action should fall on the party making such an assertion.

As a consequence of these ICC responses to NEPA, in a proceeding involving proposed increases in railroad rates, for example, the railroads, as parties to the proceedings, would file statements that an increase in rates would have no significant adverse impact on the environment. If any other parties in the rate increase proceedings asserted that an adverse environmental impact would occur if rates were increased, the ICC would require those parties to prove the correctness of their assertion. Since such a burden of proof could not be met except by a well-financed party organized to produce the kind of extensive technical evidence required, the result was that ICC proceedings would almost always produce a finding of no adverse environmental impact resulting from the action under consideration.

Indeed, after the effective date of NEPA, it became the standard practice for the ICC to insert in its decisions a finding that the agency's action would not significantly affect the quality of the human environment and that therefore no EIS was required. For two years after NEPA became binding on the federal agencies, the ICC, in fact, issued only one environmental impact statement, and that one EIS was issued only after a federal court ordered the commission to do so.

## FREIGHT RATES AND THE RECYCLING OF MATERIALS

By 1970, the United States annually produced 4.3 billion tons of solid refuse. This included 58.3 million tons of waste paper; 30 million tons of industrial fly ash; 15 million tons of scrap metal; 4 million tons of plastics; 100 million tires; 30 billion bottles; and 60 billion cans. A substantial amount of this waste material could be recycled, with significant favorable effects upon the environment. If such waste materials were recycled to produce new products, not only would the environment be cleaned up, but these recycled materials would reduce the need for primary materials. If, for example, junked automobiles were recycled to produce more steel, not only would the removal of junked automobiles beautify the environment, but the use of scrap metal from the junked autos would reduce the need for producing iron ore, a nonrenewable resource.

In enacting NEPA, Congress had recognized the importance of recycling as a means of protecting the environment and had declared that federal agencies were directed to "enhance the quality of renewable resources and approach the maximum obtainable recycling of depletable resources." Despite this requirement of NEPA, however, only a small percentage of waste materials were being recycled in the United States. One reason for the lack of recycling of materials, many argued, was that the existing railroad freight rate structure discriminated against recyclable materials. For example, it was argued that the existing railroad freight rate structure encouraged the mining and shipping of iron ore by rail but discouraged the shipment of scrap metal, since under the prevailing rate structure it was less expensive to ship iron ore than scrap metal.

The relationship between a viable recycling program and the railroad freight rate structure was called to the attention of the Interstate Commerce Commission as early as 1968 by Secretary of the Interior Stewart Udall, the Office of Emergency Planning, and the Department of Commerce. An increase in the freight rates for hauling iron and steel scrap, Udall said to the ICC, would make more difficult "the job of clearing away the junk metal which already clutters too much of our American landscape." And the Office of Emergency Planning advised the ICC that the continuation of railroad freight rate discrimination against recyclable metals would "have an adverse effect on our defense position in an emergency."

Two years later, Russell E. Train, chairman of the Council on Environmental Quality, which coordinates environmental policy in the Executive Office of the President, again pointed out to the ICC that the railroad freight rate structure had an important effect on the economic viability of recycling materials and warned that further across-the-board freight hikes increased the bias against recyclable materials. Train therefore expressed the CEQ's "hope that the Interstate Commerce Commission's actions on the key issue of scrap material transportation rates will be consistent with the Nation's environmental goals."

Despite the fact that the relationship between the freight rate structure and a successful recycling program had been repeatedly called to the ICC's attention since at least 1968, on petition of the railroads, the commission granted general, across-the-board increases in railroad freight rates in 1968, 1969, 1970, and 1971. The result was that the bias against the shipment of recyclable materials built into the existing rate structure was reinforced and exacerbated by the across-the-board increases being granted by the ICC.

## SCRAP VERSUS THE ICC

Under the Interstate Commerce Act, the railroads must give thirty days notice of any change in rates, and the ICC may suspend any proposed change in rates for a seven-month period, pending an investigation of the lawfulness and reasonableness of the new rates. If after seven months the ICC has taken no action, the railroads may implement the new rates. Citing their precarious financial condition, on December 13, 1971, most of the nation's railroads filed with the ICC a proposed temporary across-the-board surcharge on almost all freight rates of 2.5 percent, with the goal of raising $246 million in additional annual revenue. The railroads proposed that the 2.5 percent surcharge go into effect on January 1, 1972, but the ICC proposed that the surcharge be refiled so as to permit the affected public time to respond to the railroads' action. The railroads then refiled the proposed 2.5 percent surcharge on January 5, 1972, with an effective date of February 5. The surcharge was to be temporary, lasting only until June 5, 1972, at which time the railroads intended to file permanent selective rate increases.

On February 1, 1972, the ICC refused to suspend the surcharge, pointing out that "the railroads have a critical need for additional revenue from their interstate freight rates and charges to offset, in part, recently incurred increased operating costs." The ICC noted that the operating costs of the railroads had increased by one billion dollars annually and that wages for railroad workers alone had increased by $305 million.

According to its usual practice, the ICC had ordered the railroads to submit statements regarding the effect upon the environment of the surcharge, and the railroads not unexpectedly had submitted statements that there would be no important adverse environmental impact if the surcharge were imposed. In approving the surcharge, the ICC thus stated that "the involved general increase will have no significant adverse effect on... the quality of the human environment within the meaning of the National Environmental Policy Act of 1969."

Given the fact that the surcharge meant yet another across-the-board increase in freight rates, which would perpetuate and worsen the bias against the transportation of recyclable materials by rail, a variety of groups challenged the ICC's conclusion as to the probable environmental impact of the surcharge. The ICC's action approving the surcharge was thus challenged by the Environmental Defense Fund (EDF), the Izaak Walton League (IWL), and the National Parks and Conservation Association (NPCA), all groups having long-standing interests in environmental protection; and the ICC's action was also challenged by the National Association of Secondary Materials Industries, representing over 700 recycling companies.

In September of 1971, another group of Banzhaf's bandits had been organized at George Washington University's National Law Center. The new group was composed of five law students and called itself Students Challenging Regulatory Agency Procedures (SCRAP). SCRAP also attacked the ICC's approval of the railway freight surcharge and threatened to seek an injunction against the ICC in federal court on the ground that the commission had failed to comply with NEPA's requirement of an environmental impact statement regarding the surcharge.

The Council on Environmental Quality (CEQ) also called the ICC's attention to NEPA's requirement of an EIS, and the CEQ's general counsel wrote the commission that "we assume that the Commission will circulate [an environmental impact] statement, according to CEQ guidelines for agency and public comment prior to its decision on [the railroad rate surcharge]." "Because recycling yields large environmental benefits, any policy which raises the price of wastes probably reduces the level of recycling from what it would have been without the price increase," the CEQ general counsel noted. "This can have an adverse environmental effect."

Reacting to threats by SCRAP, the Environmental Defense Fund, Izaak Walton League, and the National Parks and Conservation Association to seek an injunction against its action approving the surcharge, the ICC negotiated an agreement with those groups on February 3. The ICC agreed to "issue a draft environmental [impact] statement in accordance with the requirements of NEPA, and will otherwise comply with the requirements of that Act" in regard to the surcharge. SCRAP, the EDF, and the other groups agreed, on the other hand, to postpone any suit for an injunction pending the issuance of an EIS by the commission.

The ICC's effort to comply with the EIS requirement of NEPA, however, was anemic at best. On March 6, 1972, the commission issued a six-page "environmental impact statement" which found that, as "an emergency interim measure to meet a critical need for additional revenue that the railroads have demonstrated, the imposition of the surcharge published to become effective on February 5, 1972, and to expire not later than June 5, 1972, as required by the order of the Interstate Commerce Commission, approved February 1, 1972, will have no significant adverse effect on the quality of the human environment within the meaning of the Environmental Policy Act of 1969." The statement admitted, however, that the evidence before the commission "is completely inadequate for the Commission to make a determination as to what commodities, if any, warrant special treatment." And the commission complained in the statement that it lacked sufficient personnel to prepare a thorough EIS.

The ICC's effort to comply with NEPA not unexpectedly aroused strong condemnation not only on the part of SCRAP, the EDF, and the other environmental groups, but also on the part of the Council on Environmental Quality and the Environmental Protection Agency (EPA). The EPA, for example, commented that the ICC's "statement did not provide sufficient information to permit an evaluation of the environmental impact of increased rates and charges." "We believe," the EPA said, "that NEPA intended Federal agencies to evaluate the environmental impact of their long-term policies, not to confine their evaluation to incremental action implementing the long-term policies. Thus the ICC should broaden its evaluation to examine the freight rate setting process and its possible environmental impacts." The statement by the railroads denying any adverse environmental impact from the rate surcharge, the EPA continued, was "deficient as a useful environmental statement," and the EPA noted that the "evidence definitely indicates that both recycling and rail transport are environmentally beneficial in comparison to examined alternatives. The ICC should more fully analyze the possible impact that the freight rate setting process could have on both the use of recycled materials and the demand for rail transport."

SCRAP, the EDF, and the other environmental groups also vigorously attacked the ICC's March 6 statement. The statement, they said, was so "inadequate" that "substantive comments on the contents of this document are impossible." The commission could not, SCRAP and the other groups said, "possibly fulfill its obligations under NEPA and CEQ guidelines until it undertakes to gather the necessary information to make an adequate assessment of the environmental impact and the possible alternatives. This responsibility lies with the Commission, not with the parties. . . ." "Despite accumulating evidence of the impact of increased freight rates on recycling, the Commission's response has been to continue to grant the railroads across-the-board percentage rate increases after only the most superficial examination of the impact these increases have on the secondary materials industry and ultimately on the environment," the response of SCRAP and the other groups continued. "This means that freight rates are being increased annually without regard to the broader interests of the public such as the impact on the quality of our environment." The ICC statement was "fatally superficial," and in order to comply with NEPA, the commission at a "bare minimum" must "widen its focus to include the [environmental] impact of the underlying rate structure."

Despite such criticisms, the ICC continued to take actions during the summer and fall of 1972 with little evident concern with the need to comply with the requirements of NEPA. Finally, in a letter to the chairman of the ICC, Russell Train, the chairman of the President's Council on Environmental Quality, formally chastised the commission not only regarding its failure to comply with NEPA in approving the surcharge but also for its subsequent actions largely ignoring NEPA procedures. The CEQ was "disturbed," Train said, "by the repeated references. . .to the Commission's inability. . .to adapt to the requirements of NEPA. If manpower problems are preventing effective implementation of the Act, we would have expected the Commission to be alert to this problem earlier. With almost three years having elapsed after the passage of NEPA, lack of resources no longer appears to us to justify—if ever they did—less than full compliance with the policies and procedures of NEPA, designed as they were to give content to an expressly announced commitment of this country to the protection of environmental values. . . ." The ICC, Train continued, should evaluate the impact of the railroad rate structure on the recycling of materials in "a logical, analytical and timely fashion in compliance with the requirements of the National Environmental Policy Act. The Commission's actions to date appear to be inconsistent with the objectives of NEPA, and the analyses undertaken to date by the Commission appear to offer an inadequate basis from which to draw conclusions concerning the impact of freight rates on recycling and environmental quality."

SCRAP GOES TO COURT

On April 24, 1972, however, the ICC suspended for seven months the permanent rate increases proposed by the railroads, while allowing the temporary rate surcharge to remain in effect until November 30, 1972. In taking this action, the commission made no further effort to present an environmental impact statement evaluating the surcharge's effects on the environment. SCRAP then followed through on its threat to seek an injunction against the ICC's order permitting the surcharge and filed suit in the United States District Court for the District of Columbia. SCRAP based its suit on Section 702 of the Administrative Procedure Act, which provides that a "person suffering legal wrong because of agency action, or adversely affected or aggrieved by agency action within the meaning of a relevant statute, is entitled to judicial review thereof."

SCRAP's complaint in the district court asserted that its members would be adversely affected by the ICC's approval of the surcharge since they would have to pay "more for finished products purchased in the marketplace, made more expensive by both the non-use of recycled materials in their manufacture, and the need to use comparatively more energy in the reduction of a raw material to finished products." The ICC action, the SCRAP complaint additionally alleged, would have an adverse environmental impact on "forests, rivers, streams, mountains and other natural resources" by encouraging "the destruction of virgin timber, the unnecessary extraction of raw materials, and the discharge and accumulation of large quantities of otherwise recyclable solid and liquid waste materials such as scrap iron and oil wastes." Finally, the members of SCRAP would be adversely affected, the complaint alleged, since the ICC action encouraged "the greater discharge of larger quantities of air pollutants such as flyash. . .to the detriment of plaintiffs' health and opportunities for recreation. Rate increases also foster the diversion of freight traffic from rail to motor carrier, increasing the likelihood of an unnecessary threat to human health from increased air pollution. . . ."

On the basis of these allegations, SCRAP therefore contended that it had standing to sue for an injunction prohibiting the ICC from approving the surcharge until it issued an adequate environmental impact statement under the provisions of NEPA. U.S. District Court Judge Charles R. Richey, before whom the SCRAP complaint was filed, nonetheless expressed some doubt that the complaint alleged a sufficient personal "injury in fact" as required by the Supreme Court's decision in *Sierra Club* v. *Morton*, since the Court had held in *Sierra Club* that an allegation of personal injury to an organization's members was required to meet the requirements of standing. SCRAP consequently carefully amended its complaint to assert that each member of SCRAP personally "uses the forests, rivers, streams, mountains and other natural resources surrounding the Washington Metropolitan area and at his legal residence, for camping, hiking, fishing, sightseeing, and other recreational aesthetic purposes." Since the ICC's action approving the surcharge would allegedly adversely affect these natural resources, the theory of the SCRAP complaint was that each member of SCRAP was also personally injured in fact by the commission's action.

Judge Richey thereupon refused to grant the government's motion to dismiss the *SCRAP* case, and instead requested the chief judge of the Court of Appeals for the District of Columbia Circuit to convene a three-judge court to hear the case. A three-judge district court, composed of Court of Appeals Judge J. Skelly Wright and District Court Judges Charles Richey and Thomas Flannery was thus convened to hear the case. The Environmental Defense Fund, the Izaak Walton League, and the National Parks and Conservation Association had in the meantime joined SCRAP as plaintiffs in the case, adopting essentially the same language as was used by SCRAP in their complaints. The Aberdeen and Rockfish Railroad Company, joined by over four hundred of the nation's railroads, also joined the ICC as defendants in the case.

The government and the railroads filed a motion seeking the dismissal of the *SCRAP* case in the three-judge court, arguing that SCRAP and the other plaintiffs lacked standing to maintain the suit and that the court lacked jurisdiction to hear the case. The plaintiffs had failed to allege a sufficiently direct, personal stake in the litigation to give them standing, the government and the railroads argued. And additionally, it was argued that in *Arrow Transportation Co.* v. *Southern Railway Co.*, decided by the Supreme Court in 1963, it had been held that the federal courts could not, under the Interstate Commerce Act, interfere via injunctions with the ICC's exclusive power to decide whether or not to suspend a proposed change in railroad rates. Under the *Arrow* case, the government and the railroads thus argued, the three-judge court lacked jurisdiction to enjoin the ICC's action approving the surcharge even if the plaintiffs had standing. Finally, on the merits, the government and the railroads argued that the ICC's action approving the surcharge as a temporary measure was not a "major Federal action significantly affecting the quality of the human environment" and therefore did not fall within NEPA's requirement of a full environmental impact statement.

## THE DECISION OF THE THREE-JUDGE COURT

On July 10, 1972, however, the three-judge court rejected all these arguments in a rather caustically worded opinion and granted SCRAP and the other plaintiffs an injunction against the ICC's action approving the surcharge. The court noted that the defendants "vigorously contest [SCRAP's] standing to bring this action. They argue that [SCRAP] has no more than a general interest in seeing that the law is enforced and that [SCRAP's] members have failed to distinguish themselves from other citizens who are also concerned with the environment." In its amended complaint, the court noted on the other hand, SCRAP "alleges that its members use the forests, streams, mountains, and other resources in the Washington area for camping, hiking, fishing, and sightseeing, and that this use is disturbed by the adverse environmental impact caused by nonuse of recyclable goods. It is clear that plaintiff organization has standing to raise the rights of its members, . . .and we think [SCRAP] has alleged the kind of 'injury in fact' to those members which would give them standing to sue."

SCRAP's allegation, the court held, "that its members actually use the environmental resources adversely affected by the Commission action is sufficient to distinguish this case from *Sierra Club* v. *Morton*. . . ." Indeed, the court pointed out, SCRAP "has followed the Supreme Court's suggestion and amended its complaint to conform to *Sierra Club* requirements. Consequently, it is not surprising that it meets the *Sierra Club* test for standing." "The mere fact that [SCRAP's] allegations do not distinguish its members from a great many others who use our natural resources does not disqualify it as a party," the court declared. "*Sierra Club* also makes plain that '[a]esthetic and environmental well-being, like economic well-being, are important ingredients of the quality of life in our society, and the fact that particular environmental interests are shared by the many rather than the few does not make them less deserving of legal protection through the judicial process.' "

Having sustained SCRAP's standing to sue, the three-judge court then turned to the contention that, under the Supreme Court's *Arrow Transportation Co.* decision, it lacked jurisdiction to enjoin the ICC's approval of the surcharge under the Interstate Commerce Act. The court conceded that under the *Arrow* decision a federal court could not second-guess the ICC's judgment as to the lawfulness or reasonableness of proposed rates by enjoining the implementation of rates the ICC had refused to suspend. On the other hand, the court held that in its opinion "NEPA implicitly confers authority in the federal courts to enjoin *any* federal action taken in violation of NEPA's procedural requirements, even if jurisdiction to review this action is otherwise lacking." The court thus concluded that, while it could not interfere injunctively with the ICC's substantive judgment as to the lawfulness or reasonableness of the proposed surcharge, under NEPA it could require the commission to comply with NEPA's procedural requirement of an EIS before approving of the surcharge.

Having concluded that it possessed jurisdiction to act in the case, the three-judge court finally examined the extent to which the ICC had complied with the requirements of NEPA, and it denounced in rather caustic terms the commission's performance. The statement which the ICC had solicited from the railroads on the environmental impact of the surcharge, the court said, could not take the place of a commission-prepared environmental impact statement. "We need hardly point out that this self-serving statement by one of the parties cannot take the place of a NEPA impact statement which," the court noted, "according to the statute, must be prepared 'by the responsible official.' "

The fact that the ICC had found in its order approving the surcharge that there would be no adverse environmental impact was "no more than glorified boilerplate," the court said. "Clearly NEPA would be rendered meaningless if an agency could avoid its mandate by baldly asserting that it 'finds' no need to comply with it." And the six-page impact statement filed by the ICC on March 6 was equally condemned by the court. "The Commission has never adequately explained why it bothered to prepare a draft impact statement premised on facts it knew to be false," the court said of the March 6 statement, "and the reason why the ICC finds itself with the resources necessary to prepare draft statements based on false hypotheses while it is assertedly without resources to prepare impact statements as required by NEPA based on real facts remains one of the enduring mysteries of this case."

The court noted that both the CEQ and the EPA had found the March 6 statement "inadequate," and it declared that "this assessment is a charitable one." The ICC's statement, the court continued, "fails to discuss in any detail the possible environmental effects of the higher freight rates, fails to discuss the alternatives to an across-the-board increase, and impermissibly relies on the parties instead of the Commission's own investigative apparatus to uncover possible environmental effects of [the approval of the surcharge]. It should go without saying that the mere filing of a document labelled 'final impact statement' is insufficient to shield an agency from judicial review if the document fails to comply with the standards outlined in NEPA."

"We hold that [SCRAP] is entitled to a preliminary injunction against implementation of the ICC's April 24 order permitting an extension of the 2.5 percent surcharge until November 30, 1972," the three-judge court concluded. "We further hold that the Commission should be preliminarily enjoined from permitting the railroads to collect the surcharge until an adequate environmental impact statement has been issued." The court limited its injunction, however, to the surcharge affecting recyclable materials, thus allowing the railroads to continue to collect the surcharge on the shipment of all other commodities.

## THE APPEAL TO THE SUPREME COURT

Refusing to accept the defeat in the district court, the government and the railroads filed notices of appeals to the Supreme Court, and the Court agreed to hear the appeal in the *SCRAP* case on December 18, 1972. Representing the government and the ICC, Solicitor General Erwin Griswold attacked the standing of SCRAP and the other environmental groups to bring the case, arguing that the "holding [by the three-judge court] below that [SCRAP] had standing to obtain...relief on the basis of the allegations here thus abandons altogether the 'injury in fact' test reaffirmed in *Sierra Club,* and permits suits by organizations seeking 'to do no more than vindicate their own value preferences through the judicial process.'"

Arguing the case orally before the Supreme Court, Solicitor General Griswold expressed dismay regarding the district court's upholding of SCRAP's standing, and he warned of dire consequences if the Court affirmed the district court's ruling on the standing issue. "We have a rather remarkable situation here—five law school students, though I'm told they are a changing group..., proceeding not as lawyers but as plaintiffs..., have tied up all the railroads in the country, and with the aid of the district court, have prevented the railroads from collecting from 500,000 to a million dollars a month for the past eight months on shipments of recyclable materials," Griswold told the Court. Quoting the allegations in SCRAP's complaint, the solicitor general pointed out that "it will be seen that these allegations are entirely general. It is not said which forest, river, stream or mountain—we don't even have a particular valley as we did in the Mineral King [*Sierra Club*] case last year—which forest, stream, river or mountain is used by any member of SCRAP. It's obvious that these allegations could be made by any member of the public who wishes to make them.... There is no evidence to support their standing...."

"There are those who feel that standing is no longer a relevant argument, though I wonder if our predecessors were always that wrong," the solicitor general continued. The virtual abandonment of the requirement of standing in federal cases might be "the wave of the future, but it's a serious step the implications of which should be carefully explored and considered. Before going further, I may observe, that if there is standing in this case, it would be helpful, I think, and a contribution to candor, if this Court would indicate that standing is no longer required, [rather than for the Court] to say that standing is required and that there is standing in this case...."

"Standing is not a fiction and never has been and should not be," Griswold declared. "If anyone has standing to bring a suit like this, it will mark a substantial shift in the balance under our traditional and constitutional separation of powers, for this is what the Constitution meant by cases and controversies to which the judicial power is extended. If everyone is a private attorney general, free to raise any public question at his whim, or because of his academic or abstract interest, more and more questions will be thrown into the courts, and we can readily have a situation where every facet of our governmental operation depends on the let or hindrance of the courts—where in effect the courts would take over all the details of the administration of the government." "In my view," the solicitor general continued, "that would not be good for the courts, and it would not be good for the country. Perhaps more pertinent, it's not the sort of division of function which was intended by the framers, as I see it, when they established the Constitution...."

"It may seem very fine to some today to have the courts decide all the legal questions—often pretty much in advance and in the absence of concrete facts, as is the situation here," Griswold continued. "For the courts today are progressive and forward-looking and innovative, but it has not always been so. There have been times when the courts were felt by many to be backward-looking and obstructive, and serious attacks on the courts have occurred." "Of course, the courts should do their duty, they should exercise the judicial power without fear or favor, but the judicial power does not authorize a general overriding sort of oversight of all legal questions arising in the government—a sort of ombudsman to whom all may resort when they feel so impelled," the solicitor general concluded. "It was for this reason that the judicial power was extended to cases and controversies, and that should mean bona fide disputes by a party who has a real stake and who can show how he has been hurt. That is not this case with respect to any of the appellees."

In addition to the standing issue in the *SCRAP* case, the solicitor general and the railroads contended that, even if *SCRAP* had standing the district court lacked the power to enjoin the rate surcharge under an amendment to the Interstate Commerce Act in 1927. In construing this amendment in *Arrow Transportation Co.* v. *Southern Railway Co.* in

1963, the Supreme Court, they argued, had held that the federal courts were without power to suspend railroad rates the ICC had chosen not to suspend. Even if SCRAP had standing, it was therefore argued, the district court had exceeded its powers by enjoining the rate surcharge.

SCRAP and the other environmental groups responded to the attack on their standing with the argument that the allegations in the *SCRAP* case were carefully tailored to meet the Court's decision requiring an allegation of an injury in fact in the *Sierra Club* case. If the position of the solicitor general and the railroads on the standing issue prevailed, the environmental groups argued, the result "would be to preclude judicial review in situations involving some of the most important administrative actions, where courts historically have found standing." SCRAP and the other environmental groups additionally argued that the Interstate Commerce Act had been modified by the passage of NEPA to allow the federal courts to enjoin railroad rates when the ICC had not complied with the requirement of an environmental impact statement as part of its decision-making process relative to whether or not to suspend proposed rates. The *Arrow Transportation Co.* case, it was therefore argued, was inapplicable to the situation involved in the *SCRAP* case.

The Supreme Court announced its decision in the *SCRAP* case on June 18, 1973. A bare majority of five members of the Court agreed that SCRAP had standing to sue in the case, but a six-member majority held that the three-judge district court did not have jurisdiction to issue the injunction against the temporary railroad rate surcharge under the doctrine enunciated in the *Arrow Transportation Co.* case.

*United States* v.
*Students Challenging Regulatory Agency Procedures (SCRAP)*
412 U.S. 669. Argued February 28, 1973. Decided June 18, 1973.
Mr. Justice Stewart delivered the opinion of the Court.

[Justice Stewart first summarized the facts in the case, including the proceedings before the Interstate Commerce Commission which had led the Commission to approve the 2.5% railroad rate surcharge.]

On May 12, 1973, SCRAP filed the present suit against the United States and the [Interstate Commerce] Commission in the District Court for the District of Columbia seeking, along with other relief, a preliminary injunction to restrain enforcement of the Commission's February 1 and April 24 orders allowing the railroads to collect the 2.5% surcharge. SCRAP stated in its amended complaint that it was "an unincorporated association formed by five law students. . .in September, 1971. Its primary purpose is to enhance the quality of the human environment for its members, and for all citizens. . . ." To establish standing to bring this suit, SCRAP repeated many of the allegations it had made before the Commission. . . . It claimed that each of its members "suffered economic, recreational and aesthetic harm directly as a result of the adverse environmental impact of the railroad freight [rate] structure, as modified by the Commission's actions to date. . . ." Specifically, SCRAP alleged that each of its members was caused to pay more for finished products, that each of its members "uses the forests, rivers, streams, mountains, and other natural resources surrounding the Washington Metropolitan area and at his legal residence, for camping, hiking, fishing, sightseeing, and other recreational [and] aesthetic purposes," and that these uses have been adversely affected by the increased freight rates, that each of its members breathes the air within the Washington metropolitan area and the area of his legal residence and that this air has suffered increased pollution caused by the modified rate structure, and that each member has been forced to pay increased taxes because of the sums which must be expended to dispose of otherwise reusable waste materials.

The main thrust of SCRAP's complaint was that the Commission's decisions of February 1 and April 24, insofar as they declined to suspend the 2.5% surcharge, were unlawful because the Commission had failed to include a detailed environmental impact statement as required by Sec. 102(2)(c) of the National Environmental Policy Act of 1969. . . . NEPA requires such a statement in "every recommendation or report on proposals for legislation and other major Federal actions significantly affecting the quality of the human environment. . . ." SCRAP contended that because of its alleged adverse impact upon recycling, the Commission's action with respect to the surcharge constituted a major federal action significantly affecting the environment.

Three additional environmental groups, also appellees here, were allowed to intervene as plaintiffs, and a group of railroads, appellants here, intervened as defendants to support the 2.5% surcharge. After a single district judge had denied the defendants' motion to dismiss and SCRAP's motion for a temporary restraining order, a statutory three-judge district court was convened. . .to decide the motion for a preliminary injunction and the cross-motion to dismiss the complaint.

[At this point in his opinion, Justice Stewart summarized the three-judge court's decision to issue the injunction barring the implementation of the surcharge insofar as it affected recyclable materials.]

The appellants challenge the appellees' standing to sue, arguing that the allegations in the pleadings as to standing were vague, unsubstantiated, and insufficient under our recent decision in Sierra Club v. Morton. . . . The appellees respond that unlike the petitioner in Sierra Club, their pleadings sufficiently alleged that they were "adversely affected" or "aggrieved" within the meaning of the Administrative Procedure Act (APA), . . .and they point specifically to the allegations that their members used the forests, streams, mountains, and other resources in the Washington metropolitan area for camping, hiking, fishing, and sightseeing, and that this use was disturbed by the adverse environmental impact caused by the nonuse of recyclable goods brought about by a rate increase on those commodities. The District Court found these allegations sufficient to withstand a motion to dismiss. We agree.

The petitioner in Sierra Club, "a large and long-established organization, with a historic commitment to the cause of protecting our Nation's natural heritage from man's depredations" . . .sought a declaratory judgment and an injunction to restrain federal officials from approving the creation of an extensive ski-resort development in the scenic Mineral King Valley of the Sequoia National Forest. The Sierra Club claimed standing to maintain its "public interest" lawsuit because it had " 'a special interest in the conservation and the sound maintenance of the national parks, game refuges and forests of the country' " . . .We held those allegations insufficient.

Relying on our prior decisions in Data Processing Service v. Camp. . . and Barlow v. Collins. . . , we held that Sec. 702 of the APA conferred standing to obtain judicial review of agency action only upon those who could show "that the challenged action had caused them 'injury in fact,' and where the alleged injury was to an interest 'arguably within the zone of interests to be protected or regulated' by the statutes that the agencies were claimed to have violated". . . .

In interpreting "injury in fact" we made it clear that standing was not confined to those who could show "economic harm," although both Data Processing and Barlow had involved that kind of injury. Nor, we said, could the fact that many persons shared the same injury be sufficient reason to disqualify from seeking review of an agency's action any person who had in fact suffered injury. Rather, we explained: "Aesthetic and environmental well-being, like economic well-being, are important ingredients of the quality of life in our society, and the fact that particular environmental interests are shared by the many rather than the few does not make them less deserving of legal protection through the judicial process". . . . Consequently, neither the fact that the appellees here claimed only a harm to their use and enjoyment of the natural resources of the Washington area, nor the fact that all those who use those resources suffered the same harm, deprives them of standing.

In Sierra Club, though, we went on to stress the importance of demonstrating that the party seeking review be himself among the injured, for it is this requirement that gives a litigant a direct stake in the controversy and prevents the judicial process from becoming no more than a vehicle for the vindication of the value interests of concerned bystanders. No such specific injury was alleged in Sierra Club. In that case the asserted harm "will be felt directly only by those who use Mineral King and Sequoia National Park, and for whom the aesthetic and recreational values of the area will be lessened by the highway and ski resort, . . .yet "[t]he Sierra Club failed to allege that it or its members would be affected in any of their activities or pastimes by the. . .development". . . . Here, by contrast, the appellees claimed that the specific and allegedly illegal action of the Commission would directly harm them in their use of the natural resources of the Washington Metropolitan Area.

Unlike the specific and geographically limited federal action of which the petitioner complained in Sierra Club, the challenged agency action in this case is applicable to substantially all of the Nation's railroads, and thus allegedly has an adverse environmental impact on all the natural resources of the country. Rather than a limited group of persons who used a picturesque valley in California, all persons who utilize the scenic resources of the country, and indeed all who breathe its air, could claim harm similar to that alleged by the environmental groups here. But we have already made it clear that standing is not to be denied simply because many people suffer the same injury. Indeed some of the cases on which we relied in Sierra Club demonstrated the patent fact that persons across the Nation could be adversely affected by major governmental actions. . . . To deny standing to persons who are in fact injured simply because many others are also injured, would mean that the most injurious and widespread Government actions would be questioned by nobody. We cannot accept that conclusion.

But the injury alleged here is also very different from that at issue in Sierra Club because here the alleged injury to the environment is far less direct and perceptible. The petitioner there complained about the construction of a specific project that would directly affect the Mineral King Valley. Here, the Court was asked to follow a far more attenuated line of causation to the eventual injury of which the appellees complained—a general rate increase would allegedly cause increased use of nonrecyclable commodities as compared to recyclable goods, thus resulting in the need to use more natural resources to produce such goods, some of which resources might be taken from the Washington area, and resulting in more refuse that might be discarded in national parks in the Washington area. The railroads protest that the appellees could never prove that a general increase in rates would have this effect, and they contend that these allegations were a ploy to avoid the need to show some injury in fact.

Of course, pleadings must be something more than an ingenious academic exercise in the conceivable. A plaintiff must allege that he has been or will in fact be perceptibly harmed by the challenged agency action, not that he can imagine circumstances in which he could be affected by the agency's action. And it is equally clear that the allegations must be true and capable of proof at trial. But we deal here simply with the pleadings in which the appellees alleged a specific and perceptible harm that distinguished them from other citizens who had not used the natural resources that were claimed to be affected. If, as the railroads now assert, these allegations were in fact untrue, then the appellants should have moved for summary judgment on the standing issue and demonstrated to the District Court that the allegations were sham and raised no genuine issue of fact. We cannot say on these pleadings that the appellees could not prove their allegations which, if proved, would place them squarely among those persons injured in fact by the Commission's action, and entitled under the clear import of Sierra Club to seek review. The District Court was correct in denying the appellants' motion to dismiss the complaint for failure to allege sufficient standing to bring this lawsuit. . . .

[Having held that SCRAP had standing to sue, Justice Stewart nonetheless held that the district court should not have enjoined the temporary 2.5% surcharge, since it lacked power to do so under the Supreme Court's decision in the *Arrow Transportation Co.* case. NEPA had not, Stewart said, amended the Interstate Commerce Act which prohibited the federal courts from enjoining railroad rates that the ICC had refused to suspend. "Accordingly," Stewart concluded, "because the District Court granted a preliminary injunction suspending railroad rates when it lacked the power to do so, its judgment must be reversed and the cases remanded to that court for further proceedings consistent with this opinion."]

Mr. Justice Powell took no part in the consideration or decision of these cases.

Mr. Justice Blackmun, with whom Mr. Justice Brennan joins, concurring.

I join the Court's judgment and its opinion, but. . .to avoid any misunderstanding as to my posture, I add a few words.

For the reasons stated in my dissenting opinion in Sierra Club v. Morton. . . , I would hold that the appellees here have standing to maintain this action based on their allegations of harm to the environment resulting from the Commission's order of April 24, 1972. And in evaluating whether injunctive relief is warranted, I would not require that the appellees, in their individual capacities, prove that they in fact were injured. Rather, I would require only that appellees, as responsible and sincere representatives of environmental interests, show that the environment would be injured in fact and that such injury would be irreparable and substantial.

Mr. Justice Douglas, dissenting in part.

. . .I agree with the Court that appellees have standing, but like Mr. Justice Blackmun, I would not require appellees, in their individual capacity, to prove injury in fact. As Mr. Justice Blackmun states, it should be sufficient if appellees, "as responsible and sincere representatives of environmental interests, show that the environment would be injured in fact. . . ."

[Justice Douglas, however, dissented from the Court's holding that the *Arrow Transportation Co.* case prohibited the district court from issuing an injunction compelling the ICC to comply with NEPA.]

Mr. Justice White, with whom The Chief Justice and Mr. Justice Rehnquist join, dissenting in part.

I would reverse the judgment of the District Court and order the complaint dismissed because appellees lack standing to bring this suit. None of our cases, including inferences that may be drawn from dicta in Sierra Club v. Morton. . . , where we denied standing to petitioner there, are sufficient to confer standing on plaintiffs in circumstances like these. . . .

As I see the allegations in this case, they are in reality little different from the general-interest allegations found insufficient and too remote in Sierra Club. If they are sufficient here, we are well on our way to permitting citizens at large to litigate any decisions of the Government which fall in an area of interest to them and with which they disagree. . . .

[Mr. Justice White, joined by Chief Justice Burger and Justice Rehnquist, agreed with the majority of the Court, however, that the district court lacked the power to issue the injunction under the principles of the *Arrow Transportation Co.* case.]

[Justice Marshall, concurring in part and dissenting in part, agreed with the majority that the appellees had standing to sue, but dissented from the Court's ruling that the district court lacked the power to enjoin the 2.5% surcharge.]

A majority of the Court, Justices Stewart, Brennan, Blackmun, Douglas, and Marshall, thus agreed that SCRAP had standing to attack the ICC's decision not to suspend the surcharge. There was disagreement among these justices, however, as to how SCRAP's allegations of injury in fact should be proven. Justices Blackmun, Brennan, and Douglas would have required only a showing that the environment was adversely affected by the ICC's action, while the other members of the majority would have required SCRAP to demonstrate that the damage to the environment resulting from the ICC's action would adversely affect the members of SCRAP. With only Justices Douglas and Marshall dissenting, on the other hand, the Court nevertheless held that the three-judge district court had lacked the power to interfere with the ICC's power to suspend or not suspend proposed railroad rates.

The Court's decision, however, was only one round in a continuing battle between the ICC and SCRAP regarding the commission's compliance with NEPA. While the SCRAP case was being appealed to the Supreme Court, the issue of permanent rate increases for the railroads was pending before the ICC, and on October 4, 1972, the ICC issued an order approving almost all the permanent rate increases proposed by the railroads. Although the commission discussed environmental issues generally in its decision, it concluded that the increases would not significantly affect the environment. There was thus no need, the commission concluded, to issue an environmental impact statement regarding the rate increase.

The ICC's October 4 decision approving the increase and its continued refusal to issue an EIS provoked a storm of criticism of the commission by the Council on Environmental Quality, the Environmental Protection Agency, SCRAP, and other environmental groups. SCRAP also reacted to the ICC's action by filing a motion in the U.S. District Court for the District of Columbia for an injunction against the increases the ICC had approved on recyclable materials, again arguing that the commission had failed to meet the requirements of NEPA. On the same day that SCRAP filed its motion for an injunction, however, the ICC announced that it was suspending the rate increases on recyclables until June, 1973, and that it was reopening its investigation of those rates for the purpose of evaluating their impact upon the environment. In light of the ICC's action, the district court refused SCRAP's motion for an injunction, pending the outcome of the reopened ICC proceedings.

The ICC finally prepared and presented for comment by the public and other federal agencies a draft environmental impact statement regarding the increases of freight rates for recyclables on March 5, 1973. SCRAP, the Environmental Defense Fund, and other environmental groups were extremely critical of this draft EIS, and these groups were joined in their criticisms by the CEQ, EPA, General Services Administration, Department of Interior, and the Department of Commerce. Despite these criticisms from both environmental groups and federal agencies, on May 1, 1973, the

ICC issued a final EIS that was essentially the same as the draft statement it had issued on March 5. Instead of responding to the criticisms of its draft EIS, the commission merely added the criticisms to the final statement, appended its original order approving the rate increases to the final statement, and terminated the proceedings.

## SCRAP STRIKES AGAIN

SCRAP and the other environmental groups on May 30 again challenged the adequacy of the ICC's compliance with NEPA in the U.S. District Court for the District of Columbia. A three-judge court was again convened, and it issued a temporary injunction prohibiting the collection of the rate increases on recyclable materials on June 7. On appeal by the government, the Supreme Court in *United States* v. *SCRAP* vacated the injunction and remanded the case to the three-judge court with instructions that the court examine its jurisdiction in the case.

On February 19, 1974, the three-judge court ruled that it possessed jurisdiction to review the adequacy of the ICC's compliance with NEPA, and it again found the commission's performance to be seriously deficient. The court held that the ICC had already decided to approve the rate increases before it considered their impact on the environment, and the commission had thus ignored NEPA's command that environmental impacts be a factor considered by federal agencies in their decision-making processes. The court also noted that the ICC's impact statement was characterized by "combative, defensive and advocatory language," and that the "statement's defensiveness, and the Commission's insensitivity to its NEPA responsibilities are even manifested at one point by an assertion that NEPA does not require any balancing of environmental costs."

The three-judge court therefore directed the commission to prepare another draft EIS, which must include an analysis of the impact of the underlying rate structure on recyclables. This draft EIS, the court further ordered, must be circulated for comment by interested parties and agencies, and a hearing on the EIS must be held by the ICC. Then, the court said, the commission should prepare a final impact statement and issue another order regarding the rate increases embodying an analysis of the relationship of the environmental impact of the railroad rate structure to the national transportation policy.

## SCRAP II IN THE SUPREME COURT

This decision of the three-judge court, however, was appealed by the government to the Supreme Court, and on June 24, 1975, the Court reversed the decision of the district court in *Aberdeen and Rockfish Railroad Co.* v. *SCRAP* and held that the ICC had adequately considered the environmental effects of its action in compliance with NEPA. The Court pointed out that, in deciding whether to suspend proposed rate increases, the ICC was primarily concerned with the narrow issue of the lawfulness of the rates. Given the narrow focus of ICC proceedings on whether to suspend proposed rate increases, the Court found that such proceedings raised "few environmental issues and none which is claimed in this case to have been inadequately addressed in the impact statement."

The Court also held that the three-judge court had erred in directing the ICC to reopen its proceedings and to fully evaluate the environmental impact of the underlying rate structure before deciding whether to suspend the proposed general rate increase. The Court noted that the ICC had begun in another proceeding to explore comprehensively the environmental impact of the underlying railroad rate structure, and it therefore held that the Commission need not duplicate that process by reopening the proceedings involving whether or not to suspend the general rate increase. "Thus even if NEPA. . .were read to require the ICC to address comprehensively the underlying rate structure at least once before approval of a facially neutral general rate increase," the Court said, "no purpose could have been served by ordering it to thoroughly explore the question in the confined and inappropriate context of a railroad proposal for a general rate increase when it was already doing so in a more appropriate proceeding." The Court thus concluded that, even assuming "that some rudimentary examination into the underlying rate structure and into the reasonableness of the new rates on particular recyclables was required [of the ICC], the consideration of environmental factors in connection therewith was more than adequate."

Dissenting from the Court's decision holding that the ICC compliance with NEPA had been adequate, Justice Douglas pointed out that the litigation in the *SCRAP* case "presents a history of foot dragging by the ICC, as other parties to proceedings before it, including other federal agencies, have attempted to prod it into compliance with the National Environmental Policy Act (NEPA)." "NEPA is more than a technical statute of administrative procedure," Douglas declared. "It is a commitment to the preservation of our national environment." One purpose of NEPA was to "force agencies to *acquire* expertise in environmental matters, even if attention to parochial matters in the past had not demanded this capacity,"

Douglas concluded. "The Court today excuses the Commission's performance. The District Court, following the spirit of NEPA, told the Commission to do better. I would affirm its judgment."

As the dissent by Justice Douglas indicated, SCRAP was not successful either in *SCRAP I* or *SCRAP II* in forcing the ICC to formulate more elaborate environmental impact statements as a part of the process of deciding whether or not to suspend proposed railroad rates. In *SCRAP I,* however, SCRAP had established that the Court's holding in the *Sierra Club* case, that there must be an allegation of an injury in fact as a prerequisite to obtaining standing to challenge administrative action under Section 702 of the APA, did not constitute a very serious hurdle as far as meeting the requirement of standing was concerned. In upholding SCRAP's standing in *SCRAP I,* despite the "attenuated line of causation" linking the decision of the ICC not to suspend the 2.5 percent surcharge and the alleged injury in fact to SCRAP's members, the Court seemingly made the *Sierra Club* requirement of injury in fact a largely technical or formal requirement which could be rather easily met by most parties seeking to challenge administrative action. The result was that the *Sierra Club* decision, contrary to some of the initial reactions to it, did not constitute a major retreat from the liberalization of standing requirements that has occurred in recent years.

Although the solicitor general and the railroads had engaged in dire warnings that the requirement of standing was being abandoned in *SCRAP I,* the Court has retained standing as a part of the cases and controversies requirement. Indeed, in recent cases, the Supreme Court has rejected allegations of rather indirect injuries, similar to those asserted in *SCRAP I,* as failing to meet the standing requirement. In *Simon* v. *Eastern Kentucky Welfare Rights Organization,* decided in 1976, a welfare rights organization challenged a ruling by the Internal Revenue Service (IRS) which granted favorable tax treatment to nonprofit hospitals even though the hospitals did not provide the maximum feasible services for indigent persons. The IRS ruling, the welfare rights organization alleged, had the effect of encouraging nonprofit hospitals to deny care to indigents, or to provide only limited care for indigents, and therefore the members of the welfare rights organization had suffered an injury in fact under Section 702 of the APA as a consequence of the IRS ruling.

The Supreme Court ruled in the *Simon* case, however, that the plaintiffs challenging the IRS ruling lacked standing to sue, since it was mere speculation as to whether a changed ruling would result in greater hospital care for indigent persons. The Court held that "unadorned speculation will not suffice to invoke the federal judicial power," and that "indirectness of injury, while not necessarily fatal to standing, 'may make it substantially more difficult to meet the minimum requirement of Art. III: to establish that, in fact, asserted injury was the consequence of the defendant's actions, or that prospective relief will remove the harm.'"

In *Laird* v. *Tatum*, decided in 1972, the Court also ruled that plaintiffs lacked standing to challenge the army's surveillance of lawful civilian political activities on the ground such surveillance "chilled" or inhibited the exercise of First Amendment rights such as freedom of speech and freedom of association. "Allegations of a subjective 'chill,'" the Court said, "are not an adequate substitute for a claim of specific present objective harm or a threat of specific future harm. . . ."

Similarly, in *United States* v. *Richardson,* the Court ruled in 1974 that an individual, asserting his status as a citizen and taxpayer, did not have standing to maintain a suit seeking a court order requiring the disclosure of the budget of the Central Intelligence Agency (CIA) under the provision of the Constitution that "a regular Statement and Account of the Receipts and Expenditures of all public Money shall be published from time to time." The plaintiff, the Court said, was not challenging a spending program but rather the statute allowing the CIA budget to be kept secret, and therefore under *Flast* v. *Cohen* there was no nexus between his status as a taxpayer and the program he was attacking. And as a citizen, the Court held, the plaintiff had alleged only an injury which he shared with the public generally and not a concrete, personal injury. The plaintiff, the Court concluded, "is seeking 'to employ a federal court as a forum in which to air his generalized grievances about the conduct of the government.'"

Also, in *Schlesinger* v. *Reservists to Stop the War,* decided in 1974, the Court held that the Incompatibility Clause of the Constitution, which prohibits members of Congress from holding "any Office under the United States," was unenforceable in the federal courts because no one had standing to maintain a suit enforcing its provisions. The Reservists to Stop the War filed suit seeking judicial orders directing the Secretary of Defense to remove all members of Congress from the rolls of reserved officers in the military, arguing that for members of Congress to hold reserved officer commissions was violative of the Incompatibility Clause.

The Supreme Court held that the Reservists to Stop the War had alleged a mere "injury in the abstract." Standing to sue, the Court said, "may not be predicated upon an interest of the kind alleged here which is held in common by all members of the public, because of the necessarily abstract nature of the injury all citizens share. Concrete injury, whether actual or threatened, is that indispensable element of a dispute which serves in part to cast it in a form traditionally capable of judicial resolution. It adds the essential dimension of specificity to the dispute by requiring that the complaining party have suffered a particular injury caused by the action challenged as unlawful. This personal stake is what the Court has consistently held enables a complainant authoritatively to present to a court a complete perspective upon the adverse consequences flowing from the specific set of facts undergirding his grievance."

Despite the predictions of the imminent demise of the requirement of standing which were made by the solicitor general in *SCRAP I,* therefore, the requirement remains alive. And, indeed, in such decisions as *Simon, Richardson,* and *Reservists to Stop the War,* the Court has appeared to be tightening the standing requirement. Although Justice Douglas once said, probably correctly, that "[g]eneralizations about standing to sue are largely worthless as such," it seems safe to say that, despite the recent tightening of the standing requirement by the Court, the kinds of interests that may be asserted in challenges to administrative action, as well as the numbers of persons potentially having standing to challenge administrative action, have rather dramatically increased in recent years. The result is that more issues may be raised and more administrative actions challenged in litigation than at any time in the past.

## SOVEREIGN IMMUNITY, OFFICIAL IMMUNITY, AND SUITS FOR DAMAGES

Individuals whose rights have been violated or injured by governmental or administrative action sometimes file suits for damages in the courts seeking compensation for the harm done them. In seeking damages for governmentally or administratively inflicted harm or injury, however, the individual again encounters some formidable barriers to the achievement of his objectives. One such barrier encountered in suits for damages is the doctrine of sovereign immunity. Inherited in the United States as a part of the common law, sovereign immunity was originally based upon the English concept that "the king can do no wrong," and consequently that the government may not be sued for damages without its consent. Under the doctrine of sovereign immunity, therefore, the state and federal governments cannot, absent their consent, be sued for damages by individuals whose rights have been injured by governmental or administrative action.

As implemented in the United States, the doctrine of sovereign immunity has long been the subject of attack. A legal doctrine based upon the concept that the king can do no wrong, it has been argued, seems incompatible with a republic that began its existence with a revolution that repudiated a king. More importantly, it is argued that injuries to the rights of individuals are an inevitable part of modern government, and it is unjust to require the individual with limited resources to bear the costs of such injuries because the government cannot be sued for damages. A more just system, it is argued, would require the government with its vast resources to bear the costs of the inevitable injuries to the rights of individuals resulting from governmental action, and the government should therefore be liable for damages in the courts.

As a consequence of these and other criticisms of the doctrine of sovereign immunity, it has suffered rather steady erosion as a legal principle. Legislative waivers of the right of the government not to be sued have been increasingly enacted, such as the Tucker Act of 1855 and the Federal Tort Claims Act of 1946, in which Congress consented to a variety of suits against the federal government. And in many states, the doctrine of sovereign immunity has been repudiated altogether or in part by either legislative or judicial action. Where it remains in effect, however, sovereign immunity prevents individuals from suing the government for damages as a result of injuries or harm inflicted by governmental action.

### SUITS FOR DAMAGES AGAINST GOVERNMENTAL OFFICERS

If the doctrine of sovereign immunity bars suits for damages by individuals directly against the government, a way around the doctrine is for the individual to sue not the government but the governmental officers responsible for the action that resulted in an injury to the individual's rights. Within the federal system, there are two sets of judicial remedies that may be pursued by individuals suing governmental officers for damages to redress violations of their rights. Under the common law as administered by the state courts, individuals can maintain tort actions for damages against governmental officers who violate their rights in the state courts.

If federal constitutional rights are violated by governmental officers, there are in addition damage remedies that may be pursued in the federal courts. State officers who, acting under the authority of their offices, violate the rights protected by the Fourteenth Amendment of the Constitution may be sued for damages under Title 42 of the United States Code, Section 1983. Federal officers who violate constitutional rights may be sued under the general federal question jurisdiction of the federal courts. The federal courts may also of course issue injunctions against both federal or state officials who are threatening to violate an individual's rights but have not yet done so.

## THE ELEVENTH AMENDMENT AND SOVEREIGN IMMUNITY

The Eleventh Amendment to the Constitution, in conjunction with the doctrine of sovereign immunity, prohibits the federal courts from entertaining suits by individuals against the states. At first glance, therefore, it would appear that for a federal court to entertain a suit for damages against state officers under Section 1983 would violate the command of the Eleventh Amendment and the doctrine of sovereign immunity. In *Ex parte Young,* decided in 1908, however, the Supreme Court held that, when a state officer violates the federal Constitution, he is stripped of his official character and may be treated as a private individual for purposes of a suit in the federal courts. A suit against a state officer in such circumstances, the Court held, was not a suit against the state itself as prohibited by the Eleventh Amendment and sovereign immunity.

Although an injunction prohibiting state officers from taking certain actions effectively prevents the state itself from acting, the fiction of *Ex parte Young* is that the suit against the state officers in the federal court resulting in the issuance of an injunction is not a suit against the state as prohibited by the Eleventh Amendment and sovereign immunity. Similarly, suits for damages against state officers who violate federal rights are considered not to be barred by the Eleventh Amendment and sovereign immunity, since the suits are against the officers in their personal capacities and not against the states themselves.

*Ex parte Young* thus created one of the most useful fictions in American constitutional law, but problems arise when the federal courts forget the fiction of the *Young* case and realize that a suit against state officers is in reality a suit against the state. When the fiction of the *Young* case is not adhered to, the federal courts will hold that a suit against state officers is barred by the Eleventh Amendment and sovereign immunity, since such a suit is a suit against the state. The successful maintenance of suits for damages against state officers under Section 1983 thus depends upon the federal courts' adhering to the fiction of the *Young* case, and the federal courts are not always willing to do that.

## OFFICIAL IMMUNITY

While the useful fiction of *Ex parte Young* provides a way around the Eleventh Amendment and sovereign immunity, the doors of the federal courts may nevertheless still be closed to suits for damages against governmental officers under the doctrine of official immunity. Official immunity has been recognized under the common law, and under Supreme

Court decisions interpreting Section 1983, to mean that governmental officers performing certain types of functions are absolutely immune from suits for damages with regard to actions undertaken in the performance of their official duties. Other governmental officers, on the other hand, are held to have only a qualified or limited immunity in like situations. If a governmental officer has absolute immunity, he may not be sued for damages regardless of what kinds of injuries may occur as a consequence of his performance of his official duties. Those officers with only qualified or limited immunity may, in contrast, be sued for damages in appropriate cases.

Among those officials who have absolute immunity from damage suits for actions performed in their official capacities are judges, prosecutors, and legislators. The justification for extending immunity from damage suits to these kinds of officials is that the public interest is served by the fearless performance of their duty by these officials, and if they were subject to suits for damages, they might hesitate to take actions that the public interest requires. In a 1967 decision, *Pierson* v. *Ray,* the Supreme Court thus held that the traditionally recognized absolute immunity of judges prohibited suits for damages against state judges under Section 1983 in the federal courts. "It is a judge's duty to decide all cases within his jurisdiction that are brought before him, including controversial cases that arouse the most intense feelings in the litigants," the Court said. "His errors may be corrected on appeal, but he should not have to fear that unsatisfied litigants may hound him with litigation charging malice or corruption. Imposing such a burden on judges would contribute not to principled and fearless decision-making but to intimidation." In *Stump* v. *Sparkman,* decided in 1978, the Court thus held a state judge to be absolutely immune from a suit for damages under Section 1983 even though the judge had ordered a woman sterilized without her knowledge or consent.

Prosecutors have similarly been granted traditional immunity for their actions taken as a part of their prosecutorial responsibilities, and in *Imbler* v. *Pachtman* in 1976 the Supreme Court held that state prosecutors were immune from suits for damages under Section 1983. "Attaining the system's goal of accurately determining guilt or innocence requires that both the prosecution and the defense have wide discretion in the conduct of the trial and the presentation of evidence. . . ," the Court held. "If prosecutors were hampered in exercising their judgment as to the use of. . .witnesses by concern about resulting personal liability, the triers of fact in criminal cases often would be denied relevant evidence."

Under both the common law and Section 1983, legislators are also absolutely immune from suits for damages growing out of the performance of their legislative duties. The immunity of members of Congress is indeed constitutionally based, since Article I, Section 6, of the Constitution provides that "Senators and Representatives shall...in all Cases, except Treason, Felony and Breach of the Peace, be privileged from Arrest during their Attendance at the Session of their respective Houses, and in going to and returning from the same; and for any Speech or Debate in either House, they shall not be questioned in any other Place." And in *Tenny* v. *Brandhove,* decided in 1951, the Supreme Court extended a similar immunity from suits for damages under Section 1983 to state legislators. "One must not expect uncommon courage even in legislators," the Court said. "In times of political passion, dishonest and vindictive motives are readily attributed to legislative conduct and as readily believed. Courts are not the place for such controversies. Self-discipline and the voters must be the ultimate reliance for discouraging or correcting such abuses."

In contrast to the absolute official immunity that legislators, judges, and prosecutors enjoy, executive officers have traditionally not been accorded absolute immunity from damage suits by the courts. Police officers, for example, may be sued for damages, and if they cannot demonstrate that they acted in good faith and reasonably in the circumstances, they are liable for damages for their official actions.

The qualified or limited immunity from damage suits which the Court has recognized for executive officers, such as police officers, was nonetheless challenged in litigation growing out of the tragic shootings of students at Kent State University by the Ohio National Guard in May of 1970. The Kent State tragedy produced a substantial amount of litigation, both civil and criminal, in the state and federal courts. And in this litigation questions relating to the doctrine of political questions, sovereign immunity, and official immunity for executive officers were raised and explored by the courts. We shall now therefore examine the Kent State litigation in detail.

### CASE STUDY
### SUING THE BASTARDS
#### The *Kent State* Case

On the evening of April 30, 1970, President Richard Nixon announced to the nation that he had ordered United States troops into Cambodia. By thus widening the war in Indochina, the president further enraged a substantial portion of the public already strongly opposed to the war in Vietnam. Protests against Nixon's action quickly spread across the country and were particularly strong on college campuses.

At Kent State University, located in the city of Kent, Portage County, Ohio, the president's order of the invasion of Cambodia was protested peacefully throughout the day of May 1, but during the evening protesters inflicted about ten thousand dollars in property damages to approximately fifteen business buildings in downtown Kent. There was also some relatively minor property damage on the Kent State campus, two policemen were injured by rocks or other missiles, and fifteen protesters were arrested.

On May 2, an injunction was secured prohibiting any further damage or destruction of property, but the injunction did not prohibit assemblies or rallies. The mayor of Kent nevertheless requested that the governor of Ohio, James Rhodes, dispatch National Guard troops to Kent. Governor Rhodes had issued a proclamation on April 29 calling out the National Guard to assist local authorities in controlling violence associated with a wildcat truckers' strike in northeastern Ohio, and although the April 29 proclamation had not mentioned Portage County (where Kent State was located) nor campus violence, the governor apparently felt the proclamation sufficient to cover his dispatch of National Guard troops to Kent State. Under the terms of the proclamation, the adjutant general, Sylvester Del Corso, was given complete authority to use whatever National Guard units he wished "to take action necessary for the restoration of order throughout the State of Ohio" without consultation with civilian authorities. National Guard troops bivouacked at Akron, ten miles from Kent, were consequently put on alert.

Some Kent State University officials were aware of the mayor of Kent's request for National Guard troops, but they were under the impression that the troops were to be used for the maintenance of order in the city of Kent. No university official requested troops for the purpose of policing the campus. On the evening of May 2, however, a crowd of approximately one thousand persons gathered on the Kent State campus and marched on the ROTC building, and the building was subsequently set afire. Only after firemen arrived and were forced to withdraw did campus police disperse the crowd with the aid of tear gas. The mayor of Kent had meanwhile requested and obtained National Guard troops for the city of Kent, and after conferring with the mayor, Adjutant General Del Corso sent troops onto the Kent State campus. Using tear gas, the troops cleared and secured the campus by midnight. Del Corso had not consulted with nor received permission from any university official regarding the need of sending troops onto the campus. University officials, including Kent State president Robert White, assumed their authority over the campus had been preempted by the National Guard.

Governor Rhodes, who was engaged in a hotly contested primary election campaign for the U.S. Senate, arrived in Kent on Sunday, May 3, and held a news conference in which he vehemently denounced the perpetrators of the disorders on the Kent State campus. Rhodes allegedly compared the campus demonstrators to "brownshirts, nightriders and communists," and promised to "eradicate the problem." The governor's language was thus similar to that of President Nixon, who denounced those demonstrating against the Cambodian invasion as "bums." On the same day as the governor's press conference, the National Guard dispersed a crowd from the campus commons, an event that led to two hours of nonviolent demonstrations followed by some rock throwing, minor injuries, and additional arrests.

In response to Governor Rhodes's remarks, twenty-three "concerned faculty" members at Kent State issued a statement proclaiming that they "[h]ere and now repudiate the inflammatory inaccuracies expressed by Governor Rhodes in his press conference today. We urge him to remove the troops from our campus. No problem can be solved so long as the campus is under martial law. . . ." The faculty members also declared that the "appearance of armed troops on the campus of Kent State University is an appalling sight. Occupation of the town and campus by National Guardsmen is testimony to the domination of irrationality in the policies of our government."

"The President of the United States commits an illegal act of war and refers to his opposition as 'bums,'" the faculty statement continued. "That students and faculty and, indeed, all thinking people reject his position is not only rational but patriotic." The burning of the ROTC building on the campus was to be condemned, the statement said, but it also must be "viewed in the larger context of the daily burning of buildings and people by our government in Vietnam, Laos, and now Cambodia." There was only one course which would restore the faith of the American people in their leaders, the faculty members concluded: "The war must stop." And the constitutional "rights of all must be defended against any challenge, even from the Department of Justice itself. If Mr. Nixon instead continues his bankrupt, illegal course, the Congress must be called upon to impeach him."

## THE KILLINGS

On Monday, May 4, classes were held as scheduled at the university, but at about 11:45 A.M. five hundred persons gathered on the campus commons in a peaceful demonstration. The National Guard troop commander, Assistant Adjutant General Robert Canterbury, nonetheless ordered that the crowd be dispersed. The guardsmen were ordered to "lock and load" their weapons, which meant that the weapons had live ammunition in their chambers, ready to fire. The guardsmen also fixed bayonets and began dispersing the crowd on the commons by firing tear gas. During the following thirty minutes the air was filled with name-calling, tear gas, and rocks.

One group of guardsmen herded a part of the crowd past the administration building and down a hill onto a football practice field, where the guardsmen and demonstrators confronted one another and exchanged rocks and tear gas cannisters across a chain link fence. At one point, some of the guardsmen knelt and aimed their rifles at the demonstrators but did not fire. The guardsmen were finally ordered to return up the hill, but as they did so, members of Troop G, 107th Armored Calvary, turned back toward the football practice field and adjacent parking lot and began firing. Other guardsmen then also joined in the approximately eleven- to thirteen-second fusillade of about sixty shots.

Four Kent State students, Jeff Miller, Allison Krause, William Shroeder, and Sandy Scheuer, were killed, while nine other students were wounded, three seriously. Although some guardsmen subsequently claimed that they had felt their lives to be endangered, a Department of Justice summary of the findings of an FBI investigation of the shootings concluded that there had been no such justification for the shootings. The Justice Department summary noted that the bodies of those killed were found from 85 to 130 yards from the guardsmen, and that no student who was shot was closer than 20 yards from the guardsmen.

## THE INVESTIGATIONS

The tragedy at Kent State was subsequently the subject of an investigation by the President's Commission on Campus Unrest, which reported to the president on September 26, 1970. The commission concluded that the rally on the campus commons just prior to the shootings on May 4 had been peaceful, and that violence had occurred only after the National Guard had attempted to disperse the crowd, an action the legality of which the commission called "at least debatable." "The indiscriminate firing of rifles into a crowd of students and the deaths that followed," the commission concluded, "were unnecessary, unwarranted, and inexcusable."

The Kent State shootings were also extensively investigated by the FBI, which compiled some eight thousand pages of evidence. The Justice

Department's summary of this FBI evidence indicated that the National Guard had begun firing without having given any verbal warning to the students; that no permission was requested or given to any guardsman to fire his weapon; that the guardsmen were not surrounded when the firing began, nor had any guardsmen been hit by rocks immediately prior to the shootings; that, despite rumors to the contrary, there was no sniper on the campus and the guardsmen were not fired upon. "Aside entirely from any question of specific intent on the part of the Guardsmen or a predisposition to use their weapons," the Justice Department summary concluded, "we do not know what started the shooting."

An investigation by a state grand jury, on the other hand, came to rather different conclusions. At the direction of Governor Rhodes, the Ohio attorney general appointed three attorneys as special counsel to conduct a state grand jury investigation of the Kent State tragedy. The report of the state grand jury was written by the chief special counsel, Robert Balyeat, in collaboration with the foreman of the grand jury. The grand jury report absolved the National Guard of blame for the events at Kent State, although never directly mentioning the killings. Kent State University, the university administration, faculty, and students, on the other hand, were strongly condemned in the grand jury report.

"It should be made clear that we do not condone all of the activities of the National Guard on the Kent State University campus on May 4, 1970," the grand jury report said. "We find, however, that the members of the National Guard who were present on the hill adjacent to Taylor Hall on May 4, 1970, fired their weapons in the honest and sincere belief and under circumstances which would have logically caused them to believe that they would suffer serious bodily injury had they not done so. They are not, therefore, subject to criminal prosecution under the laws of this state for any death or injury resulting therefrom."

The grand jury, however, found the university's responsibility for the events of May 4 to be an entirely different matter. "The administration at Kent State University has fostered an attitude of laxity, over-indulgence, and permissiveness within its students and faculty," the grand jury said, "to the extent that it can no longer regulate the activities of either and is particularly vulnerable to any pressure applied from radical elements within the student body or faculty." One of the conditions that had led to the tragedy of May 4, the grand jury concluded, was the "over-emphasis which [the university] has placed and allowed to be placed on the right to dissent." "Although we fully recognize that the right of dissent is a basic freedom to be cherished and protected," the grand jury stated, "we cannot agree that the role of the University should be to continually foster a climate in which dissent becomes the order of the day to the exclusion of all normal behavior and expression."

The grand jury thus declared that "the major responsibility for the incidents occurring on the Kent State University campus on May 2nd, 3rd, and 4th rests clearly with those persons who are charged with the administration of the University." "The evidence presented to us," the grand jury continued, "has established that Kent State University was in such a state of disrepair, that it was totally incapable of reacting to the situation in any effective manner. We believe that it resulted from policies formulated and carried out by the University over a period of several years. . . ." The grand jury also concluded that the faculty statement issued in response to Governor Rhodes's news conference on May 3 had been an "irresponsible act" and that those issuing the statement bore some responsibility for "the tragic consequences of May 4, 1970."

## THE LITIGATION

In addition to issuing its report, the state grand jury also returned thirty indictments charging some forty-three offenses against twenty-five individuals. The charges consisted primarily of offenses such as arson, rioting, and inciting to riot, and of the twenty-five persons indicted, seventeen were indicted for offenses they were alleged to have committed on the day of the shootings, May 4.

During the grand jury's deliberations, the judges of the Portage County Court of Common Pleas issued injunctions prohibiting witnesses summoned by the grand jury from commenting on the grand jury's work and additionally prohibiting any demonstrations, picketing, distribution of leaflets, etc., in the area around the courthouse where the grand jury was meeting. The effect of these injunctions was to prohibit those most likely to be critical of the grand jury's investigation and report from commenting publicly on them, or demonstrating their disagreement through picketing or distributing leaflets in the vicinity of the courthouse. One of the special counsel representing the state was thus permitted to hold a press conference and present the grand jury's report to the news media, while Kent State president Robert White had to seek permission from the common pleas court to comment on the grand jury report. The court granted permission to White to hold two meetings on the report, but he was admonished to "refrain from any critical comment regarding the report of the special grand jury."

The report of the state grand jury and the gag orders accompanying the grand jury's deliberations caused two lawsuits to be filed in the U.S. District Court for the Northern District of Ohio. The first suit challenged the gag orders issued by the judges of the Portage County Court of

Common Pleas as violations of the freedom of expression guaranteed by the First and Fourteenth Amendments of the federal Constitution. And on November 3, 1970, U.S. District Judge Ben C. Green upheld these contentions and enjoined the further enforcement of the gag orders.

The gag orders, Judge Green held, prevented those persons with the most complete knowledge of the events at Kent State from "answering the social and philosophical arguments of the Grand Jury, which, in this Court's opinion, represent essentially but one side of the argument." Continuation of the gag orders, he said, would "muzzle the rights of debate and dissent guaranteed by the First Amendment of the United States Constitution." Judge Green additionally held that the ban on demonstrations, picketing, etc., around the Portage County courthouse was also violative of freedom of expression.

In the second suit filed in the U.S. district court relating to the grand jury's report, some of those indicted by the grand jury and some faculty members at Kent State sought injunctions against state authorities who were about to prosecute those indicted and also an injunction ordering the expunging of the grand jury's report from the records of the Portage County Court of Common Pleas. The U.S. district court refused to enjoin the prosecution of those indicted, holding that there had been no showing that the prosecutions were undertaken in bad faith or for purposes of harassment.

On the other hand, the district court found that the grand jury report declared some of those indicted to be guilty "beyond doubt," and also tended to inhibit free expression and academic freedom at Kent State. The report thus interfered with the right of those indicted to a fair trial under the Due Process Clause of the Fourteenth Amendment, the court held, as well as interfering with First Amendment rights. Under Ohio law, the court also found, grand juries were not authorized to issue the kind of report issued by the grand jury in this instance. Since the grand jury's report violated federal constitutional rights and was unauthorized by state law, the district court ordered that most of the report be expunged from the records of the Portage County Court of Common Pleas.

While the report of the state grand jury was thus expunged, the U.S. district court refused to enjoin the prosecution of those indicted by the grand jury. Of those indicted, two pleaded guilty, one was tried and found guilty of a misdemeanor related to the burning of the ROTC building at Kent State, and two were tried and acquitted. On December 7, 1971, the state entered a motion to dismiss the charges against the remaining twenty defendants indicted by the grand jury on the ground of lack of evidence. Included among those against whom the charges were dismissed were all seventeen persons indicted in connection with the events of May 4, the day of the shootings.

In contrast to these criminal proceedings initiated by the State of Ohio, U.S. Attorney General John Mitchell refused to convene a federal grand jury to investigate the Kent State shootings. By 1973, however, Elliott L. Richardson had become attorney general, and a new head of the Civil Rights Division of the Department of Justice, J. Stanley Pottinger, had been appointed, and Pottinger announced in August of 1973 that the Justice Department investigation of the Kent State shootings was being reopened.

As a result of the Department of Justice's reopened investigation, a federal grand jury was convened in Cleveland to evaluate the evidence related to the Kent State shootings. In March of 1974, the grand jury indicted eight members of the Ohio National Guard who had been at Kent State, charging them with acting under color of law with the willful intent to deprive the killed and wounded students of their federally protected rights. The grand jury indictment was based on Title 18, Section 242, of the United States Code, which makes it a criminal offense for anyone acting under color of state law to willfully deprive any person of his federally protected rights. In order to prosecute successfully under Section 242, the government must not only prove that a federally protected right has been violated by someone acting under color of state law, but it must also prove that the action was taken with the willful intent to deprive the individual affected of a federally protected right. In the Kent State case, therefore, the government was required to prove not only that the guardsmen, acting under state authority, had shot the students, but also that the guardsmen had shot the students with the specific intent of depriving them of their federal rights.

The trial of the guardsmen began on October 29, 1974, in the U.S. district court in Cleveland. When the government had concluded presenting its evidence against the defendants to the jury in early November, however, U.S. District Judge Frank J. Battisti granted a motion by the defendants' lawyers to dismiss the charges and to acquit the defendants. The government, Judge Battisti said, had failed to prove beyond a reasonable doubt that the guardsmen had acted with the willful intent to deprive the students of their federal rights. At best, the judge said, the evidence indicated that the guardsmen had used excessive and unjustified force with the intent of frightening or harming the students, but there was no evidence that the guardsmen had "any actively formulated intention to punish or otherwise deprive any students of their constitutional rights." While he was thus legally required to acquit the defendants, Judge Battisti declared that the "events at Kent State University were made up of a series of tragic blunders and mistakes of judgment," and he warned that it was "vital that state officials and National Guard officials not regard this decision as authorizing or approving the use of force against demonstrators, whatever the occasion or the issue involved. Such use of force is, and was, deplorable."

Assistant U.S. Attorney General Stanley Pottinger expressed disappointment with Judge Battisti's ruling, but he noted that the Department of Justice was "not disappointed with our efforts to see that justice was done." "The decision to reopen the case was right," Pottinger declared. "The grand jury's decision to indict was honest. The Department of Justice has done everything in its power to air the cause of this tragedy and to enforce the law. The court's ruling. . .ends the Federal Government's prosecution in the Kent State case."

Although the guardsmen could not be convicted of having willfully deprived the Kent State students of their federal rights, Judge Battisti suggested in his opinion granting the acquittal that state authorities "might wish to pursue criminal prosecutions against various persons responsible for the events at Kent State." The Ohio attorney general's response to Judge Battisti's suggestion indicated that a state prosecution of the guardsmen was highly unlikely. "I don't know what he's talking about," he said. "I'd have to read the [judge's] statement in its totality. After all, we've just defended [the guardsmen]." And James Rhodes, who had been reelected governor of Ohio, said of Judge Battisti's ruling, "Justice has prevailed." Despite Judge Battisti's suggestion, therefore, it was clear that the criminal proceedings involving the Kent State tragedy in either the state or the federal courts had come to an end.

## GILLIGAN v. MORGAN

The civil litigation arising out of the Kent State shootings, however, was far from over. On October 15, 1970, the American Civil Liberties Union filed suit in the U.S. district court on behalf of the president of the Kent State University student body, Craig Morgan, the vice-president of the student body, and the president pro tem of the student senate, as well as all Kent State students as a class. The suit sought an injunction prohibiting the governor of Ohio from using troops on the Kent State campus unless there was an actual invasion or absolute breakdown of civilian authority. The suit also sought an injunction prohibiting the governor of Ohio from using the National Guard in civilian disturbances "unless such troops have been competently trained in techniques of civilian disorder control, have been provided with the best available non-lethal equipment for use in civilian disorder control, have been specifically ordered and instructed not to use deadly force except in the case of actual self-defense or upon persons who have actually used or threatened the use of deadly force and have been ordered not to carry live ammunition loaded in their guns when engaged in such control of civilian disorders, and declaring the use of the Ohio National Guard troops contrary to these requirements to be unlawful."

The U.S. district court, however, dismissed the suit, and the U.S. Court of Appeals for the Sixth Circuit affirmed the dismissal in part, but remanded the case to the district court for consideration of the question of whether there was and continued to be "a pattern of training, weaponry and orders in the Ohio National Guard which singly or together require or make inevitable the use of fatal force in suppressing civilian disorders when the total circumstances at the critical time are such that lethal force is not reasonably necessary."

The State of Ohio, however, appealed the decision of the court of appeals to the Supreme Court, and the Court reversed the decision of the court of appeals in *Gilligan* v. *Morgan,* decided on June 21, 1973. Writing for the majority of the Court, Chief Justice Burger held that the order remanding the case to the district court would involve the district court in a nonjusticiable, political question and involve the federal judiciary in a continuing role of supervising the training of the Ohio National Guard. "It would be difficult to think of a clearer example of the type of governmental action that was intended by the Constitution to be left to the political branches, directly responsible—as the Judicial Branch is not—to the elective process," Burger said. "Moreover, it is difficult to conceive of an area of governmental activity in which the courts have less competence. The complex, subtle, and professional decisions as to the composition, training, equipping, and control of a military force are essentially professional military judgments, subject *always* to civilian control of the Legislative and Executive Branches. The ultimate responsibility for these decisions is appropriately vested in branches of the government which are periodically subject to electoral accountability."

## SOVEREIGN IMMUNITY AND THE STATE COURTS

The attempt to subject the future employment and training of the Ohio National Guard to federal judicial supervision thus failed, but this did not end the civil litigation related to the Kent State tragedy. Arthur Krause, the father of one of the slain students, Allison Krause, sued the State of Ohio for damages in the Court of Common Pleas of Cuyahoga County, but the court dismissed the suit on the ground that the state enjoyed sovereign immunity from suits for damages. The Court of Appeals for

Cuyahoga County, however, ruled that the action of the court of common pleas was unjustified, since the doctrine of sovereign immunity should no longer apply to the State of Ohio. "Governmental immunity," the court of appeals said, "is an anachronism. It represents a vestige of the ancient apotheosis of the state in the person of a king. That the king can do no wrong is a dubious concept in a nation whose very founding repudiated kings."

On appeal of this ruling by the state, however, the Ohio Supreme Court reversed the state court of appeals and held that the state enjoyed sovereign immunity from suits for damages under the state constitution, and that only the legislature or the people through a constitutional amendment could repeal sovereign immunity in Ohio. And in a concurring opinion, one of the judges of the Ohio Supreme Court condemned the decision of the court of appeals for having "unsettled the stability of Ohio law on sovereign immunity with the widespread publicity given to their misleading, unwarranted and erroneous opinion and judgment in newspapers, magazines, law journals, legal periodicals, and in the news media."

The result of this ruling by the Ohio Supreme Court was thus to close the doors of the Ohio courts to suits for damages against the State of Ohio itself regarding the events at Kent State University. Under Title 42 of the United States Code, Section 1983, however, suits either for damages or for injunctions may be maintained in the U.S. district courts against any person who, acting under color of state law, violates or is about to violate an individual's federally protected rights. Although the doctrine of sovereign immunity thus barred suits in the Ohio courts against the State of Ohio, Ohio officials remained subject to suits for violation of federal rights in the federal courts.

## SCHEUER v. RHODES

Accordingly, on September 8, 1970, the American Civil Liberties Union filed suit in the U.S. District Court for the Northern District of Ohio on behalf of Sarah Scheuer, mother and administratrix of the estate of Sandra Lee Scheuer, one of the students killed at Kent State. The complaint in the *Scheuer* case charged that Governor Rhodes, Kent State president Robert White, Ohio National Guard Adjutant General and Assistant Adjutant General Sylvester Del Corso and Robert Canterbury, and various officers and enlisted men of the Ohio National Guard had, "acting in concert and under color of state law, subjected, and caused to be subjected," Sandra Lee Scheuer to "the deprivation of rights, privileges and immunities secured by the Constitution and laws of the United States and the deprivation of life without due process of law" as guaranteed by the Fourteenth Amendment. Through their disposition and use of the Ohio National Guard troops at Kent State University, the complaint charged, the defendants had "intentionally, recklessly, wilfully and wantonly" violated Sandra Scheuer's federal rights. The U.S. district court was requested to adjudge one million dollars in compensatory damages against all the defendants and also to award "just and proper" punitive damages. In addition to the complaint in the *Scheuer* case, similar suits were filed in the U.S. district court on behalf of Arthur Krause, father and administrator of the estate of Allison Krause, and Elaine B. Miller, mother and administratrix of the estate of Jeffrey Glenn Miller, both of whom had also been killed on May 4 at Kent State.

Governor Rhodes and the other defendants subsequently filed motions to dismiss the suits against them on the grounds that the suits were barred by the doctrine of sovereign immunity and the Eleventh Amendment of the federal Constitution. It was apparent, the motion to dismiss on behalf of Governor Rhodes said, that Rhodes was being "sued in his capacity as Governor of the State of Ohio, and in that capacity, he is clothed with the immunity of the sovereign, the action being essentially against the State of Ohio, which has not in any manner consented to be sued by waiving its constitutional right to sovereign immunity." "Government can function only by uninhibited, fearless and honest exercise of the best judgment of its executives and administrators," the motion to dismiss continued. "If a Governor is to be subjected to civil liability for the far-flung and unpredictable consequences of his act in moving to avoid and suppress riotous conduct, the effect on government can only be chaotic."

Arguing against the defendants' motions to dismiss the suits against them, counsel for the plaintiffs pointed out to the court that the suits had arisen "out of one of the gravest tragedies in American history. Never before has this nation witnessed such a gruesome bloodletting on a college campus. Never before have members and officers of a state militia fired upon unarmed student civilians, wantonly inflicting death and injury without just cause." The Kent State cases, plaintiffs' counsel argued, therefore called "upon the Federal Judiciary to exercise its historic function of providing a place where issues involving the most basic rights of our people can be aired." "It is the practical need to encourage and provide redress in a court which underlies the Civil Rights Act [Section 1983], to provide a peaceful channel for the airing and resolution of our conflicts, no matter how fundamental they may be," counsel for the plaintiffs concluded. "Indeed, it is this kind of case—one which addresses itself to fundamentals—which the Civil Rights Act is designed to cover."

United States District Judge James C. Connell nevertheless sustained the defendants' motions to dismiss the cases on June 2, 1971, holding that the plaintiffs' suits were barred by sovereign immunity and the Eleventh Amendment. "The Eleventh Amendment to the United States Constitution prohibits this court from exercising jurisdiction in this case and this court so finds," Judge Connell said. "All defendants, including President White, are sued in their official capacities and sovereign immunity so extends. The...cases are dismissed as to all defendants." Judge Connell's decision to grant the defendants' motions to dismiss the cases was an example of a federal court's failure to heed the fiction of *Ex parte Young*, which had held that a suit against state officers for violating federal rights was not a suit against the state within the meaning of the Eleventh Amendment and the doctrine of sovereign immunity.

In ruling on the defendants' motions to dismiss, Judge Connell was of course also taking an action before any evidence had been offered to either prove or disprove the assertions of the plaintiffs that the defendants had wantonly violated federally protected rights. The general rule in the federal courts is therefore that, in ruling on motions to dismiss, federal judges should construe the facts alleged in the complaint favorably to the plaintiffs, and should grant a motion to dismiss only if, upon a construction of the facts most favorable to the plaintiffs, it still appears that the plaintiffs could not prevail if the case were tried. Judge Connell, however, in sustaining the defendants' motions to dismiss, appeared to rely upon facts favorable to the defendants, even though no evidence of any kind had been submitted to the court at this stage in the proceedings.

Judge Connell thus held in his opinion sustaining the motions to dismiss that Governor Rhodes "had determined in good faith that on the basis of the facts as they appeared that riot and mob rule existed at Kent State University" and that the emergency thus existing had compelled "the Governor to act decisively in suppressing this most dangerous activity, and the citizens of Ohio so demand it." "The purpose of the Eleventh Amendment is to enable the sovereign to act without fear of lawsuit in preventing mob action," Judge Connell continued. "Quelling riot is the duty of the state, and its actions in preventing an unrestrained mob bent on violating the rights of its citizens is the act of the State of Ohio." Judge Connell thus based his ruling at least in part on an assumption that Governor Rhodes had acted in "good faith" in the face of "riot" and "mob rule" at Kent State, despite the fact that no proof was before the court on the state of the governor's mind or conditions at Kent State when the National Guard had been ordered there.

Counsel for the plaintiffs challenged Judge Connell's decision to sustain the defendants' motions to dismiss in an appeal to the U.S. Court of

Appeals for the Sixth Circuit, but on November 17, 1972, the court of appeals affirmed Judge Connell's ruling. The court held that it was the duty of the executive departments of state governments to protect the "general public from domestic as well as foreign enemies." "It would not be conducive to good government to require the Chief Executive of either the nation or the state to defend himself in court, in a multitude of protracted actions, because he called out troops to suppress riots or disorders which resulted in injury," the court said. "It would surely take a hardy executive to exercise his discretion by calling out troops to suppress riot or insurrection, if he knew that in so doing the wisdom of his action could later be challenged in the courts. And since the courts have granted to themselves absolute immunity, it would seem incongruous for them not to extend the same privilege to the Executive."

"We hold," the court of appeals continued, "that the actions against the Governor, the officers of the National Guard, and the President of Kent State University, are in substance and effect actions against the State of Ohio. Suits against the State are prohibited by the Eleventh Amendment. The Governor, the officers of the Guard, and the President of Kent State University all have executive immunity." "We ought not to deter the Chief Executive of either the state or the nation in the *unflinching* performance of their duty to protect the public," the court concluded, "nor should we make their actions in this respect in times of emergency, subject to judicial review."

In a concurring opinion, Judge O'Sullivan charged the plaintiffs with "dissembling" and using "obvious contrivances" in their complaint against Governor Rhodes and the other defendants. And like Judge Connell in the district court, Judge O'Sullivan assumed facts which were not in the record or which had been subject to proof in the trial court. "I believe... that what had been going on at Kent State and its environs preceding the tragic deaths of these young people is so widely and publicly known across the nation that the Court may take judicial notice of such events...," he said. "The pleadings [in the plaintiffs' complaint] make no mention of the burning down of the ROTC building on the campus of the University and the continued threats to persons and property—all a part of a state of insurrection that preceded and continued up to the very instant of the tragedy with which we deal." "For the Governor of Ohio to have refused to send the National Guard to the scene of these events," Judge O'Sullivan concluded, "and for the Guard and its men to have refused to deal with the situation confronting them, would have been dereliction of duty."

Judge Celebrezze dissented from the decision of his colleagues on the court of appeals, and charged that the court's ruling on the Eleventh Amendment and executive immunity issues would "destroy Section 1983 as a tool by which federal courts are to guard against state interference with constitutional rights." "It is difficult to envision," Judge Celebrezze declared, "what, if any, remedy would remain under Section 1983 if, in addition to those persons who can bring themselves under legislative or judicial immunity, the broad class of persons who might be characterized as state executive officials is also immune from suit under the statute."

Having encountered yet another setback with the decision of the court of appeals, counsel for the plaintiffs filed a petition for a writ of certiorari in the U.S. Supreme Court seeking a reversal of that decision. Charging that both Judge Connell in the district court and at least Judge O'Sullivan in the court of appeals had assumed facts not in the record, counsel for the plaintiffs declared to the Supreme Court that it was "incredible that such blatant factual assertions are advanced by federal magistrates without the benefit of applicable sworn testimony, relying presumably instead upon presentations of this incident in the news media. Not only are these assertions legally incorrect, but they are factually incorrect. The fact that a lawsuit arises out of a controversial incident does not warrant a radical departure from the basic rule of law that on a motion to dismiss a complaint the allegations of that complaint must be assumed as true." "The real question presented here," counsel for the plaintiffs told the Court, "is whether in a matter as critical in our national life as the killing and wounding of students at Kent State University on May 4, 1970, there will be no legal avenue for redress because courts of review have made findings of fact based upon news media reports. . . . This case presents an outrageous record of judicial abuse, so shocking in magnitude that on this ground alone certiorari should be granted." The Supreme Court's response was to grant certiorari in *Scheuer* v. *Rhodes* on June 25, 1973, thus giving the plaintiffs another chance to win a day in court.

## THE SCHEUER CASE BEFORE THE SUPREME COURT

In urging the Supreme Court to reverse the decision of the court of appeals, counsel for the plaintiffs first pointed out that this decision was contrary to the Court's decision in *Ex parte Young* in 1908 on the issue of the Eleventh Amendment. In the *Young* decision, it was noted, the Court had held that a suit in a federal court for an injunction against a state official was not a suit against the state itself, which was barred by the Eleventh Amendment. "Thus, in 1908, the Supreme Court settled the law that a suit not naming the State as a party, which charges individual wrongdoing or deprivation of constitutional rights, is not a suit against the State," counsel for the plaintiffs said. "This Court, and the lower courts have continued to recognize the viability of the 'fiction' created by *Ex parte Young....*" Both the district court and the court of appeals had therefore been incorrect, plaintiffs' counsel contended, in their rulings that the suits against Governor Rhodes and the other defendants were barred by the Eleventh Amendment.

Counsel for Governor Rhodes and the other defendants replied that *Ex parte Young* was inapplicable to the facts in *Scheuer* v. *Rhodes*. The *Young* case, it was argued, involved a suit for an injunction against a state official who had no authority from the state to enforce an unconstitutional statute, while Governor Rhodes and the other defendants in the *Scheuer* case had "acted at Kent State University pursuant to statutory authority not challenged as being repugnant to the Federal Constitution." Unlike the *Young* case, therefore, the defendants in the *Scheuer* case had authority from the state to act, and the *"Ex parte Young* rule is not relevant to the Eleventh Amendment issue now before this Court." The district court and the court of appeals, it was thus argued, had properly disregarded *Ex parte Young* in holding the *Scheuer* case to be barred by the Eleventh Amendment.

The alternative basis for the decisions of the district court and court of appeals—that Governor Rhodes and the other defendants sued in the *Scheuer* case were clothed with executive immunity—was also vigorously attacked by the counsel for the plaintiffs. The theory of the suit against Rhodes and the other defendants, it was noted, was grounded on the contention that the Fourteenth Amendment protected individuals from being deprived of life without due process of law. The killing of the Kent State students thus involved the violation of their federal rights and justified a suit for damages under Section 1983, which conferred jurisdiction on the federal courts to entertain suits for damages or injunctions against state officials who violated federally protected rights. If the decisions of the district court and the court of appeals, holding that state executive officials were absolutely immune from suits for damages in such situations, were upheld by the Court, counsel for the plaintiffs argued, such a ruling would "work a *pro tanto* repeal of that provision of [Section 1983] which specifically authorizes liability 'to the party injured in an action at law,' i.e., money damages from the wrongdoer."

For the Court to hold that state executive officials had absolute immunity from suits for damages for violation of federal constitutional rights, plaintiffs' attorneys contended, would also involve "a profound policy conclusion which this Court should not embrace." That policy conclusion would be that *"in all circumstances,* affording governmental officials freedom from the restraint of potential liability for misconduct of even the worst kind in office is a higher value than the value or interest of individuals sought to be protected by the substantive provisions of the Constitution opposed to it," counsel pointed out. "In this case, to uphold the court of appeals' decision, the Court must categorize the individual's interest in not being deprived of life without due process of law as of lesser importance than the freedom of government officials to act without restraint. If it does so, the Court will erect a value judgment over the framers of the Constitution, who chose to erect a right to be free of arbitrary taking of life as part of the...Fourteenth [Amendment] and nowhere mentioned officials' freedom from suit as one of the inviolate tenets of our governmental system."

Replying to this attack on absolute executive immunity, the attorneys for Governor Rhodes and the other Ohio officials relied on the decisions of the Court in which it had held that state legislators and judges were immune from suits for damages under Section 1983 and argued that a similar immunity should be conferred upon state executive officials. If the Court ruled in favor of the plaintiffs, it was argued, state executive officials "in the future would find themselves subject to the whims of a vindictive plaintiff's pen, while the judge who rules upon their cases and the legislator who creates the laws under which they act would be immune."

The public interest would be best served, counsel for the defendants continued, by an executive immunity from harassing lawsuits. Otherwise, the bold, courageous executive action upon which the public was dependent would be inhibited by the fear of suits for damages. "If in times of insurrection and emergency demanding discretionary acts, Ohio's public officials, functioning under their unchallenged obligation to the state, could, at the stroke of a vindictive plaintiff's pen, be subjected to the threats of hindsight and *ex post facto* speculation, Ohio would be hard pressed to find responsible officials to act," the defendants' counsel concluded. "This reality, manifest in the trial court and the court of appeals, prohibited the federal courts from acquiring subject matter jurisdiction over [the defendants'] actions. If this Court were to determine the doctrine of executive immunity not available to shield Ohio's executive officials from the inevitable lawsuits, the adverse effects upon the State become even more demonstrable."

The *Scheuer* case was argued on December 4, 1973, and on April 17, 1974, the Court announced its unanimous opinion holding that state executive officers were not entitled to absolute immunity.

*Scheuer* v. *Rhodes*

416 U.S. 232. Argued December 4, 1973. Decided April 17, 1974.

Mr. Chief Justice Burger delivered the opinion of the Court.

We granted certiorari in these cases to resolve whether the District Court correctly dismissed civil damage actions, brought under 42 USC Sec. 1983. . . , on the ground that these actions were, as a matter of law, against the State of Ohio, and hence barred by the Eleventh Amendment to the Constitution and, alternatively, that the actions were against state officials who were immune from liability for the acts alleged in the complaints. These cases arise out of the same period of alleged civil disorder on the campus of Kent State University in Ohio during May 1970 which was before us, in another context, in Gilligan v. Morgan. . . .

In these cases the personal representatives of the estates of three students who died in that episode seek damages against the Governor, the Adjutant General, and his assistant, various named and unnamed officers and enlisted members of the Ohio National Guard, and the president of Kent State University. The complaints in both cases allege a cause of action under the Civil Rights Act of 1871, 42 USC Sec. 1983. . . .

The District Court dismissed the complaints for lack of jurisdiction over the subject matter on the theory that these actions, although in form against the named individuals, were, in substance and effect, against the State of Ohio and thus barred by the Eleventh Amendment. The Court of Appeals affirmed the action of the District Court, agreeing that the suit was in legal effect one against the State of Ohio and, alternatively, that the common-law doctrine of executive immunity barred action against the state officials who are respondents here. . . . We are confronted with the narrow threshold question whether the District Court properly dismissed the complaints. We hold that dismissal was inappropriate at this stage of the litigation and accordingly reverse the judgments and remand for further proceedings. We intimate no view on the merits of the allegations since there is no evidence before us at this stage.

The complaints in these cases are not identical but their thrust is essentially the same. In essence, the defendants are alleged to have "intentionally, recklessly, willfully and wantonly" caused an unnecessary deployment of the Ohio National Guard on the Kent State campus and, in the same manner, ordered the Guard members to perform allegedly illegal actions which resulted in the death of plaintiffs' decedents. Both complaints allege that the action was taken "under color of state law" and that it deprived the decedents of their lives and rights without due process of law. Fairly read, the complaints allege that each of the named defendants, in undertaking such actions, acted either outside the scope of his respective office or, if within the scope, acted in an arbitrary manner, grossly abusing the lawful powers of office.

The complaints were dismissed by the District Court for lack of jurisdiction without the filing of an answer to any of the complaints. The only pertinent documentation before the court in addition to the complaints were two proclamations issued by the respondent Governor. The first proclamation ordered the Guard to duty to protect against violence arising from wildcat strikes in the trucking industry; the other recited an account of the conditions prevailing at Kent State University at that time. In dismissing these complaints for want of subject matter jurisdiction at that early stage, the District Court held, as we noted earlier, that the defendants were being sued in their official and representative capacities and that the actions were therefore in effect against the State of Ohio. The primary question presented is whether the District Court acted prematurely and hence erroneously in dismissing the complaints on the stated ground, thus precluding any opportunity for the plaintiffs by subsequent proof to establish a claim.

When a federal court reviews the sufficiency of a complaint, before the reception of any evidence either by affidavit or admissions, its task is necessarily a limited one. The issue is not whether a plaintiff will ultimately prevail but whether the claimant is entitled to offer evidence to support the claims. Indeed it may appear on the face of the pleadings that a recovery is very remote and unlikely but that is not the test. Moreover, it is well established that, in passing on a motion to dismiss, whether over the subject matter or for failure to state a cause of action, the allegations of the complaint should be construed favorably to the pleader.

"In appraising the sufficiency of the complaint we follow, of course, the accepted rule that a complaint should not be dismissed for failure to state a claim unless it appears beyond doubt that the plaintiff can prove no set of facts in support of his claim which would entitle him to relief". . . .

The Eleventh Amendment to the Constitution of the United States provides: "The Judicial power of the United States shall not be construed to extend to any suit in law or equity, commenced or prosecuted against one of the United States by Citizens of another State. . . ." It is well established that the Amendment bars suits not only against the State when it is the named party but also when it is the party in fact. . . .

However, since Ex parte Young. . . , it has been settled that the Eleventh Amendment provides no shield for a state official confronted by a claim that he had deprived another of a federal right under the color of state law. Ex parte Young teaches that when a state officer acts under a state law in a manner violative of the Federal Constitution, he "comes into conflict with the superior authority of that Constitution, and he is in that case stripped of his official or representative character and is subjected *in his person* to the consequences of his individual conduct. The State has no power to impart to him any immunity from responsibility to the supreme authority of the United States". . . .

Ex parte Young. . .involved a question of the federal courts' injunctive power, not, as here, a claim for monetary damages. While it is clear that the doctrine of Ex parte Young is of no aid to a plaintiff seeking damages from the public treasury, . . .damages against individual defendants are a permissible remedy in some circumstances notwithstanding the fact that they hold public office. . . . In some situations a damage remedy can be as effective a redress for the infringement of a constitutional right as injunctive relief might be in another.

Analyzing the complaints in light of these precedents, we see that petitioners allege facts that demonstrate they are seeking to impose individual and personal liability on the *named defendants* for what they claim—but have not yet established by proof—was a deprivation of federal rights by these defendants under color of state law. Whatever the plaintiffs may or may not be able to establish as to the merits of their allegations, their claims, as stated in the complaints, given the favorable reading required by the Federal Rules of Civil Procedure, are not barred by the Eleventh Amendment. Consequently, the District Court erred in dismissing the complaints for lack of jurisdiction.

The Court of Appeals relied upon the existence of an absolute "executive immunity" as an alternative ground for sustaining the dismissal of the complaints by the District Court. If the immunity of a member of the executive branch is absolute and comprehensive as to all acts allegedly performed within the scope of official duty, the Court of Appeals was correct; if, on the other hand, the immunity is not absolute but rather one that is qualified or limited, an executive officer may or may not be subject to liability depending on all the circumstances that may be revealed by evidence. The concept of the immunity of government officers from personal liability springs from the same root considerations that generated the doctrine of sovereign immunity. While the latter doctrine—that the "King can do no wrong"—did not protect all government officers from personal liability, the common law soon recognized the necessity of permitting officials to perform their official functions free from the threat of suits for personal liability. This official immunity apparently rested, in its genesis, on two mutually dependent rationales: (1) the injustice, particularly in the absence of bad faith, of subjecting to liability an officer who is required, by the legal obligations of his position, to exercise discretion; (2) the danger that the threat of such liability would deter his willingness to execute his office with the decisiveness and the judgment required by the public good.

In this country, the development of the law of immunity for public officials has been the product of constitutional provision as well as legislative and judicial processes. The Federal Constitution grants absolute immunity to Members of both Houses of the Congress with respect to any speech, debate, vote, report or action done in session. . . . This provision was intended to secure for the Legislative Branch of the Government the freedom from executive and judicial encroachment which had been secured in England in the Bill of Rights of 1689 and carried to the original Colonies. . . . Immunity for the other two branches—long a creature of the common law—remained committed to the common law. . . .

Although the development of the general concept of immunity, and the mutations which the underlying rationale has undergone in its application to various positions are not matters of immediate concern here, it is important to note, even at the outset, that one policy consideration seems to pervade the analysis: the public interest requires decisions and action to enforce laws for the protection of the public. . . . Public officials, whether governors, mayors or police, legislators or judges, who fail to make decisions when they are needed or who do not act to implement decisions when they are made do not fully and faithfully perform the duties of their offices. Implicit in the idea that officials have some immunity—absolute or qualified—for their acts, is a recognition that they may err. The concept of immunity assumes this and goes on to assume that it is better to risk some error and possible injury from such error than not to decide or act at all. . . .

For present purposes we need determine only whether there is an absolute immunity, as the Court of Appeals determined, governing the specific allegations of the complaint against the chief executive officer of a State, the senior and subordinate officers and enlisted personnel of that State's National Guard, and the president of a state-controlled university. If the immunity is qualified, not absolute, the scope of that immunity will necessarily be related to facts as yet not established either by affidavits, admissions or a trial record. Final resolution of this question must take into account the functions and responsibilities of these particular defendants in their capacities as officers of the state government, as well as the purposes of 42 USC Sec. 1983. . . .In neither of these inquiries do we write on a clean slate. It can hardly be argued, at this late date, that under no circumstances can the officers of state government be subject to liability under this statute. In Monroe v. Pape. . . , Mr. Justice Douglas, writing for the Court, held that the section in question was meant "to give a remedy to parties deprived of constitutional rights, privileges and immunities by an official's abuse of his position". . . . Through the Civil Rights statutes, Congress intended "to enforce provisions of the Fourteenth Amendment against those who carry a badge of authority of a State and represent it in some capacity, whether they act in accordance with their authority or misuse it". . . .

Since the statute relied on thus included within its scope the " '[m] isuse of power, possessed by virtue of state law and made possible only because the wrongdoer is clothed with the authority of state law,' ". . .government officials, as a class, could not be totally exempt, by virtue of some absolute immunity, from liability under its terms. Indeed, as the Court also indicated in Monroe v. Pape. . .the legislative history indicates that there is no absolute immunity. Soon after Monroe v. Pape, Mr. Chief Justice Warren noted in Pierson v. Ray. . .that the "legislative record [of Sec. 1983] gives no clear indication that Congress meant to abolish wholesale all common-law immunities". . . . The Court had previously recognized that the Civil Rights Act of 1871 does not create civil liability for legislative acts by legislators "in a field where legislators traditionally have power to act. . . ."

In similar fashion, Pierson v. Ray. . .examined the scope of judicial immunity under this statute. . . .the Court concluded that, had the Congress intended to abolish the common-law "immunity of judges for acts within the judicial role". . .it would have done so specifically. . . .

The Pierson Court was also confronted with whether immunity was available to that segment of the executive branch of state government that is most frequently and intimately involved in day-to-day contacts with the citizenry and, hence, most frequently exposed to situations which can give rise to claims under Sec. 1983—the local police officer. . . . The Court noted that the "common law has never granted police officers an absolute and unqualified immunity,". . .but that "the prevailing view in this country [is that] a peace officer who arrests someone with probable cause is not liable for false arrest simply because the innocence of the suspect is later proved". . . .the Court went on to observe that a "policeman's lot is not so unhappy that he must choose between being charged with dereliction of duty if he does not arrest when he has probable cause, and being mulcted in damages if he does". . . .

When a court evaluates police conduct relating to an arrest its guideline is "good faith and probable cause". . . . In the case of higher officers of the executive branch, however, the inquiry is far more complex since the range of decisions and choices—whether the formulation of policy, of legislation, of budgets, or of day-to-day decisions—is virtually infinite. In common with police officers, however, officials with a broad range of duties and authority must often act swiftly and firmly at the risk that action deferred will be futile or constitute virtual abdication of office. Like legislators and judges, these officers are entitled to rely on traditional sources for the factual information on which they decide and act. When a condition of civil disorder in fact exists, there is obvious need for prompt action, and decisions must be made in reliance on factual information supplied by others. While both federal and state laws plainly contemplate the use of force when the necessity arises, the decision to invoke military power has traditionally been viewed with suspicion and skepticism since it often involves the temporary suspension of some of our most cherished rights—government by elected civilian leaders, freedom of expression, of assembly, and of association. Decisions in such situations are more likely than not to arise in an atmosphere of confusion, ambiguity, and swiftly moving events and when, by the very existence of some degree of civil disorder, there is often no consensus as to the appropriate remedy. In short, since the options which a chief executive and his principal subordinates must consider are far broader and far more subtle than those made by officials with less responsibility, the range of discretion must be comparably broad. . . .

These considerations suggest that, in varying scope, a qualified immunity is available to officers of the executive branch of government, the variation being dependent upon the scope of discretion and responsibilities of the office and all the circumstances as they reasonably appeared at the time of the action on which liability is sought to be based. It is the existence of reasonable grounds for the belief formed at the time and in light of all the circumstances, coupled with good-faith belief, that affords a basis for qualified immunity of executive officers for acts performed in the course of official conduct. . . .

Under the criteria developed by precedents of this court, Sec. 1983 would be drained of meaning were we to hold that the acts of a governor or other high executive officer have "the quality of a supreme and unchangeable edict, overriding all conflicting rights of property and unreviewable through the judicial power of the Federal Government". . . . In Sterling [v. Constantin], Mr. Chief Justice Hughes put it in these terms: "If this extreme position could be deemed to be well taken, it is manifest that the fiat of a state Governor, and not the Constitution of the United States, would be the supreme law of the land; that the restrictions of the Federal Constitution upon the exercise of state power would be but impotent phrases, the futility of which the State may at any time disclose by the simple process of transferring powers of legislation to the Governor to be exercised by him, beyond control, upon his assertion of necessity. Under our system of government, such a conclusion is obviously untenable. There is no such avenue of escape from the paramount authority of the Federal Constitution. When there is a substantial showing that the exertion of state power has overriden private rights secured by that

Constitution, the subject is necessarily one for judicial inquiry in an appropriate proceeding directed against the individuals charged with the transgression. . . ."

Gilligan v. Morgan, by no means indicates a contrary result. Indeed, there we specifically noted that we neither held nor implied "that the conduct of the National Guard is always beyond judicial review or that there may not be accountability in a judicial forum for violations of law or for specific unlawful conduct by military personnel, whether by way of damages or injunctive relief". . . .

These cases, in their present posture, present no occasion for a definitive exploration of the scope of immunity available to state executive officials nor, because of the absence of a factual record, do they permit a determination as to the applicability of the foregoing principles to the respondents here. The District Court acted before answers were filed and without any evidence other than the copies of the proclamations issued by respondent Rhodes and brief affidavits of the Adjutant General and his assistant. In dismissing the complaints, the District Court and the Court of Appeals erroneously accepted as a fact the good faith of the Governor, and took judicial notice that "mob rule existed at Kent State University." There was no opportunity afforded petitioners to contest the facts assumed in that conclusion. There was no evidence before the courts from which such a finding of good faith could be properly made and, in the circumstances of these cases, such a dispositive conclusion could not be judicially noticed. We can readily grant that a declaration of emergency by the chief executive of a State is entitled to great weight but it is not conclusive. . . .

The documents properly before the District Court at this early pleading stage specifically placed in issue whether the Governor and his subordinate officers were acting within the scope of their duties under the Constitution and laws of Ohio; whether they acted within the range of discretion permitted the holders of such office under Ohio law and whether they acted in good faith both in proclaiming an emergency and as to the actions taken to cope with the emergency so declared. Similarly, the complaints place directly in issue whether the lesser officers and enlisted personnel of the Guard acted in good-faith obedience to the orders of their superiors. Further proceedings, either by way of summary judgment or by trial on the merits, are required. The complaining parties are entitled to be heard more fully than is possible on a motion to dismiss a complaint.

We intimate no evaluation whatever as to the merits of the petitioners' claims or as to whether it will be possible to support them by proof. We hold only that, on the allegations of their respective complaints, they were entitled to have them judicially resolved.

The judgments of the Court of Appeals are reversed and the cases are remanded for further proceedings consistent with this opinion.

It is so ordered.

Mr. Justice Douglas took no part in the decision of these cases.

The Supreme Court thus rejected the proposition that state executive officials were absolutely immune from suits for damages for their actions, holding rather that executive officials were entitled only to a qualified immunity. In "varying scope, a qualified immunity is available to officers of the executive branch of government, the variation being dependent upon the scope of discretion and responsibilities of the office and all the circumstances as they reasonably appeared at the time of the action on which liability is sought to be based," the Court had held. "It is the existence of reasonable grounds for the belief formed at the time and in light of all the circumstances, coupled with good-faith belief, that affords a basis for qualified immunity of executive officers for acts performed in the course of official conduct."

As the Court's opinion indicated, the plaintiffs were entitled to attempt to prove whether Governor Rhodes and the other defendants had been acting beyond the scope of their duties under Ohio law, whether they had acted beyond the range of discretion of their offices under Ohio law, whether they had acted in bad faith, and whether the members of the National Guard had not acted in good faith obedience to the orders of their superiors. Although the Court's decision in the *Scheuer* case did not necessarily require a trial of these issues, on remand to the district court a jury trial was in fact ordered. The legislature of Ohio appropriated $850,000 to be used in the defense of the defendants, and the trial lasted almost four months during the spring and summer of 1975. At its conclusion, the jury returned verdicts favorable to Governor Rhodes and the other defendants.

As the trial was reaching its conclusion, however, one of the jurors reported to the court that he had been threatened and even assaulted by a person pressuring him to vote a certain way in the case. The juror also reported that he had received threats that his house would be blown up if he failed to vote correctly. The response of the trial judge was to inform the entire jury of the threats and to sequester the jury for the remainder of the trial. Although the trial judge had assured counsel for the plaintiffs and the defendants that he would excuse the threatened juror, he did not do so, with the result that the threatened juror participated in the decision of the case. "I feel," the trial judge said, "even though he was approached and threatened something was going to happen, being assured that protection was forthcoming, he no longer has to consider that, and I am quite sure that he will be able to put these extraneous things out of his mind and decide the case on the basis of the law and the evidence."

The plaintiffs challenged the validity of the verdict in an appeal to the U.S. Court of Appeals for the Sixth Circuit, and on September 12, 1977, the court of appeals reversed the verdict. The court of appeals pointed out that the general rule was that private communications between jurors and third parties regarding the subject matter of a trial invalidated a verdict, unless such communications were shown to be harmless. And the court pointed out that the trial judge had not questioned the threatened juror to determine if his judgment would be affected by the threats, nor had the judge attempted to determine the effect of the threats on the other jurors.

"The intrusion in this case represents an attempt to pervert our system of justice at its very heart," the court of appeals said. "No litigant should be required to accept the verdict of a jury which has been subjected to such an intrusion in the absence of a hearing and determination that no probability exists that the jury's deliberations or verdict would be affected." "Although we are reluctant to do so, particularly in the face of the obvious good faith efforts of the trial judge to deal with a most difficult problem which arose near the conclusion of an exhausting trial," the court of appeals continued, "we conclude that reversal for a new trial is required."

Petitions for a rehearing and for a rehearing *en banc* in the Kent State case were rejected by the court of appeals. A petition for a writ of certiorari was thereupon filed in the U.S. Supreme Court seeking its review of the case, but the Court denied certiorari on March 20, 1978. The result was that the Kent State litigation was back where it had begun with the filing of the original complaints in September of 1970.

As a result of the court of appeals's decision, a new trial in the Kent State case was begun in December of 1978, but on January 4, 1979, it was announced that the plaintiffs and the defendants had agreed to a settlement of the case. The State of Ohio agreed to pay the plaintiffs $675,000 to settle the case, and Governor Rhodes and twenty-seven National Guard officers and men issued what an American Civil Liberties Union attorney called a "formal apology." In the statement Governor Rhodes and the guardsmen expressed deep regret regarding the shooting of the students at Kent State. "Hindsight suggests that another method would have resolved the confrontation," the statement said. "Better ways must be found to deal with such confrontations."

The American Civil Liberties Union applauded the settlement of the Kent State case, pointing out that the "admission of wrongdoing will make a difference the next time there is a confrontation between police and citizens exercising their rights." And the plaintiffs also issued a statement noting that one of the objectives of the litigation had been to hold the State of Ohio responsible for the shootings. "The State of Ohio, although protected by the doctrine of sovereign immunity and consequently not legally responsible in a technical sense," the plaintiffs said, "has now recognized its responsibility by paying a substantial amount of money in damages." Another objective of the litigation, the plaintiffs said, was "to demonstrate that the excessive use of force by the agents of government would be met by a formidable citizen challenge." "We have learned through a tragic event," the plaintiffs concluded, "that loyalty to our nation and its principles sometimes requires resistance to our government and its policies—a lesson many young people, including the children of some of us, had learned earlier."

Not everyone, however, was satisfied with the outcome of the Kent State litigation. Elaine Miller Holstein, mother of Jeffrey Miller, who had been killed at Kent State, remained embittered. "No amount of settlement is enough for me, because there is only one thing that can satisfy me," she said. "How can I replace my son? The state and the governor can pay their money, but it is little comfort—none really. I guess you could say I've had my faith shaken."

Most of the money from the settlement was given to Dean Kahler, who was paralyzed and confined to a wheelchair as a result of being wounded by the guardsmen at Kent State. "Since that time, I have tried my hardest to understand something out of all of it," Kahler said. "And I think that I have changed to where I can forgive." Kahler had graduated from Kent State in 1977 and was employed by the Industrial Commission of Ohio as a consultant on the handicapped. "I will use [the money from the settlement] to survive," he said. "If the money helps me to live a little longer, then that will be a little longer that I have to understand life around me." "I want to live," Kahler concluded. "I want to be an old man."

Since the Court's decision in *Scheuer* v. *Rhodes,* it has continued to apply the standard of qualified immunity to various state executive officials who have been sued for damages under Section 1983. The *Scheuer* standard of qualified immunity has thus been held to be applicable to school administrators and school board members, to a superintendent of a state hospital, and to prison administrators. Officials serving on state parole boards, which must decide whether to release individuals on parole from prison, the Court has held on the other hand, may be given by the states complete immunity from suits for damages arising out of the actions of individuals they have paroled.

## SUITS AGAINST FEDERAL OFFICERS

Although the *Scheuer* v. *Rhodes* litigation arose under Section 1983, which is applicable only to state officers, the qualified immunity of executive officers enunciated by the Court in the *Scheuer* case has since been applied also to federal executive officers. In *Bivens* v. *Six Unknown Agents,* decided in 1971, the Supreme Court held that federal officers who

violate the Fourth Amendment's prohibition of unreasonable searches and seizures could be sued for damages in the federal courts. And in *Butz* v. *Economou,* decided in 1978, the Court held that the qualified immunity of executive officers recognized in the *Scheuer* case was equally applicable to federal officers who are sued for damages for violations of constitutional rights.

In the absence of "congressional direction to the contrary, there is no basis for according to federal officials a higher degree of immunity from liability when sued for a constitutional infringement as authorized by Bivens than is accorded state officials when sued for the identical violation under Section 1983," the Court said in the *Butz* case. "The constitutional injuries made actionable by Section 1983 are of no greater magnitude than those for which federal officials may be responsible. The pressures and uncertainties facing decision makers in state government are little if at all different from those affecting federal officials." "We see no sense in holding a state governor liable," the Court continued, "but immunizing the head of a federal department; in holding the administrator of a federal hospital immune where the superintendent of a state hospital would be liable; in protecting the warden of a federal prison where the warden of a state prison would be vulnerable; or in distinguishing between state and federal police participating in the same investigation. Surely, *federal* officials should enjoy no greater zone of protection when they violate *federal* constitutional rules than do *state* officers." "To create a system," the Court concluded, "in which the Bill of Rights monitors more closely the conduct of state officials than it does that of federal officials is to stand the constitutional design on its head."

While applying the *Scheuer* principle of qualified immunity to federal executive officers in the *Butz* case, the Court nevertheless held that administrative officers exercising judicial powers, such as administrative law judges, were entitled to absolute immunity, since such officials exercised powers "comparable to those of a trial judge. . . ." Additionally, the Court held in the *Butz* case that administrative officers exercising powers analogous to those of a prosecutor should also have absolute immunity. The result of the *Butz* case was thus to apply the *Scheuer* standard of qualified immunity from damage suits to federal executive officers, but to extend to federal administrative officers exercising judicial or prosecutorial powers the absolute immunity traditionally enjoyed by prosecutors and judges in the judicial process.

# 2

## THE ADMINISTRATIVE EXERCISE OF JUDICIAL POWER
### Adjudication

The exercise of judicial power by administrative agencies is called adjudication. Whereas rule making by administrative agencies involves the making of policy applicable to relatively large segments of the population, adjudication usually involves the application of administrative policy to an individual or a relatively small group of individuals based upon facts peculiar to those individuals. The result of the administrative resort to rule making is a rule or regulation; the result of an administrative adjudication is an "order" which normally directs an individual or group of individuals to perform or not to perform certain actions.

Just as legislatures were constrained to delegate legislative, rule-making powers to administrative agencies in light of the complexity of the problems of modern governmental regulation, it was also found to be convenient to delegate judicial powers to the agencies as well. Among the most important reasons for the delegation of judicial power to administrative agencies are these: (1) the volume of cases arising under contemporary governmental programs, which is so great that the regular law courts would be overwhelmed if all such cases had to be resolved via the judicial process; (2) the feeling that the rather inflexible and slow-moving procedures of the law courts were ill adapted to the processing of the great volume of administrative cases requiring adjudication and that more flexible and speedier procedures for the processing of these cases could be obtained in the administrative process; (3) the judgment that law court judges, being generalists, were not sufficiently versed in the complexities of administrative programs and that therefore administrative adjudication would be informed by an expertise unavailable in the regular law courts; and (4), at least until the 1930s, the belief among supporters of many innovative administrative programs that the courts were bastions of laissez faire conservatism and were thus hostile to progressive governmental programs, and that therefore the enforcement of such programs must be placed in the hands of administrative agencies rather than in the hands of the law courts.

A traditional criticism of the delegation of judicial power to administrative agencies is that, as modern agencies evolved, they came to possess not only judicial power but also legislative and executive powers; and that the agencies thus had the power not only to declare legislatively what the law was and to enforce their declarations of law through prosecutorial proceedings, but also the power to adjudicate the cases that they themselves brought against violators of agency-made law. Given the fact that, in the exercise of their judicial powers, agencies were judging—in cases brought by the agencies themselves—whether or not violations of their own regulations had occurred, critics have argued that individuals could not possibly obtain fair hearings in agency adjudicatory proceedings.

Despite such arguments, the courts have readily upheld congressional delegations of judicial power to administrative agencies. In addition to the judicial power conferred upon the federal courts under Article III of the Constitution, the courts have held, Congress may create and delegate judicial power under Article I of the Constitution. And while Article III judicial power may be exercised only by judges possessing life tenure, Article I judicial power may be conferred upon non-life tenured officials such as those employed by administrative agencies. The source of the adjudicative power of federal administrative agencies is therefore Article I rather than Article III of the Constitution.

In creating and delegating judicial power under Article I, Congress has generally opted, not to create a system of administrative courts, but rather to delegate judicial power to administrative agencies. Exceptions to this generalization are the Court of Military Appeals and the Tax Court, specialized courts hearing appeals arising under the Uniform Code of Military Justice and the internal revenue code respectively. Administrative adjudicative power in the United States is nonetheless typically exercised by institutions organized along the bureaucratic lines of administrative agencies rather than along the lines of the judiciary.

## ADMINISTRATIVE ADJUDICATION AND THE RIGHT TO A HEARING

One of the key questions of administrative law in relation to the administrative exercise of judicial power is when and under what circumstances an individual is entitled to a hearing as a part of the adjudicative process. The right to a hearing as a part of administrative adjudication may be provided for by statute or it may be required by the Constitution. In creating an administrative agency, and conferring upon it adjudicative power, Congress frequently requires by statute that the adjudicative power possessed by the agency may be exercised only after the agency has extended a hearing to affected individuals.

The Constitution, on the other hand, also requires in many instances that agencies must hold hearings in the exercise of their powers of adjudication. The sources of the constitutional right to a hearing are the Due Process Clauses of the Fifth and Fourteenth Amendments. The Due Process Clauses provide that no person shall be deprived of life, liberty, or property without due process of law, and the courts have held in many instances that agencies in exercising their adjudicative powers must afford individuals a hearing in order to comply with due process of law.

On the other hand, the courts have also traditionally interpreted the content of procedural due process flexibly, varying the procedures that must be followed by the government according to the nature of the governmental action involved and the likely impact that action will have upon the individual. How elaborate a hearing may be required by due process will thus vary considerably depending upon the kind of governmental action involved. Due process, for example, requires a very elaborate hearing for those facing a criminal charge, when individual liberty or even life may be at stake, while in noncriminal, administrative proceedings due process has been interpreted to require fewer procedural safeguards than those that would have to be met in a criminal trial.

A good example is the right to counsel. In any criminal proceeding in which a loss of liberty is possible, the Supreme Court has held not only that the defendant has the right to retain a lawyer but also that, if the defendant is indigent, counsel must be appointed for the defendant and paid for by the government. In administrative proceedings, on the other hand, the Court has never held that due process guarantees an absolute right to appointed counsel when the proceedings involve indigent individuals.

## LEGISLATIVE AND ADJUDICATIVE FACTS

A long-standing rule of due process is that an administrative agency must hold a hearing prior to taking action when the facts upon which the action is based are characterized as adjudicative facts. Adjudicative facts are facts that relate to the circumstances or the status of a specific individual or a relatively few individuals. When an administrative agency, on the other hand, bases an action or decision on legislative facts, due process does not require a hearing. Legislative facts are facts that relate to the society as a whole, or a large segment thereof, rather than to the condition of a specific individual or a few individuals. Due process therefore does not ordinarily require a hearing before an administrative agency issues rules and regulations based on legislative facts, but it does often require a hearing when agency action is based on adjudicative facts, such as whether a particular individual has violated the agency's rules or regulations.

## THE DECLINE OF THE RIGHT-PRIVILEGE DICHOTOMY

Another traditional rule governing the right to an administrative hearing, the so-called right-privilege dichotomy, has undergone drastic alteration in recent years. Under the right-privilege dichotomy, as traditionally applied by the courts, due process often required a hearing if a "right" were affected by governmental action. If, however, only a "privilege" were affected, no hearing was required by due process. The right-privilege dichotomy was based on the concept that the Due Process Clauses protected only the rights of life, liberty, and property, but not those benefits individuals might receive from the government that were not recognized as legally protected rights. Until recently, for example, a welfare recipient was not entitled to a due process hearing prior to having his welfare benefits terminated. Since no one had a legal right to welfare benefits, the courts reasoned, but rather such benefits were in the nature of a privilege bestowed upon individuals by the government, due process did not restrict the method or manner in which such privileges were revoked by the government.

As long as the role of government was relatively limited and most governmental action affected traditional legal rights, the Due Process Clauses guaranteed hearings to individuals when governmental power was brought to bear against them, despite the right-privilege dichotomy. But with the rise of positive government, particularly after the New Deal, large segments of the public became dependent upon governmental subsidies, contracts, welfare benefits, unemployment compensation, and pensions, all of which fell within the traditional classification of privileges to which the procedural requirements of due process did not apply.

Given this increasing dependence of society upon governmental privileges, governmental action extending or withdrawing such privileges could have as important an impact upon individuals as governmental action affecting what were traditionally classified as legal rights. The question thus became, as one commentator said, whether in an era "when rights are mass produced, can the quality of their protection against arbitrary official action be as high as the quality of the protection afforded in the past to traditional legal rights less numerous and less widely dispersed among the members of the society?"

Beginning in the late 1950s, the response of the Supreme Court to such questions was increasingly in the affirmative, as it began to undermine the right-privilege dichotomy in its decisions. Although under the right-privilege dichotomy as traditionally interpreted, welfare benefits, unemployment compensation, and tax exemptions were classified as privileges, the Court held in a series of cases that the government could not condition or withdraw such privileges in a manner violative of substantive constitutional rights of the individual. In *Speiser* v. *Randall,* decided in 1958, the Court thus held that a state tax exemption could not be conditioned upon the surrender of the right of free speech; in *Sherbert* v. *Verner,* decided in 1963, the Court held that unemployment compensation benefits could not be withheld in a manner that penalized an individual's religious freedom; and in *Shapiro* v. *Thompson,* decided in 1969, the Court held that welfare benefits could not be conditioned by residency requirements that violated the right to travel interstate and the right to the equal protection of the laws.

The teaching of these and similar cases was that governmental action involving the granting or withholding of privileges was limited by the relevant substantive constitutional rights of individuals. And if violations of substantive constitutional rights were alleged, the Court was clearly ignoring whether a right or a privilege was involved and was focusing upon the harm being done to the constitutional rights of the individual. But if the so-called privileges could not be conditioned or withdrawn in ways that violated such substantive constitutional rights as freedom of speech and religion, the question arose as to whether administrative action affecting privileges was not also restricted by the requirements of procedural fairness imposed by the Due Process Clauses. That is, if the government was constitutionally compelled to respect such substantive constitutional rights as freedom of speech in administering programs conferring privileges upon individuals, why was it not also required to respect the individual right to fair procedure under the Due Process Clauses, such as the right to a fair hearing before administrative action affecting the individual was undertaken?

Questions of this nature came to a head before the Supreme Court in the litigation involving *Goldberg* v. *Kelly* in 1970, and the result was a landmark Supreme Court decision on the right to a hearing in the administrative process that seriously eroded the viability of the right-privilege dichotomy in administrative law. We shall now examine the litigation in *Goldberg* v. *Kelly* in detail.

## CASE STUDY
# MR. KELLY AND THE BUREAUCRACY IN THE BIG APPLE
Due Process Comes to Welfare

Before the 1930s, welfare benefits for the poor were provided by a myriad of both private and public agencies largely within local communities. The benefits thus distributed, characterized as the dole, were regarded as charity for the "worthy poor," and legal standards were almost nonexistent in regard to either the selection of recipients of welfare or the reasons for the extension to or withdrawal of benefits from recipients. As far as the courts were concerned, poor relief was an act of charity, the granting or termination of which was within the discretion of those administering such relief.

With the depression and the coming of the New Deal, however, both state and federal governments assumed major responsibilities for the administration of welfare programs, and statutes creating various welfare programs for the first time set legal criteria which created legal entitlements for welfare benefits. Welfare administration thus became a regular and bureaucratic function of government, with specific legal criteria defining those among the public who were entitled to benefits.

Under the Social Security Act of 1935, Congress thus created several categorical welfare assistance programs, including aid to the blind, aid to crippled children, Aid to Families with Dependent Children (AFDC), and old age assistance. Under the act, federal money was appropriated to support the categorical assistance programs, while the administration of the programs was undertaken by state welfare agencies. The state agencies, however, were required to administer the programs in accordance with rules and regulations promulgated at the federal level. At the same time, state governments established and funded their own welfare programs to assist those who did not qualify for the categorical assistance programs under the Social Security Act.

In the State of New York during the late 1960s, for example, all welfare programs were under the state Department of Social Services, which supervised the administration of welfare by county welfare agencies, and, in New York City, the city's Department of Social Services. These agencies administered not only the categorical assistance programs under the Social Security Act, such as AFDC, but also New York State's own welfare program, which was called home relief. The New York welfare agencies were thus responsible for the expenditure of massive amounts of not only federal funds but also state welfare funds. In the 1967-68 fiscal year, the New York City Department of Social Services, the largest welfare agency in the nation, thus had a budget of over $839,000,000 for the state home relief program alone.

Since both the Social Security categorical assistance programs and the state home relief program were administered by the same state agencies, the programs were largely indistinguishable from an administrative standpoint. One procedural difference between the administration of the categorical assistance programs and the state home relief program, however, stemmed from the Social Security Act, which provided that a person whose benefits were terminated under one of the categorical assistance programs must be provided a "fair hearing" by the state agency at which the termination could be contested. The fair hearing occurred only after termination of benefits, and while the hearing was supposed to be held within sixty days of the termination of benefits, in reality most hearings were held well beyond the sixty-day limit. In New York State, for example, most fair hearings were not held for at least three months after the termination of benefits.

Under the New York home relief program, however, there was no provision for a hearing either before or after benefits were terminated. Because hearings were not granted to recipients prior to the termination of their benefits, the crucial decision in regard to the termination of benefits was more often than not that of the welfare caseworker. Yet the typical caseworker in New York was not a trained professional social worker, and the turnover rates among caseworkers were extremely high. During a typical year, from one-fourth to one-half of the caseworkers in New York City quit to seek employment elsewhere. One consequence of this high turnover rate and lack of training was a high percentage of error in the denial or termination of benefits to welfare recipients. According to the Department of Health, Education, and Welfare (now the U.S. Department of Health and Human Services), erroneous terminations or denials of benefits under the AFDC program occurred in 6.3 percent of the cases nationwide during the late 1960s, while in New York the rate was 7.9 percent. And in those cases involving categorical assistance in which fair hearings were held in New York, terminations of assistance were reversed in 37 percent of the cases during 1967-1968.

As the 1960s drew to a close, however, the problems of the New York welfare bureaucracy were only beginning. Welfare recipients were becoming not only more militant but also better organized into such groups as the National Welfare Rights Organization. In the fall of 1967, this new militancy on the part of welfare recipients became evident in New York City when the Citywide Coordinating Committee of Welfare Groups began a campaign for fair hearings for welfare recipients. The impact of such activity was soon felt by the New York welfare bureaucracy when the demand for fair hearings regarding terminations of benefits under the categorical assistance programs increased dramatically. In 1964, for example, there had been a total of only 188 requests for fair hearings in the entire state; in 1967, there were 4,233 requests for fair hearings, almost all from New York City. The state Department of Social Services, however, employed only eight hearing officers to conduct fair hearings, and, as the official in charge of fair hearings admitted, the increased demand for such hearings made it clear that "drastic revisions of procedure were needed." "We are still in a state of flux," he added, "with reference to establishing a definitive set of underlying procedures governing the processing of requests for fair hearings."

## THE WELFARE SYSTEM CHALLENGED

Challenges to New York welfare administration procedures soon came to focus, however, upon the lack of any *prior* hearing before benefits were terminated in both the categorical assistance and home relief programs. The issue of the lack of pretermination hearings came to a head when several welfare recipients were terminated by the New York City Department of Social Services in early 1968, and these former recipients sought legal help in challenging the administrative procedures of the department.

One of those who was terminated was John Kelly, who was twenty-nine years old and had been a recipient of home relief benefits since August of 1967. Kelly had been the victim of a hit-and-run accident in June of 1967 that had injured him so seriously that he was unable to work. Under the home relief program he received $160.10 monthly plus his rent, and in December of 1967 he was living in the Broadway Central Hotel. Kelly's caseworker, however, ordered him to move to the Barbara Hotel. He complied with the order but moved from the Barbara Hotel after only a brief stay, since he found the hotel to be populated by drunks and drug addicts and he feared for his safety. Kelly began living at a friend's apartment, but on January 8, 1968, he was informed by the desk clerk at the Barbara Hotel, where he received his mail, that his caseworker had terminated his benefits. He attempted to see his caseworker at the Gramercy Welfare Center but was refused an interview, although welfare officials at the center informed him that he had been terminated for failure to follow his caseworker's instructions and live at the Barbara Hotel. As a result of his termination, Kelly was forced to live on the limited charity of his friends.

The Department of Social Services later challenged Kelly's version of the events leading to his termination and contended that Kelly changed addresses so frequently that it was almost impossible to keep contact with him. As a result of his frequent moves, the department said, welfare officials were forced to "chase after the checks sent to him at his last known addresses where he did not stay long enough to pick them up and for all of which he was issued replacement funds." Kelly had not been ordered to live at the Barbara Hotel, the department insisted, but had simply been told by his caseworker to obtain a permanent address so that his benefits could continue steadily. His case had been closed, the department added, only because it had been reclassified to fall within the Presumptive Aid to Disabled program.

In addition to John Kelly, Randolph Young, Juan DeJesus, Pearl Frye, Pearl McKinney, and Altagracia Guzman also had either their home relief or AFDC benefits terminated without a hearing by the Department of Social Services in early 1968. Such terminations were of course routine occurrences, but in these instances the terminated recipients sought and received legal help in challenging the procedures of the Department of Social Services that had resulted in their terminations.

At the time of the termination of the welfare benefits of John Kelly and his fellow recipients, legal services for the poor were more readily available than at any time in the past. As a part of the "war on poverty" during the 1960s, the federal Office of Economic Opportunity funded neighborhood legal services programs which provided legal aid for the first time to many of the nation's poor. When their benefits were terminated, therefore, Kelly and his fellow welfare recipients were able to turn to such agencies in New York City as the Mobilization for Youth and the Williamsburg and Morrisania Neighborhood Legal Services, all legal aid societies funded by OEO. Some of those whose benefits had been terminated also sought and received assistance from the Legal Aid Society, which had for many years been one of the few sources of legal aid for the poor in New York City.

The termination of the benefits of Kelly and his fellow recipients also coincided with decisions by the Columbia Center on Social Welfare Policy and Law and the Roger Baldwin Foundation of the American Civil Liberties Union to initiate test cases challenging the validity of welfare benefit terminations without hearings. The Center on Social Welfare Policy and Law, affiliated with the schools of law and social welfare at Columbia University, was a part of the Legal Services Program of the Office of Economic Opportunity. The center conducted research regarding legal rights of the poor as well as supporting OEO legal services programs in the preparation of litigation testing aspects of poverty law in the courts. Lee A. Albert, the director of the center, thus coordinated the efforts of attorneys and social workers affiliated with Mobilization for Youth, the Williamsburg and Morrisania Neighborhood Legal Services, and the Legal Aid Society in documenting the circumstances surrounding the terminations of John Kelly and his fellow welfare recipients in preparation for challenging the terminations in court.

On January 29, 1968, a complaint was filed in the U.S. District Court for the Southern District of New York on behalf of John Kelly and five other welfare recipients whose benefits had been terminated without hearings. Named as defendants were State Department of Social Services Commissioner George K. Wyman, the state Board of Social Welfare, and the New York City Department of Social Services Commissioner, Jack R. Goldberg. The complaint sought a declaratory judgment by the court holding invalid the statutes and rules under which the Department of Social Services refused to grant hearings to welfare recipients prior to the termination of their benefits. This failure to grant pretermination hearings, the complaint alleged, deprived the "plaintiffs of the due process of law guaranteed by the Fourteenth Amendment to the United States Constitution," and the court was requested to issue an injunction prohibiting the defendants from terminating welfare recipients without hearings. Finally, the complaint asked that a three-judge court be convened to hear the case on the merits.

The complaint filed in the *Kelly* case was backed by the Columbia Center on Social Welfare Policy and Law, the Mobilization for Youth, the Williamsburg and Morrisania Neighborhood Legal Services, the Legal Aid Society of New York, and the Roger Baldwin Foundation of the ACLU. When the complaint was filed, Martin Garbus of the Roger Baldwin Foundation pointed out that approximately three million welfare recipients were terminated without hearings nationwide and that the *Kelly* case was only a part of a series of suits that would be filed around the nation in an attempt to obtain judicial recognition of a welfare "bill of rights." And, indeed, suits similar to the *Kelly* case were filed in California and Mississippi.

## THE BUREAUCRACY COUNTERATTACKS

The reaction in New York to the filing of the *Kelly* case was a flurry of activity by the state and city welfare bureaucracies, and it was soon apparent that the strategy of New York welfare officials was to moot the issues in the *Kelly* case. The New York officials and their attorneys were obviously convinced that the traditional doctrine that welfare benefits were privileges, the termination of which was not limited by the Due Process Clauses, had been sufficiently undermined by the decisions of the Supreme Court that it was extremely likely that the *Kelly* case would result in a ruling that terminations of welfare benefits had to meet due process standards. Since cases similar to the *Kelly* case had been filed in California and Mississippi, the New York officials quickly contacted the welfare officials in those states to learn how they had dealt with the cases in their states. The New York officials learned that in both California and Mississippi the welfare departments had adopted pretermination procedures in the face of the pending lawsuits.

Following the lead of California and Mississippi, within two weeks after the complaint in the *Kelly* case was filed, the New York State Department of Social Services announced that the right to a fair hearing would henceforth be available to recipients of home relief as well as recipients of categorical assistance. The fair hearing procedure of course occurred only after the termination of benefits, but the department also soon announced that under regulation 351.26, effective March 1, 1968, welfare recipients were additionally entitled to a prior "administrative hearing" before their benefits were terminated.

Under regulation 351.26, this administrative hearing involved written notice to the recipient seven days prior to the proposed termination of benefits that his benefits were about to be terminated for the reasons stated in the notice. If the recipient requested a hearing, a hearing would be held at which the recipient could appear personally and be informed of the reasons why he was being terminated, while the recipient was entitled to present oral or written evidence as to why termination should not occur. The recipient could be represented at this hearing by an attorney or other representative, and the welfare official presiding at the hearing had to be superior to the supervisor who initially approved the termination of benefits. A written notice of the final decision of the hearing officer was also required to be furnished to the recipient.

Having thus changed their procedures in an attempt to moot the issues in the *Kelly* case, the New York welfare officials filed a motion to dismiss the complaint in the *Kelly* case in late February. While admitting that at the time of the filing of the complaint, "no provisions of the New York State Welfare Law gave recipients notification of their suspension or termination prior to such suspension or termination, nor was a hearing authorized to be conducted prior to the date of discontinuance," the motion to dismiss pointed out that, "after conferring with the Welfare Departments in the States of California and Mississippi," the New York State Department of Social Services had amended the regulations to extend pretermination hearings to welfare recipients as well as posttermination fair hearings to all recipients. The new rules, the motion to dismiss asserted, "conclusively show that plaintiff's claim as to the unconstitutionality of the procedures which the New York State Department of Social Services follows when a recipient's aid is suspended or terminated, is utterly without merit," since the new procedures gave the plaintiffs "precisely the relief they requested. . . ." The issues in the *Kelly* case were therefore moot, the motion to dismiss concluded, and the complaint should be dismissed by the district court.

Unfortunately for the strategy of the state welfare officials to moot the issues in the *Kelly* case, their hasty amendment of the procedures regarding the termination of benefits caught the New York City Department of Social Services completely unprepared to implement the new regulations. The New York City department received word of the state department's proposed action on February 16, but while the new procedures were effective March 1, the city department continued to terminate welfare recipients without the benefit of pretermination hearings as required by regulation 351.26 throughout March and April. The New York City department argued that the new procedures had been suddenly imposed and that the state department had not supplied it with the funds needed to comply with the new regulations.

With the strategy of mooting the issues in the *Kelly* case being undermined by the city department's noncompliance with the new regulations, further action was clearly needed to head off a decision in the federal court. On Thursday, April 25, 1968, therefore, leading officials of the state and city departments of social services along with their attorneys met in a six hour session to deal with the city department's noncompliance with regulation 351.26. It was decided at the meeting that a new regulation 351.26 would be adopted by the state department, and under the new regulation there would be an option (a) and an option (b) regarding pretermination procedures. Option (a) retained the procedures originally contained in regulation 351.26, but option (b), for the benefit of the New York City department, contained alternative pretermination procedures that local departments could adopt rather than option (a).

The new option (b) procedures, which were adopted by the New York City department, retained the requirement of a notice of suspension or termination of a recipient's benefits seven days prior to such action. The primary difference between option (a) and option (b) was that option (b) did not provide for a hearing at which the recipient could appear personally and contest the termination of his benefits. Rather, option (b) only allowed the recipient to submit "in writing a statement or other evidence" demonstrating why his benefits should not be terminated. Even with the somewhat relaxed procedural standards under option (b), however, Commissioner Jack R. Goldberg of the city department estimated that the city department could not begin to comply with option (b) until approximately June 1, 1968.

In order to meet the argument of the defendants that the new regulations providing pretermination hearings rendered the issues in the *Kelly* case moot, the attorneys for the plaintiffs were constrained to amend their complaint in the case. In their amended complaint, instead of arguing that New York was terminating welfare benefits without pretermination hearings in violation of due process, the attorneys for the plaintiffs attacked the pretermination hearings provided under regulation 351.26 (a) and (b) as lacking in essential elements of due process. They particularly attacked option (b) as violative of due process because it failed to afford adequate notice and a chance to reply to recipients and especially because it did not afford a recipient the right to appear personally at his pretermination hearing, to present oral as well as documentary evidence, and to confront and cross-examine the witnesses and evidence against him. The issues in the *Kelly* case had thus shifted from the question of whether due process required any pretermination hearing at all to the adequacy under due process of the pretermination hearings now being provided by the New York welfare bureaucracy.

Not only did the attorneys for the plaintiffs complain to the federal court regarding the attempt of the welfare bureaucracy to moot the issues in the *Kelly* case, but they especially attacked what they perceived to be the recalcitrant attitude of the New York City welfare officials toward any change in termination procedures. Lee Albert, as one of the plaintiff's counsel, thus charged that when the state department of social services promulgated regulation 351.26, the state department "had gone much too far for the City. The City, in an astonishing display of lawlessness, failed to heed the binding state regulation and continued terminations apace without prior review during March and April, when the state regulation was in full force and effect." In addition, Albert charged, soon after the plaintiffs' original complaint was filed, "counsel for the City began a newsletter to the Court, relating the attempts of the City to deprive plaintiffs of what the State said was everything wanted by the plaintiffs. The city suggested that the Court delay decision until the City and the State could determine just what the law should be anyway." Finally, Albert said, the city obtained a revision of regulation 351.26, but even then "non-compliance is still the rule in some, if not all, counties in New York City."

The attempt by New York welfare officials to moot the *Kelly* case by changing the procedures regarding termination of benefits, however, was not the only problem faced by attorneys for the plaintiffs on that score. The New York City department also attempted to moot the issues in the case by restoring the original plaintiffs to the welfare rolls. Assistant Corporation Counsel Luis M. Neco, an attorney representing Commissioner Jack Goldberg of the New York City department, thus informed the federal court on February 29 that John Kelly and all the other original plaintiffs, except Randolph Young, had been restored to the welfare rolls.

Young, Neco informed the court, was "presently in Manhattan State Hospital undergoing treatment for detoxification of narcotics, and is not presently entitled to public assistance benefits." "Thus," Neco concluded, "there is no longer any controversy between plaintiffs and defendant Goldberg, and the instant proceeding is moot."

To meet this additional attempt to moot the issues in the *Kelly* case, the attorneys for the plaintiffs recruited new plaintiffs from among those welfare recipients who had been terminated without hearings by the New York City department and filed new complaints on behalf of these recipients. On February 22, therefore, an additional complaint was filed on behalf of two additional recipients who had been terminated without a hearing, and on June 17 another complaint was filed on behalf of twelve terminated recipients.

One of these additional plaintiffs, Mrs. Esther Lett, had had an especially harrowing experience at the hands of the New York City department. Mrs. Lett received AFDC benefits to support four dependent nieces and nephews, who ranged in ages from three months to fifteen years. Her benefits were terminated on February 1, 1968, by the city department on the ground that she had concealed assets by not reporting her salary as a teacher's aid in the New York City school system. Mrs. Lett sought assistance from a Legal Aid attorney who determined that she was not employed by the New York school system and that the city department of social services had been misinformed. Nevertheless, the city department refused to reinstate Mrs. Lett's assistance, and she and her four dependents were near starvation as a result. Indeed, Mrs. Lett fainted from lack of food while waiting for emergency aid at the Melrose Welfare Center, and she and her dependents were hospitalized after eating spoiled food. The frustration of the Legal Aid attorney who had attempted to assist Mrs. Lett was evident in an affidavit he filed to support her complaint in the federal court. "The obvious insensitivity of the officials I have dealt with and their unwillingness to make any meaningful efforts to alleviate grievous human suffering is literally beyond belief," he told the court. "The physical and emotional injury being wreaked on Mrs. Lett and her four dependents can never be fully ameliorated. . . ."

The filing of complaints on behalf of Mrs. Lett and the other additional plaintiffs was of course an attempt to demonstrate the continuing availability of plaintiffs to the federal court and that the issues in the *Kelly* case should not be declared moot. Because the "treatment of Mrs. Lett was so outrageous, and the suffering caused so severe," the plaintiffs' attorneys said, they not only asked for injunctive relief in her case but money damages in the amount of $50,000 because of the violation of her Fourteenth Amendment due process rights by the city welfare officials.

The request for money damages in Mrs. Lett's case was also additional insurance that the due process issues in the *Kelly* case could not be mooted, since even her restoration to the welfare rolls would not moot her claim for money damages against the city welfare officials.

A crucial hurdle from the standpoint of the plaintiffs' attorneys in the *Kelly* case was reached on May 17, 1968, when U.S. District Judge Frederick vanPelt Bryan issued his ruling on whether a three-judge court should be convened in the case. The attorneys for the New York welfare officials had argued not only that the *Kelly* case should be dismissed because the issues in the case were moot but also that the plaintiffs had failed to exhaust the administrative remedies available to them within the New York welfare bureaucracy. Fortunately for the plaintiffs, Judge Bryan rejected both these contentions.

In a suit alleging the violation of Fourteenth Amendment rights by state officials acting under color of law, Judge Bryan ruled, there was no requirement that available state administrative remedies be exhausted by the plaintiffs. And, although many of the plaintiffs had been restored to the welfare rolls, Judge Bryan rejected the mootness argument, noting that judicial "determination of questions of this importance cannot thus be evaded...." Finally, Bryan ruled that the *Kelly* case raised substantial constitutional issues and that a three-judge court should be convened to decide them.

### THE THREE-JUDGE COURT DECIDES

Pursuant to Judge Bryan's ruling, Chief Judge J. Edward Lumbard of the Second Circuit U.S. Court of Appeals convened a three-judge court in the *Kelly* case, the court being composed of Judge Bryan, District Judge Edward C. Helsan, and Court of Appeals Judge Wilfred Feinberg. After hearing arguments in the case, the three-judge court announced its decision on November 26, 1968, and handed the plaintiffs an important victory.

The court noted that the defendants had not pressed the right-privilege dichotomy in their arguments and had not thus argued "that welfare benefits are a 'privilege,' rather than a right, and that therefore they may fix the procedures of termination as they see fit." Conceding that due process did impose some constraints upon the procedures governing the suspension or termination of welfare benefits, the defendants had argued that the pretermination procedures under regulation 351.26 (a) and (b), taken together with the posttermination fair hearings, met the standards of due process.

While the court agreed that New York's fair hearings met due process standards, and that their availability was relevant to evaluating the validity of the state's welfare termination procedures, it nonetheless insisted that the crucial issue in the *Kelly* case was the adequacy under due process of the pretermination hearings under regulation 351.26. "While post-termination review is relevant," the court said, "there is one overpowering fact which controls here. By hypothesis, a welfare recipient is destitute, without funds or assets." "Suffice it to say," the court continued, "that to cut off a welfare recipient in the face of this kind of 'brutal need' without a prior hearing of some sort is unconscionable, unless overwhelming considerations justify it."

The court acknowledged that the defendants had argued that more elaborate pretermination hearings and a requirement that benefits to recipients continue until a pretermination hearing was held would add to the costs of welfare administration. "Against the justified desire to protect public funds," the court nevertheless held, "must be weighed the individual's overpowering need in this unique situation not to be wrongfully deprived of assistance, and the startling statistic that post-termination fair hearings apparently override prior decisions to terminate benefits in a substantial number of cases." "While the problem of additional expense must be kept in mind," the court said, "it does not justify denying a hearing meeting the ordinary standards of due process. Under all the circumstances, we hold that due process requires an adequate hearing before termination of welfare benefits, and the fact that there is a later constitutionally fair proceeding does not alter the result."

Having concluded that due process required a pretermination hearing, the court then evaluated the pretermination hearings provided for by regulation 351.26 (a) and (b) in light of due process standards. "While the Supreme Court has been solicitious to assure 'traditional forms of fair procedure' in administrative hearings . . . ," the court noted, "we do not believe that every person directly affected by administrative action must be afforded all of the procedural rights guaranteed in a full-fledged judicial trial. . . . Rather we are called upon to determine what minimum procedural safeguards are required here in the context of the welfare system. . . ." Examining option (a) of regulation 351.26 from this standpoint, the court found it to conform to the requirements of due process if the hearing under its terms were construed not only to permit the recipient to appear personally and present oral or documentary evidence but also to confront and cross-examine adverse witnesses and evidence. Since option (a) did not specifically provide for confrontation and cross-examination, the court construed it to contain these elements of due process in order to save it from invalidation.

The counsel for the plaintiffs had also attacked the provisions for hearing officers under both options (a) and (b) on the ground that the hearing officers were often welfare officials who had approved proposed terminations in advance or may even have initiated the termination under review. On this point, the court held that some "degree of previous familiarity and informal contact with a case by a hearing officer is a common phenomenon in many administrative agencies" and that this, in itself, would not disqualify a hearing officer on the grounds of bias under due process. The court did hold, however, that the officers conducting pretermination hearings must not have previously approved or initiated the termination being reviewed and that they must be superior to the supervisors who approved the proposed terminations.

Regarding option (b) of regulation 351.26, which was in force in New York City, the court held that it failed to meet minimum due process standards and was thus invalid under the Due Process Clause of the Fourteenth Amendment. Noting that under option (b) the recipient could submit evidence in writing but could not appear personally at the pretermination hearing, the court held that a "hearing on a proposed termination of welfare benefits is, of course, a classic instance of determination of what have been called 'adjudicative facts—facts pertaining to a particular party,'" and that on "an issue of such immediate and crucial impact as termination of welfare benefits, we conclude that the right to be heard means the right to be heard in person. . . ." The court also held that option (b)'s provision for recipients to submit evidence only in writing was "cruelly ironic," since the burden of "marshalling and writing down persuasive arguments in opposition to frequently vague or cryptic charges would discourage even a relatively well-educated layman. In fact, many welfare recipients clearly lack the education or sophistication either to understand the reason for their proposed termination or to prepare an adequate written defense. . . ."

The next "most glaring deficiency of option (b)," the court continued, was its failure "to require disclosure to the recipient of the real basis of the case against him. It merely provides for notice of proposed discontinuance 'together with the reasons for the intended action.' This procedure clearly falls far short of giving the recipient sufficient notice of the case against him so that he may ascertain its basis and contest it effectively. . . ." Option (b) must be revised, the court ruled, to provide for adequate notice of the case against the recipient, to allow the recipient to appear personally at the hearing and present evidence, oral or written, justifying the continuation of his benefits, and, where termination of benefits "depends upon information supplied by a particular person whose reliability or veracity is brought into question by the [recipient], confrontation and the right of cross-examination should be afforded."

In light of "the shattering effect of wrongful termination of benefits upon a recipient," the court concluded, "we believe that the procedures called for here are minimum requirements of due process. Accordingly, therefore, we conclude that option (b) is constitutionally inadequate and that plaintiffs' application for a preliminary injunction against the use of the option in New York City must be granted. . . ."

## NEW YORK CITY APPEALS

With the victory in the three-judge court, the counsel for the plaintiffs had thus established that due process required hearings before welfare benefits could be terminated, but the decision of the three-judge court was directly appealable to the Supreme Court. The division between the state welfare officials and the New York City Department of Social Services, which was apparent in the conflict over appropriate pretermination procedures, continued in regard to whether an appeal should be taken. Initially, both the state and city officials filed notices of an appeal, but on February 25, 1969, State Commissioner Wyman and the members of the State Board of Social Welfare withdrew from the appeal, indicating a willingness on their part to live with the decision of the three-judge court. New York City Commissioner of Social Services Jack R. Goldberg and his department, on the other hand, continued their opposition to the new pretermination procedures and prosecuted the appeal to the Supreme Court. The litigation on appeal to the Court thus became *Goldberg* v. *Kelly*, and the Court agreed to hear the appeal in the case on April 21, 1969.

## ARGUMENTS BEFORE THE SUPREME COURT

In the briefs and arguments in the *Kelly* case in the Supreme Court, the traditional argument, based on the right-privilege dichotomy, that welfare benefits were privileges beyond the reach of due process, was largely ignored by the counsel for the New York City welfare officials. Because the litigation in the *Kelly* case involved termination procedures under the Social Security Act, however, the U.S. solicitor general filed an amicus curiae brief in the case on invitation of the Court, and there were echoes of the right-privilege dichotomy in the solicitor general's brief.

While conceding that due process applied to the termination of welfare benefits, the solicitor general did allege that welfare benefits were not property in the classic sense and that the interest of welfare recipients in their benefits was perhaps "more tentative" than a person's interest in his "property." The solicitor general's brief thus seemed to suggest that, while due process applied to the termination of welfare benefits, the elements of due process applicable in such cases should be less stringent than those applicable when governmental action adversely affected traditional property rights. The solicitor general's brief was consequently denounced on this point by the attorneys for the welfare recipients in the *Kelly* case as engaging in "opaque legalisms" which were "variations on the theme of rights and privileges and invocation of the doctrine that the latter are not entitled to traditional constitutional safeguards against revocation."

While the right-privilege dichotomy was therefore not much pressed by counsel for the New York City welfare officials or the solicitor general, counsel for the welfare recipients pressed the Court to repudiate the right-privilege distinction in the *Kelly* case. It "may no longer be seriously contended that the capricious or invidious revocation of government benefits may be justified by simple characterization of their receipt as a 'privilege' rather than a 'right,' " counsel for the recipients argued. "The notion that whatever the government undertakes to afford it can precipitiously and arbitrarily revoke has played no significant role in this Court's resolution of questions of the requirements of procedural due process."

The National Institute for Education in Law and Poverty filed an amicus curiae brief with the Court supporting the welfare recipients in the *Kelly* case, and it too strongly urged the Court to repudiate the right-privilege dichotomy. The National Institute thus urged the Court "to deal the final and finishing blow to the 'rights vs. privileges' dichotomy which still haunts and distorts the administration of justice in the lower courts and administrative agencies. The protections of due process are available wherever government would act to impair the interests of any of its citizens, whether those interests be characterized as privileges or rights." Strict due process standards should apply, the National Institute argued, "where the government would withdraw the bare means of subsistence from [welfare] recipients who by definition have been previously found eligible on the basis of a primitive and dire need."

Although counsel for New York City, Assistant Corporation Counsel John J. Loflin, Jr., again did not press the distinction between rights and privileges during oral argument of the *Kelly* case, Justice Black did question Lee A. Albert, counsel for the recipients, on that point during his argument. Albert argued that due process applied to prevent any arbitrary or capricious governmental action adversely affecting individuals, but Justice Black characterized Albert's definition of due process as "latitudinarian" and asked, "Are you arguing that it's arbitrary and capricious for the government to cut off a gift or a gratuity?" "I gather from your argument," Black continued, "that it would be hard to repeal a gratuity once you'd given it on the ground it would be too arbitrary and capricious." Albert responded that he was not arguing that the government was required to maintain welfare programs, but once such programs were established and benefits extended to individuals, revocation of the benefits was governed by the standards of fairness required by the Due Process Clauses.

Given the abandonment of any reliance on the right-privilege distinction by counsel for New York City, the central point of contention between the parties in the *Kelly* case was whether or not the termination procedures used by the New York City Department of Social Services met due process standards. Arguing on behalf of the city, John Loflin pointed out that under state regulation 351.26(b) and city department regulation 68-18 implementing regulation 351.26(b), the welfare recipient whose benefits were terminated received elaborate procedural safeguards. These procedural safeguards involved, Loflin pointed out to the Court, discussion by a caseworker with the recipient of the reasons for a proposed discontinuance of benefits; a report by the caseworker to his unit supervisor recommending termination; approval of the caseworker's recommendation by the unit supervisor; a notice to the recipient of the termination, the reasons therefor, and notification that within seven days the recipient could contest the termination, including the submission of written documents demonstrating his continuing eligibility for benefits; if the termination were contested by the recipient, the case was reviewed by a review officer, who was superior to the unit supervisor who had approved the termination; if the review officer upheld the termination, written notice of the decision was furnished to the recipient along with notification that the recipient could request a posttermination fair hearing; if the fair hearing were requested, it was held by state hearing officers, and if the termination of benefits were affirmed after a fair hearing, the recipient could petition for judicial review of the decision.

These procedures, Loflin argued, met the flexible due process standards traditionally imposed upon administrative adjudications by the Court. They struck a reasonable balance, he argued, between the rights of welfare recipients and the interest of the state and city in controlling the costs of administering their welfare programs.

As counsel for the recipients, however, Lee Albert argued that the New York pretermination procedures were inadequate for failure to afford the right of a recipient to present oral testimony at a pretermination hearing or to confront and cross-examine adverse witnesses. "Rarely, if ever, does administrative action, adjudicatory in nature, in revoking a statutory right," he argued, "result in such irremediable and wholesale harms upon individuals, certainly without first affording notice and an opportunity to contest the basis of the decision causing such grievous injury." The fact that under the New York procedures a recipient received a full due process hearing after termination of his benefits was largely irrelevant, Albert argued, since the "issue of what is constitutionally compelled cannot be addressed or resolved by indiscriminately viewing a combination of a constitutionally inadequate hearing before termination with a constitutionally untimely one afterwards."

Saving money was not an adequate justification for denying welfare recipients a full due process pretermination hearing, Albert continued. Such a hearing could be provided from one to two weeks after notice of proposed termination, and this would entail perhaps one additional welfare benefit payment to a possibly ineligible recipient prior to the hearing. The cost of affording a full due process hearing would therefore be negligible, he argued, and would involve a "miniscule part" of the welfare budget. Denial of full hearings prior to termination could also not be justified, Albert continued, because of "wholly unsubstantiated fear of frivolous requests for review" by recipients. Such fears were based "on the stubborn prejudice or myth that the poor cannot be trusted with rights, procedural or substantive. . . . The fear is quite belied by actual experience. The fact is not that the poor abuse their legal rights, but that they do not use them." During a four-and-one-half month period in New York City, Albert pointed out, over sixty thousand welfare cases were closed, yet just over one thousand persons requested a review of their terminations. "It is not likely," Albert said, "that any infusion of legal process will overcome the erosion of spirit and the destruction of self-image and personality resulting from welfare's pervasive distrust of the poor."

There were those, Albert concluded, who believed that "our traditional legal institutions and precepts of fairness cannot respond to the needs of the poor and disadvantaged. There may be some truth in this. Due process of law is not a panacea to the problems inherent in our ossified and bureaucratic system of public assistance administration. Errors will continue apace and due process will not rectify all of them. But until legislative or administrative ingenuity creates something better, the time-honored procedures afforded by reflex to our more advantaged citizens in dealing with the government can no longer be denied to the poor. Appellees are not asking for any special or novel constitutional rule because of their circumstances. They seek only traditional constitutional safeguards, safeguards which themselves embody the government's respect for the elementary rights of individuals."

The oral arguments in *Goldberg* v. *Kelly* were held on October 13, 1969. Some five months later, on March 23, 1970, the Supreme Court announced its landmark decision holding that the termination of welfare benefits must meet the standards of procedural fairness required by the Due Process Clauses of the Constitution.

*Goldberg* v. *Kelly*
397 U.S. 254. Argued October 13, 1969. Decided March 23, 1970.
Mr. Justice Brennan delivered the opinion of the Court.

[Justice Brennan first summarized the facts in the case and the decision of the three-judge district court.]

The constitutional issue to be decided, therefore, is the narrow one whether the Due Process Clause requires that the recipient be afforded an evidentiary hearing *before* the termination of benefits. The District Court held that only a pre-termination evidentiary hearing would satisfy the constitutional command, and rejected the argument of the state and city officials that the combination of the post-termination "fair hearing" with the informal pre-termination review disposed of all due process claims. . . .

Appellant does not contend that procedural due process is not applicable to the termination of welfare benefits. Such benefits are a matter of statutory entitlement for persons qualified to receive them. Their termination involves state action that adjudicates important rights. The constitutional challenge cannot be answered by an argument that public assistance benefits are "a 'privilege' and not a 'right.' " Shapiro v. Thompson. . . . Relevant constitutional restraints apply as much to the withdrawal of public assistance benefits as to disqualifications for unemployment compensation, Sherbert v. Verner. . . , or to denial of a tax exemption, Speiser v. Randall. . . . The extent to which procedural due process must be afforded the recipient is influenced by the extent to which he may be "condemned to suffer grievous loss. . ." and depends upon whether the recipient's interest in avoiding that loss outweighs the governmental interest in summary adjudication. Accordingly, as we said in Cafeteria & Restaurant Workers Union v. McElroy. . . , "consideration of what procedures due process may require under any given set of circumstances must begin with a determination of the precise nature of the government function involved as well as of the private interest that has been affected by governmental action". . . .

It is true, of course, that some governmental benefits may be administratively terminated without affording the recipient a pre-termination evidentiary hearing. But we agree with the District Court that when welfare is discontinued, only a pre-termination evidentiary hearing provides the recipient with procedural due process. . . . For qualified recipients, welfare provides the means to obtain essential food, clothing, housing, and medical care. . . . Thus the crucial factor in this context—a factor not present in the case of the blacklisted government contractor, the discharged government employee, the taxpayer denied a tax exemption, or virtually anyone else whose governmental entitlements are ended—is that termination of aid pending resolution of a controversy over eligibility may deprive an *eligible* recipient of the very means by which to live while he waits. Since he lacks independent resources, his situation becomes immediately desperate. His need to concentrate upon finding the means for daily subsistence, in turn, adversely affects his ability to seek redress from the welfare bureaucracy.

Moreover, important governmental interests are promoted by affording recipients a pre-termination evidentiary hearing. From its founding the Nation's basic commitment has been to foster the dignity and well-being of all persons within its borders. We have come to recognize that forces not within the control of the poor contribute to their poverty. This perception, against the background of our traditions, has significantly influenced the development of the contemporary public assistance system. Welfare, by meeting the basic demands of subsistence, can help bring within the reach of the poor the same opportunities that are available to others to participate meaningfully in the life of the community. At the same time, welfare guards against the societal malaise that may flow from a widespread sense of unjustified frustration and insecurity. Public assistance, then, is not mere charity, but a means to "promote the general Welfare, and secure the Blessings of Liberty to ourselves and our Posterity." The same governmental interests that counsel the provision of welfare counsel as well its uninterrupted provision to those eligible to receive it; pre-termination evidentiary hearings are indispensable to that end.

Appellant does not challenge the force of these considerations but argues that they are outweighed by countervailing governmental interests in conserving fiscal and administrative resources. These interests, the argument goes, justify the delay of any evidentiary hearing until after discontinuance of the grants. Summary adjudication protects the public fisc by stopping payments promptly upon discovery of reason to believe that a recipient is no longer eligible. Since most terminations are accepted without challenge, summary adjudication also conserves both the fisc and administrative time and energy by reducing the number of evidentiary hearings actually held.

We agree with the District Court, however, that these governmental interests are not overriding in the welfare context. The requirement of a prior hearing doubtless involves some greater expense, and the benefits paid to ineligible recipients pending decision at the hearing probably cannot be recouped, since these recipients are likely to be judgment-proof. But the State is not without weapons to minimize these increased costs. Much of the drain on fiscal and administrative resources can be reduced by developing procedures for prompt pre-termination hearings and by skillful use of personnel and facilities. Indeed, the very provision for a post-termination evidentiary hearing in New York's Home Relief program is itself cogent evidence that the State recognizes the primacy of the public interest in correct eligibility determinations and therefore in the provision of procedural safeguards. Thus, the interests of the eligible recipient in uninterrupted receipt of public assistance, coupled with the State's interest that his payments not be erroneously terminated, clearly outweighs the State's competing concern to prevent any increase in its fiscal and administrative burdens. As the District Court correctly concluded, "[t]he stakes are simply too high for the welfare recipient, and the possibility for honest error or irritable misjudgment too great, to allow termination of aid without giving the recipient a chance, if he so desires, to be fully informed of the case against him so that he may contest its basis and produce evidence in rebuttal". . . .

We also agree with the District Court, however, that the pre-termination hearing need not take the form of a judicial or quasi-judicial trial. We bear in mind that the statutory "fair hearing" will provide the recipient with a full administrative review. Accordingly, the pre-termination hearing has one function only: to produce an initial determination of the validity of the welfare department's grounds for discontinuance of payments in order to protect a recipient against an erroneous termination of his benefits. . . . Thus, a complete record and a comprehensive opinion, which would serve primarily to facilitate judicial review and to guide future decisions, need not be provided at the pre-termination stage. We recognize, too, that both welfare authorities and recipients have an interest in relatively speedy resolution of questions of eligibility, that they are used to dealing with one another informally, and that some welfare departments have very burdensome caseloads. These considerations justify the limitation of the pre-termination hearing to minimum procedural safeguards, adapted to the particular characteristics of welfare recipients, and to the limited nature of the controversies to be resolved. We wish to add that we, no less than the dissenters, recognize the importance of not imposing upon the States or the Federal Government in this developing field of law any procedural requirements beyond those demanded by rudimentary due process.

"The fundamental requisite of due process of law is the opportunity to be heard". . . .The hearing must be "at a meaningful time and in a meaningful manner". . . . In the present context these principles require that a recipient have timely and adequate notice detailing the reasons for a proposed termination, and an effective opportunity to defend by confronting any adverse witnesses and by presenting his own arguments and evidence orally. These rights are important in cases such as those before us, where recipients have challenged proposed terminations as resting on incorrect or misleading factual premises or on misapplication of rules or policies to the facts of the particular cases.

We are not prepared to say that the seven-day notice currently provided by New York City is constitutionally insufficient per se, although there may be cases where fairness would require that a longer time be given. Nor do we see any constitutional deficiency in the content or form of the notice. New York employs both a letter and a personal conference with a caseworker to inform a recipient of the precise questions raised about his continued eligibility. Evidently the recipient is told the legal and factual bases for the Department's doubts. This combination is probably the most effective method of communicating with recipients.

The city's procedures presently do not permit recipients to appear personally with or without counsel before the official who finally determines continued eligibility. Thus a recipient is not permitted to present evidence to that official orally, or to confront or cross-examine adverse witnesses. These omissions are fatal to the constitutional adequacy of the procedures.

The opportunity to be heard must be tailored to the capacities and circumstances of those who are to be heard. It is not enough that a welfare recipient may present his position to the decision maker in writing or secondhand through his caseworker. Written submissions are an unrealistic option for most recipients, who lack the educational attainment necessary to write effectively and who cannot obtain professional assistance.

Moreover, written submissions do not afford the flexibility of oral presentations; they do not permit the recipient to mold his argument to the issues the decision maker appears to regard as important. Particularly where credibility and veracity are at issue, as they must be in many termination proceedings, written submissions are a wholly unsatisfactory basis for decision. The secondhand presentation to the decisionmaker by the caseworker has its own deficiencies; since the caseworker usually gathers the facts upon which the charge of ineligibility rests, the presentation of the recipient's side of the controversy cannot safely be left to him. Therefore a recipient must be allowed to state his position orally. Informal procedures will suffice; in this context due process does not require a particular order of proof or mode of offering evidence. . . .

In almost every setting where important decisions turn on questions of fact, due process requires an opportunity to confront and cross-examine adverse witnesses. . . . What we said in Greene v. McElroy. . .is particularly pertinent here:

"Certain principles have remained relatively immutable in our jurisprudence. One of these is that where governmental action seriously injures an individual, and the reasonableness of the action depends on fact findings, the evidence used to prove the Government's case must be disclosed to the individual so that he has an opportunity to show that it is untrue. While this is important in the case of documentary evidence, it is even more important where the evidence consists of the testimony of individuals whose memory might be faulty or who, in fact, might be perjurers or persons motivated by malice, vindictiveness, intolerance, prejudice, or jealousy. We have formalized these protections in the requirements of confrontation and cross-examination. They have ancient roots. They find expression in the Sixth Amendment. . . . This Court has been zealous to protect these rights from erosion. It has spoken out not only in criminal cases, . . .but also in all types of cases where administrative. . . actions were under scrutiny." Welfare recipients must therefore be given an opportunity to confront and cross-examine the witnesses relied on by the department.

"The right to be heard would be, in many cases, of little avail if it did not comprehend the right to be heard by counsel." Powell v. Alabama. . . . We do not say that counsel must be provided at the pre-termination hearing, but only that the recipient must be allowed to retain an attorney if he so desires. Counsel can help delineate the issues, present the factual contentions in an orderly manner, conduct cross-examination, and generally safeguard the interests of the recipient. We do not anticipate that this assistance will unduly prolong or otherwise encumber the hearing. . . .

Finally, the decisionmaker's conclusion as to a recipient's eligibility must rest solely on the legal rules and evidence adduced at the hearing. . . . To demonstrate compliance with this elementary requirement, the decisionmaker should state the reasons for his determination and indicate the evidence he relied on. . . , though his statement need not amount to a full opinion or even formal findings of fact and conclusions of law. And, of course, an impartial decision maker is essential. . . . We agree with the District Court that prior involvement in some aspects of a case will not necessarily bar a welfare official from acting as a decision maker. He should not, however, have participated in making the determination under review.

Affirmed.

[Justice Black dissented on the ground that the Due Process Clause of the Fourteenth Amendment did not, properly construed, guarantee to a welfare recipient a pretermination hearing before his benefits were terminated, since welfare benefits were not "property" within the meaning of the Due Process Clause.]

[Chief Justice Burger, joined by Justice Black, also dissented from the majority's opinion, arguing that the bureaucracy should be allowed more time to develop administrative solutions to the kinds of problems presented in this case before the Court imposed a constitutional remedy of its own.]

[Justice Stewart also dissented in a brief opinion.]

The *Goldberg* case signaled the virtual abandonment of the use of the right-privilege dichotomy as a test of whether a hearing is required before administrative action is undertaken. As the Supreme Court said later, it has "now rejected the concept that constitutional rights turn upon whether a governmental benefit is characterized as a 'right' or as a 'privilege.'"

This abandonment of the right-privilege dichotomy by the Court, however, has required the Court to first of all formulate new criteria which determine when a hearing is required by due process in the administrative process and, if so, what kind of a hearing is required. And secondly, the abandonment of the right-privilege dichotomy encouraged further litigation that required the Court to apply due process principles in a variety of administrative contexts that had previously been insulated from due process hearing requirements by the right-privilege dichotomy.

The question of whether due process requires a hearing in the administrative process and, if so, what kind of a hearing, the Court has said since the *Goldberg* case, depends first upon "the private interest that will be affected by the official action; second, the risk of an erroneous determination of such interest through the procedures used, and the probable value, if any, of additional or substitute procedural safeguards; and finally, the Government's interest, including the function involved and the fiscal and administrative burdens the additional or substitute procedural requirement would entail."

Applying this three-pronged "balancing" test, the Court has held that in certain contexts no hearing at all is required before administrative action is taken, that in other contexts at least a minimal hearing is required and in yet other contexts that rather elaborate hearings are required. The Court has thus recognized the validity of emergency administrative actions taken without hearings when they are necessary to protect an overriding public interest. The Securities and Exchange Commission (SEC), for example, may suspend the trading in the stock of a particular company for ten days without notice or a hearing in order to protect the public from fraud. And in *Securities and Exchange Commission* v. *Sloan,* decided in 1978, the Supreme Court upheld the validity of such actions by the SEC, even though they involve the exercise of "an awesome power with a potentially devastating impact on the issuer [of the stock], its shareholders, and other investors."

Similarly, the Court held in *Ingraham* v. *Wright* in 1977 that a prior hearing was not required before a student was paddled for disciplinary reasons in the public schools. No hearing was required by due process in that context, the Court said, because of the ability of the teacher to observe directly the infraction in question, the openness of the school environment, the visibility of the confrontation to other students and faculty, and the likelihood of parental reaction to unreasonable punishment. All these factors, the Court held, gave assurance that "the risk that a child will be paddled without cause is typically insignificant."

Considering the due process right to a hearing in still another context, the Court held in *Goss* v. *Lopez* in 1975 that due process did apply to even brief suspensions of students from the public schools. Reiterating its rejection of the right-privilege dichotomy, the Court held that, having extended the right to attend public schools, the states "may not withdraw that right on grounds of misconduct, absent fundamentally fair procedures to determine whether the misconduct has occurred." Weighing the governmental interest in maintaining order and discipline in the public schools, and the administrative burden hearings would impose, against the students' interest in not being wrongfully suspended from school, the Court held that "due process requires, in connection with a suspension of 10 days or less, that the student be given oral or written notice of the charges against him and, if he denies them, an explanation of the evidence the authorities have and an opportunity to present his side of the story."

In *Memphis Light, Gas & Water Division* v. *Craft,* decided in 1978, the Court held that similar minimal due process hearing requirements apply prior to an action by a publicly owned utility company terminating utility service to a customer who had failed to pay his bill on the ground that it was erroneous. Due process required, the Court held, that the utility must "provide notice reasonably calculated to apprise [customers] of the availability of an administrative procedure to consider their complaint of erroneous billing," and afford customers "an opportunity to present their complaint [of erroneous billing] to a designated employee empowered to review disputed bills and rectify error," before terminating service to customers for their failure to pay their bills.

In contrast to the rather minimal due process hearing requirements the Court has imposed with regard to suspensions from the public schools or terminations of utilities, in *Morrissey* v. *Brewer* in 1972 and *Gagnon* v.

*Scarpelli* in 1973, it required elaborate hearings before parole or probation may be revoked. Not only is an individual whose parole or probation is subject to revocation entitled to a preliminary hearing, at which there must be established probable cause to believe a violation of parole or probation has occurred, the Court held; but also the revocation proceedings themselves must include adequate, written notice, disclosure of adverse evidence, opportunity to be heard in person and to present favorable witnesses and documentary evidence, the right to confront and cross-examine adverse witnesses, a neutral and detached hearing body, and a written statement of the decision, the evidence relied on for the decision, and the reasons therefor. In addition, the Court has held, where the individual involved is indigent, and the issues are unusually complex or the individual involved appears unable to represent himself adequately, appointed counsel must be provided. Revocation of parole or probation proceedings were required to include all these procedural elements, the Court said, when the governmental interest in the incarceration of parole and probation violators, and the administrative burdens imposed by such hearings, were weighed against the potential loss of liberty for the parolee or probationer that such proceedings involve.

With the repudiation of the right-privilege dichotomy in the *Goldberg* case, the Court has thus applied the due process requirement of a hearing in a wide variety of administrative contexts previously insulated from such requirements. And it is apparent that whether due process requires a hearing and, if so, what kind, varies widely depending upon the context in which due process is being applied. Flexibility clearly is the central characteristic of due process, as the Court's decisions applying the right to a hearing since the *Goldberg* case have clearly indicated.

## BIAS AND THE RULE OF NECESSITY

An important element of the due process right to a hearing is that the hearing be conducted before an unbiased adjudicative officer. On the question of bias on the part of administrative decision makers exercising adjudicative power, it is generally conceded that the due process standards of bias applicable to judges in the regular law courts are applicable to administrative adjudicative officers. Such officials may thus be disqualified from deciding cases on the grounds of personal bias against parties appearing before them or because they have a personal stake in the outcome of particular cases.

The Supreme Court in *Berger* v. *United States* in 1921 thus held disqualified for personal bias a judge who, in presiding over a trial concerning German-Americans, stated that "one must have a very judicial mind, indeed, not to be prejudiced against the German Americans in this country" and that he knew a "safeblower," and "as between him and this defendant, I prefer the safeblower." Similarly, in *Tumey* v. *Ohio* in 1927, the Court held disqualified because of personal interest a judge whose salary was largely paid out of the fines he levied upon convicted defendants. And in *Ward* v. *Village of Monroeville,* decided in 1972, the Court held that a mayor who also sat as a traffic court judge was disqualified on the ground of personal interest because a substantial part of the village's budget was derived from fines, fees, and costs levied by the mayor's court.

An important recent case regarding bias in the administrative process is *Gibson* v. *Berryhill,* decided by the Court in 1973. In the *Gibson* case, the Alabama Optometric Association, composed entirely of independent practitioners of optometry, charged the optometrists employed by the Lee Optical Company with unprofessional conduct in a complaint filed with the Alabama Board of Optometry, the state agency having authority to issue, suspend, and revoke licenses for the practice of optometry. The Board of Optometry, however, was composed solely of members of the Optometric Association, and a U.S. district court enjoined the license revocation proceedings before the board on the ground of bias. In affirming the district court's decision, the Supreme Court noted that it was "sufficiently clear from our cases that those with substantial pecuniary interest in legal proceedings should not adjudicate these disputes. . . . It has also come to be the prevailing view that '[m] ost of the law concerning disqualification because of interest applies with equal force to. . .administrative adjudicators.' "

Even if a judge or adjudicative officer can be shown to possess personal bias or interest, he may still be required to decide the issues before him if no one else is legally qualified to decide the issues. This is called the rule of necessity. The leading case on the subject is *Evans* v. *Gore,* decided in 1920, in which the Supreme Court held that the income taxation of a federal judge's salary to be unconstitutional, even though the justices themselves stood to gain financially from the decision. Since there was no other tribunal to finally settle the constitutional issue involved, the Court decided the case despite a definite personal interest of the justices in the outcome.

## THE STATUS OF ADMINISTRATIVE LAW JUDGES

Certain provisions of the Administrative Procedure Act also address the problem of assuring fairness on the part of adjudicative officers in the administrative process. One important provision of the APA in this regard guarantees a degree of independence to administrative law judges, who frequently are the presiding officers in administrative adjudicative proceedings and who render initial or recommended decisions in administrative cases. Until 1972, the administrative law judges (ALJs) were usually referred to as hearing examiners or trial examiners, but the Civil Service Commission changed their titles in that year. The APA provides that administrative law judges may not perform inconsistent duties and may be removed by their employing agencies "only for good cause established and determined by the Civil Service Commission on the record after opportunity for hearing."

At the time of the effective date of the Administrative Procedure Act, there were 197 administrative law judges employed by eighteen agencies, but by the mid-1970s almost eight hundred ALJs were employed by twenty-two agencies. Four hundred and twenty ALJs were employed by the Social Security Administration, by far the largest agency employer of ALJs, with the next largest agency employers of ALJs being the National Labor Relations Board (employing 97 ALJ's), the Interstate Commerce Commission (employing 75 ALJ's) and the Occupational Safety and Health Review Commission (employing 41 ALJs).

Although the Administrative Procedure Act affords the ALJs a degree of insulation from pressure from the agencies for which they work, decisions of the ALJs are only initial or recommended decisions that are normally appealable within the agencies. The final agency decision thus frequently remains in the hands of the head or (as with the regulatory commissions) heads of the agency. The decisions of the ALJs, despite their appealability within the agencies, may nevertheless be crucial in the process of administrative adjudication. During the 1971 fiscal year, for example, 30 percent of the decisions of the ALJs employed by the National Labor Relations Board (NLRB) were not appealed to the board and thus became the final decisions of the NLRB in those cases. Of the decisions of the ALJs that were appealed to the NLRB, the board affirmed the ALJs decisions in full in 80 percent of the cases.

While the ALJs may be thought of to an extent as the trial judges of the administrative process, their status is not exactly analogous to that of trial judges in the judicial process. The decisions of the ALJs are technically only the initial or recommended decisions of the agencies which, if appealed, may be reversed by the agencies without any showing that their evaluations of the evidence produced at the hearings over which they preside are clearly erroneous. On the other hand, the initial or recommended decision of an ALJ, whether reversed or affirmed by his agency, does become part of the record in cases of administrative adjudication and must be considered by a reviewing court in determining whether the agency's decision rests on substantial evidence.

## THE SEPARATION OF FUNCTIONS

A traditional charge against the possession of adjudicative powers by administrative agencies has of course been that adjudicative decisions of the agencies must be inherently biased or unfair, since the agencies often not only are declaring the law through their rule-making power but also proceeding against alleged violators of agency rules in adjudicative proceedings presided over by agency employees. The APA's provisions insulating ALJs to a degree from agency pressures was one response to such problems, while other provisions of the APA and other congressional statutes requiring the "separation of functions" within agencies constitute another response. The purpose of the organizational separation of functions within administrative agencies is to separate and insulate agency personnel performing adjudicative functions from personnel performing incompatible functions, especially investigating and prosecuting functions. Although law court judges, police, and prosecutors are all employed by the government, to ensure the independence and integrity of law court judges, they are not subject to supervision or control by the police and prosecutors, who investigate and prosecute cases before the courts. Similarly, although an administrative agency may perform investigative, prosecutive, and adjudicative functions, the separation of functions within the agency attempts to insulate the adjudicative personnel from investigative or prosecutorial personnel in order to protect the integrity of the adjudicative process.

The Administrative Procedure Act thus provides that the officer who presides at an adjudicative hearing shall not "consult a person or party on a fact in issue, unless on notice and opportunity for all parties to participate," nor should the hearing officer "be responsible to or subject to the supervision or direction of an employee or agent engaged in the performance of investigative or prosecuting functions for an agency." "An employee or agent engaged in the performance of investigative or prosecuting functions for an agency in a case," the APA continues, "may not, in that or a factually related case, participate or advise in the decision, recommended decision, or agency review pursuant to [adjudicative proceedings], except as witness or counsel in public proceedings."

The extent to which a federal agency must separate the functions it performs depends upon whether the APA or similar congressional legislation requiring separation of functions applies to the agency. Thus far, the courts have generally not required the separation of functions by the agencies as an element of that fairness mandated by due process. Indeed, in *Marcello* v. *Bonds,* decided in 1955, the Supreme Court held that a deportation hearing presided over by an Immigration and Naturalization

Service officer, who was subject to the supervision, direction, and control by INS personnel engaged in prosecution and investigative functions, did not violate the due process guarantee of a fair hearing. The degree to which separation of functions is required in federal agencies is therefore almost entirely dependent upon statutory law and not constitutional requirements under due process.

## FINDINGS AND REASONS

In exercising judicial review of administrative agency adjudicative decisions over the years, the courts developed as a matter of common law doctrine the requirement that the agencies must state in their decisions findings of facts upon which the decisions are based and the reasons the agencies are relying upon for their decisions. And these judicially created requirements were codified in the Administrative Procedure Act, which provides that agencies must include in their adjudicative decisions statements of "findings and conclusions, and the reasons therefor, on all the material issues of fact, law, or discretion presented on the record." An example of the judicial imposition of the requirement of findings of facts and reasons upon administrative decision making may be found in *Goldberg* v. *Kelly,* where the Supreme Court said in regard to decisions terminating welfare benefits that "the decisionmaker should state the reasons for his determination and indicate the evidence he relied on. . . ." The failure of administrative agencies to adequately state findings of facts and reasons upon which their decisions are based results in large numbers of reversals of agency decisions by the courts on judicial review.

There appear to be two overriding reasons for the insistence by the courts upon statements of findings of fact and reasons by the agencies in their decisions. The first reason is that statements of facts upon which the agency has relied for its decision, and of the reasons by which the agency justifies its decision, facilitates judicial review of agency decision making. That is, by examining statements of facts supporting agency decisions and the reasons the agencies give for their decisions, the courts can more readily and easily determine whether agencies have acted lawfully and within their jurisdictions.

A second, and important, reason for these seemingly technical requirements is that they also are a significant check on administrative arbitrariness. Arbitrary or capricious decisions by administrators would be much more easily concealed if they were not compelled to state what evidence they relied upon for their decisions and what reasons justified their decisions. Although seemingly technical in nature, the requirements of findings of facts and reasons are one of the more important tools of the courts in checking the power of administrative agencies through the exercise of judicial review.

## THE SUBSTANTIAL EVIDENCE TEST

As governmental functions came to be increasingly performed through modern administrative agencies, there erupted a long-term debate, never finally resolved, over the proper scope of judicial review of administrative agency decisions. And a substantial part of the debate focused upon the so-called law-fact dichotomy. While most involved in the debate over the proper scope of judicial review of agency decisions agreed that, in reviewing agency decisions, the courts could properly review issues of law, a heated debate occurred over the extent to which the courts should review the facts or evidence upon which administrative decisions rested.

Opponents of the increasing power of administrative agencies generally favored the broadest possible review of administrative decisions by the courts, including extensive judicial review of the evidence or facts upon which such decisions were based. At the outermost extreme, opponents of the administrative process supported trials *de novo* when administrative decisions were challenged in the courts. That is, the courts were urged to conduct their own trials at which the factual bases of administrative decisions would be redetermined by the reviewing court as if prior administrative proceedings had not occurred. The practical effect of such an extensive scope for judicial review would of course be to make administrative proceedings and decisions mere preludes to proceedings in the courts.

Supporters of the administrative agencies and the programs they administered, on the other hand, pointed out that the agencies were created to take advantage of the expertise the agencies developed in many complex areas of governmental regulation. The expertise of the agencies, they argued, put them in a superior position to evaluate the complex evidentiary materials upon which their decisions were based, and the courts, in reviewing administrative decisions, should consequently defer to the expertise of the agencies. Generalist judges, untrained in the complexities of modern governmental regulatory programs, the proponents of the agencies argued, were not qualified to second-guess the expert judgments of the agencies, and the scope of review of agency decisions by the courts should therefore be quite restricted.

Lying behind these arguments over the proper scope of judicial review of agency decisions was the broader ideological conflict between conservatives and liberals over the role of the government in regulating the economy. Both sides recognized that, at least until the 1930s, the courts were generally hostile to governmental regulation of economic affairs and protective of property rights. And an increase in the scope of judicial review of the decisions of the administrative agencies which were implementing governmental regulatory programs was perceived as increasing conservative influence and restrictions upon such programs, while, on the other hand, a diminution of the scope of judicial review of agency decisions meant a reduction of conservative influence and restrictions upon regulatory programs.

Although this debate over the proper scope of judicial review of administrative decisions has in some respects never been resolved, the federal courts ultimately settled upon the "substantial evidence test" as the formula to guide the scope of their review of the evidence upon which administrative decisions are based. That is, when an administrative decision is based upon a record containing conflicting evidence, and review of the decision is sought in the federal courts, the reviewing court will uphold the agency's decision if it is supported by substantial evidence in the record.

The substantial evidence test is more a term of art than a mathematical formula, as the Supreme Court recognized when it noted the deficiency of any formula "to furnish definiteness of content for all the impalpable factors involved in judicial review." The substantial evidence test, the Court nevertheless held in *Universal Camera Corp.* v. *NLRB* in 1951, means that a reviewing court must reverse a decision of an agency "when it cannot conscientiously find that the evidence supporting that decision is substantial, when viewed in the light that the record in its entirety furnishes, including the body of evidence opposed to the [agency's] view." Substantial evidence, the Court said in *Consolidated Edison Co.* v. *NLRB* in 1938, "is more than a mere scintilla. It means such relevant evidence as a reasonable mind might accept as adequate to support a conclusion."

Although the substantial evidence test is most commonly applied by the courts in reviewing administrative adjudications based upon an evidentiary record produced at an administrative hearing, it should be noted that the substantial evidence test is also applicable to agency rules and regulations that may be issued only after a formal, trial type of hearing. Since most rule-making proceedings undertaken by administrative agencies are not required to take the form of formal hearings, however, the substantial evidence test is not in many instances applied by the courts in reviewing the validity of administrative rules and regulations.

In addition to its inherent vagueness, one difficulty with the substantial evidence test as a formula guiding the scope of judicial review of administrative decisions is that the courts have traditionally treated various kinds of evidence differently. "Legally competent" evidence is, from the standpoint of a court, the highest form of evidence, since legally competent evidence is admissible in a court of law before a jury. An administrative decision resting upon a largely uncontradicted body of legally competent evidence in the record would always satisfy a reviewing court in applying the substantial evidence test. Hearsay, on the other hand, is ordinarily inadmissible in a court of law because of its presumed unreliability and because it cannot effectively be cross-examined, and the opportunity for cross-examination is an important element of a fair hearing under due process. For example, if A sees B rob a bank and tells his friend C what he has seen, A's eyewitness testimony would be legally competent evidence against B in a trial for bank robbery. C's testimony about what A told him he saw would, however, be hearsay and inadmissible in a law court. Cross-examination of C would be ineffective, since the relative acuteness of A's powers of observation or his reliability as a witness could not be tested by the cross-examination of C.

Hearsay is nevertheless normally admissible in administrative proceedings. One of the principal reasons offered for the substitution of administrative agencies for the courts in the administration of many governmental programs was the belief that the agencies would be more flexible, speedier, and less bound down by the technical rules of procedure applicable in the courts. And one aspect of the freedom of the agencies from technical procedural rules applicable in the courts is their ability to consider evidence, including hearsay, that would be inadmissible in a court of law. The Administrative Procedure Act thus provides that in proceedings before federal agencies any "oral or documentary evidence may be received, but the agency as a matter of policy shall provide for the exclusion of irrelevant, immaterial, or unduly repetitious evidence."

The APA clearly contemplates the admission of hearsay evidence in proceedings before federal agencies, and most statutes creating the various federal agencies contain similar provisions. It was long open to doubt, however, whether an administrative decision resting entirely upon hearsay should be upheld by a reviewing court applying the substantial evidence test.

One rule adhered to by some state courts, and at least flirted with by some federal courts, holds that hearsay evidence cannot be substantial evidence sufficient to support an administrative decision. That rule is the "residuum rule," and it provides that an administrative decision, if it is to be upheld by a reviewing court as resting on substantial evidence, must be based upon a residuum of legally competent evidence. That is, the residuum rule prohibits administrative agencies from basing decisions entirely upon hearsay. Rather, the residuum rule provides, administrative decisions must be based at least partially upon legally competent evidence

—evidence that would be admissible in a court before a jury. The residuum rule thus allows administrative agencies to admit hearsay in their proceedings and to consider hearsay in weighing their decisions, but the rule nonetheless requires that some legally competent evidence must support the agency's final decision.

The incorporation of the residuum rule into the substantial evidence test as applied by the federal courts would of course have made the latter a stricter rule of judicial review, but for many years the question of whether the substantial evidence test in the federal courts embraced the residuum rule went unanswered by the Supreme Court. Some of the Court's statements regarding the substantial evidence test, taken somewhat out of context, appeared to disparage administrative reliance on hearsay, as when the Court declared in *Consolidated Edison Co.* v. *NLRB* in 1938 that "[m]ere uncorroborated hearsay or rumor does not constitute substantial evidence." But the weight of the decisions in the federal courts applying the substantial evidence test appeared to be against the residuum rule.

Yet, if hearsay were admissible in administrative proceedings and could constitute substantial evidence supporting an administrative decision, serious questions were raised regarding the due process right to a fair hearing in the administrative process. In discussing the right to a hearing in welfare termination cases in *Goldberg* v. *Kelly,* the Court held that due process requires an "opportunity to confront and cross-examine adverse witnesses" in "almost every setting where important decisions turn on questions of fact." Hearsay, however, cannot be effectively cross-examined. And if hearsay were admitted in administrative proceedings and could constitute substantial evidence supportive of an administrative decision, the question raised by the *Goldberg* case was whether an administrative decision supported only by hearsay would not violate the due process right to a fair hearing, which the Court had indicated must often involve the right of confrontation and cross-examination.

Such questions regarding the relation of the substantial evidence test to the residuum rule, as well as the implications of administrative agency reliance on hearsay for the meaning of the due process right to a hearing, came to a head in *Richardson* v. *Perales,* decided by the Supreme Court in 1971. The proceedings in the *Perales* case also illuminate the process of administrative adjudication, the role of administrative law judges as hearing officers, and questions regarding the proper separation of functions within administrative agencies. The litigation in the *Perales* case additionally involved echoes of the old debate between liberals and conservatives over the proper scope of judicial review of agency decisions, and revealed that some liberal groups were expressing a suspicion of the bureaucracy and support for broader judicial review of agency decisions reminiscent of earlier conservative critics of the administrative process. We shall now therefore take a detailed look at the issues and the litigation in *Richardson* v. *Perales.*

## CASE STUDY
### THE LAW, THE BUREAUCRACY, AND MR. PERALES'S BACK

In 1965, Pedro Perales, Jr., was a thirty-three-year-old truck driver supporting his wife and three children in San Antonio, Texas. Perales had worked for the Jim Walters Corporation for six years, making $75 a month as a truck driver and earning additional income from selling the shell houses the Jim Walters Corporation manufactured. On September 29, Perales was unloading a truck containing shingles, and while lifting a bundle of shingles weighing approximately sixty-five pounds, he "suddenly had a pain in his back, was paralyzed for five minutes, [and] dropped [the] bundle...which he had lifted." Such incidents are of course commonplace, but in this instance the conflict over the nature and scope of the injury to Pedro Perales's back would involve extensive bureaucratic decision making, produce conflict between the lower federal courts and the bureaucracy over the fairness of the administrative process, and finally lead to a landmark decision by the United States Supreme Court in the field of administrative law.

After the incident on September 29, Pedro Perales was treated by physicians, but he continued to complain of severe back pains. He was finally hospitalized and treated by a neurosurgeon, Dr. Ralph Munslow, who reported on November 12 that it was his conclusion "that this man [has] a protruded intervertebral disc and that he likely [is] not going to respond to conservative management." Dr. Munslow suggested to Perales that surgery was indicated, but Perales appeared to improve and was released from the hospital. Within ten days, however, Perales returned to Dr. Munslow complaining of severe pain in his back, and Munslow again concluded that "almost surely he has extruded a disc, and I wouldn't be at all surprised but that there is a free fragment lying in the middle of the lower part of the canal. Certainly, he should be admitted for myelography and surgery."

Dr. Munslow thus performed an operation on Perales's back (a hemilaminectomy) during November of 1965. Despite his diagnosis of a herniated disc, Munslow reported that during surgery "there was no protrusion of the disc identified." Munslow's postoperative diagnosis was that Perales was suffering from "nerve root compression syndrome, left." Perales, on the other hand, continued to complain of severe back pain, but

Dr. Munslow concluded that there was no neurological evidence of injury to Perales's back and reported that Perales "could return to work. I do not believe that his disability exceeds ten percent." In response to an inquiry in May of 1966 suggesting that Perales might need some home nursing care, Munslow responded that "the last time I saw him he appeared to me to be perfectly capable of taking care of himself." Perales was also examined by Dr. Morris Lampert, a specialist in neurological medicine, and Dr. Lampert reported that Perales was "a well developed, well nourished, somewhat obese. . .male who is alert and cooperative" and that there "is no objective evidence of neurologic involvement."

Since he continued to experience pain, Perales consulted with Dr. Max Morales, a family physician and general practitioner. Morales treated Perales at first with deep heat and muscle stimulation without much positive result. Dr. Morales also prescribed sleeping pills and muscle relaxant pills to alleviate Perales's pain and help him sleep. After hospitalizing Perales for over two weeks, Dr. Morales became convinced that Perales had indeed suffered an injury to the lumbosacral region of his spine which had not been corrected by surgery. Morales also concluded that Perales was permanently disabled, since, as he said later, "I feel there is something still wrong there that hasn't been fixed and you can't fix it with pills and a little treatment. I don't know what in the world I could do or I would have done it already. There is nothing I can do, nothing at all that will heal this man. . . ."

In 1956, Congress amended the Social Security Act of 1935 to provide benefits for persons who became permanently and totally disabled, and this disability benefits program was liberalized by subsequent amendments to the Social Security Act in 1958, 1960, and 1965. Under the program, a person who is unable "to engage in any substantial gainful activity by reason of any medically determinable physical or mental impairment" is entitled to federal disability insurance benefits. The disability benefits program is administered by the Social Security Administration in the Department of Health and Human Services, and HHS contracts with state agencies to make the initial determination of whether or not a claimant qualifies for disability benefits.

## PERALES APPLIES FOR DISABILITY BENEFITS

When Pedro Perales applied for Social Security disability benefits, his application was therefore initially reviewed by an agency of the State of Texas. In addition to a report by Dr. Morales supporting Perales's disability claim, the state agency obtained the hospital records relating the treatment Perales had undergone as well as the reports of Dr. Munslow and Dr. Lampert. The state agency also decided to obtain the opinion of a specialist, and Pedro Perales was thus examined on May 25, 1966, by an orthopedic surgeon, Dr. John H. Langston. Dr. Langston's report on the results of this examination was devastating in regard to Perales's claim of disability.

Perales, Langston reported, was five feet eleven inches tall and weighed 212 pounds. "This 33-year-old big physical healthy specimen," the doctor continued, "is obviously holding back and limiting all of his motions, intentionally. He walks very slowly, holds his body almost rigidly, and needs his wife to care for him by helping him get dressed and undressed. The examination of him is somewhat difficult because he will not do such motions as bending forward more than 10 or 15 degrees. He cannot stoop, nor will he try. He cannot squat. His upper extremities, though they are completely uninvolved by his injury, he holds very rigidly as though he were semi-paralyzed. His reach and grasp are very limited but intentionally so. When asked to squeeze my hand very tightly, the most he could manage was just a feeble grip on both sides."

Dr. Langston also reported that the results of a neurological examination were entirely normal. Perales, he said, complained of leg swelling, and his legs were "slightly edematous. No doubt because of his inactivity and sitting around in a chair or standing almost rigidly. Also some of the muscles of the dorsal spine are slightly tender, but this I believe is due to his poor posture, and a very mild sprain. . . , which would resolve [itself] were he actually to get a little exercise and move. . . ." Perales might have, Langston concluded, "a very mild chronic back sprain," but "it has been a long time since I have been so impressed with the obvious attempt of a patient to exaggerate his difficulties by simply just standing there and not moving—not even the uninvolved upper extremities. Thus, he has a tremendous psychological overlay to his illness, and I sincerely suggest that he be seen by a psychiatrist." Three to six months of active exercise, including walking and bicycling, would cure Perales, Langston said, assuming he "does not have any serious psychiatric disease, though he obviously does have a tremendous psychological overlay to his illness."

In light of Dr. Langston's report, Perales was not unexpectedly notified on June 6, 1966, by the Evaluation and Authorization Branch of the Social Security Administration that he was ineligible for disability benefits. The Evaluation and Authorization Branch informed Perales that in order to be disabled for Social Security purposes, "a person must be unable to engage in any substantial gainful activity due to a medical condition which has lasted or can be expected to last for a continuous period of at least 12 months," and that a person must be "unable to work not only at his usual occupation but at any other substantial gainful work considering his previous training and work experience." "After carefully studying the record in your case," Perales was advised, "including the medical evidence, and considering your statements, age, education, training, and experience, we find that your condition is not disabling within the meaning of the law."

Perales nonetheless requested that his disability claim be reconsidered, and his request for reconsideration was again supported by a report by Dr. Morales attesting that Perales was indeed disabled. He was convinced, Morales said in his report, "that this man is not malingering. I am completely convinced of his sincerity and of the genuine and truthful nature of his complaints." Morales indicated that it was his diagnosis that Perales "has indeed an injury to the lumbo-sacral region of the spine which has not been corrected by surgery. My opinion is that the injury sustained is of a permanent nature and that as things presently stand, the patient is totally, completely, and permanently disabled. It is my considered opinion that this patient in the condition in which he finds himself at this time would not be able to continue gainful employment as a common laborer."

As a part of the reconsideration of Perales's claim, he was also referred to a psychiatrist, Dr. James M. Bailey. Dr. Bailey reported that his examination revealed "a rather stocky male weighing 220 pounds. He walks slowly and stooped and uses a cane. He is oriented as to time, place and person. Memory for remote and recent events is good. Speech is logical and coherent." Perales, Dr. Bailey continued, could "read and write a small amount. He attended third grade in school and quit because he had to help the family feed the other children." Perales indicated that he was "depressed all the time," "yells at his wife and children usually using a great deal of profanity," had difficulty sleeping, and had a mood "of continuous anger and feelings of being put upon."

Perales, Dr. Bailey concluded, was "extremely hostile particularly to doctors, relating that he will get well even if he has to go to Mexico or somewhere to find a doctor smart enough to cure him." Perales had a paranoid personality, Bailey said, "manifested by hostility, feelings of persecution and a long history of strained interpersonal relationships. I do not feel that this patient has a separate psychiatric illness at this time. It appears that his personality is conducive to anger, frustrations, etc."

Finally, the hospital records and medical reports on Perales were reviewed by a board-certified specialist in neurology, Dr. Howard Moses of the Johns Hopkins Hospital. Dr. Moses noted that, except for the report of Dr. Morales, all the examinations of Perales for a disabling injury had been negative. Morales, Moses reported, had "documented no objective evidence of nerve root compression, but documented a great deal of conservative and narcotic treatment for the claimant. He was unable to offer a satisfactory reason for the claimant's complaints, but did submit a rather large bill." Dr. Moses concluded that there was no "objective evidence" that Perales had a "severe orthopedic or neurological impairment."

On October 20, 1966, the Reconsideration Branch of the Social Security Administration informed Perales that his request for reconsideration of his disability claim had been reevaluated by the state agency and had been independently evaluated by the Social Security Administration. The medical evidence indicated that Perales had no "bone or nerve impairment," the Reconsideration Branch said, and "your ability to sit, stand and walk is not seriously impaired. Although you may be nervous and concerned about your health, the evidence does not reveal any impairment of your ability to think, reason, remember and understand. Therefore, it has been determined that your condition is not so severe as to prevent you from doing the types of work which are consistent with your experience and background."

Pedro Perales had pressed his claim in the administrative process to the point at which the final disposition of the overwhelming majority of Social Security disability benefit claims occurs. In the fiscal year 1968, for example, there were 515,938 disability claims, of which all but 20,800 were resolved by this stage in the administrative process, 343,628 or almost two-thirds of the claims resulting in the granting of benefits. Perales's claim was exceptional not only because it was pressed beyond this stage in the administrative process but also because Perales was represented by an attorney, Richard Tinsman. In the mid-1960s, fewer than 20 percent of the claimants for disability benefits were represented by counsel at any stage in the administrative process, and, indeed, the Social Security Administration discouraged the retention of counsel by claimants.

## THE FORMAL ADJUDICATORY HEARING

When the Reconsideration Branch denied Perales's claim, the branch also informed him that if he disagreed with its decision, he could within six months request a hearing on his claim by the Bureau of Hearings and Appeals. Perales requested a hearing and was informed on January 2, 1967, that a hearing in his case would be held before an administrative law judge, Frank J. Buldain, at the U.S. Post Office and Courthouse Building in San Antonio on January 12. Although employed by the Social Security Administration as an administrative law judge, under the provisions of the

Administrative Procedure Act, Buldain, like all administrative law judges, was given relatively independent status within the bureaucracy, was insulated to a degree from agency influence, and was subject to dismissal only for cause established in a hearing before the U.S. Civil Service Commission.

In preparing for the Perales hearing, Buldain obtained the hospital records and the various reports of the medical examinations Perales had undergone, and this documentary file was available for inspection by Perales and his counsel, Richard Tinsman, prior to the hearing. The state agency also referred Perales to Dr. Richard H. Mattson, who conducted an electromyography study. Dr. Mattson reported that there might be "some chronic or past disturbance of function in the nerve supply" to certain muscles in Perales's back, but this was "strongly suggestive of lack of maximal effort" and was "the kind of finding that is typically associated with a functional or psychogenic component to weakness." There was no evidence, Mattson reported, of "any active process [affecting] the nerves at present."

Dr. Mattson's report, as well as the hospital records and other reports of medical examinations of Perales, constituted the greater proportion of the evidence that had to be evaluated by administrative law judge Buldain at the hearing on January 12. The use of such evidence in Social Security disability hearings, however, had led to a rapidly escalating confrontation between the administrative law judges, the Social Security Administration, and Chief Judge Adrian A. Spears of the United States District Court for the Western District of Texas. The district courts are authorized to review decisions by the Social Security Administration in disability benefits cases, and Judge Spears had strongly objected to administrative law judges basing decisions denying benefits upon written medical reports by doctors who did not appear and testify personally at the hearings. Such written reports, Judge Spears had said, were mere uncorroborated hearsay which was not subject to confrontation and cross-examination at the hearing, since the doctors writing the reports did not appear personally and testify. Such reports therefore could not, Spears said, constitute "substantial evidence" to justify the denial of a disability benefits claim by the Social Security Administration, and Spears advised all lawyers in the San Antonio area to object to the introduction of these medical reports in hearings before the administrative law judges.

Despite Judge Spears's condemnation of the reliance on hearsay to deny disability benefits, Congress rather clearly provided otherwise in the Social Security Act. In the act, Congress delegated legislative power to the Secretary of Health and Human Services to issue rules and regulations governing the procedure to be followed in disability benefits hearings, and Congress further provided that evidence "may be received at any hearing before the Secretary even though inadmissable under rules of evidence applicable to court procedure." And under the rules issued by the secretary governing disability hearings, the administrative law judges were authorized to issue subpoenas for testimony and documents and "receive in evidence the testimony of witnesses and any documents which are relevant and material. . . ." The secretary's rules also provided that evidence "may be received at the hearing even though inadmissable under rules of evidence applicable to court procedure."

At the outset of the hearing on Pedro Perales's disability claim, administrative law judge Buldain therefore pointed out that under "the administrative procedures, we are not bound by the formal rules of evidence, we are not concerned about the hearsay rule and many similar rules." Counsel for Perales, Richard Tinsman, nevertheless objected to the introduction of the medical reports into evidence at the hearing on the ground that, since their authors were not appearing personally and subject to cross-examination, the reports were hearsay. "Let me say this in regard to hearsay objections," Tinsman remarked. "Judge Spears and others have wished the lawyers to object. . .knowing the [administrative law judge] may overrule. Judge Spears says he may have a different ruling. . . ." As expected, Buldain overruled Tinsman's objections, and the medical reports on Perales's condition became a part of the evidence in the hearing.

In contrast with the written medical reports which were uniformly adverse to Perales's claim of disability, Dr. Max Morales appeared at the hearing and testified personally that it was his professional opinion that Perales was disabled due to the injury to his back. "I am a family physician and see somewhere between eight hundred or better than eight hundred patients per month," Morales said. "A good number of these patients are laborers who have hurt themselves or have genuine complaints and some are phony complaints, and I am so busy that I can't waste my time on a malingerer or someone that's just using me for his own means, so, quickly I try to discover if a man is sincere and legitimate when he has a complaint of long standing like this, and if I find that he's just using me and taking up my time, I try to get rid of him. Now at no time have I been impressed that I did not have genuine complaints here." Not at any time, Morales continued, "have I thought [Perales] has been lying to me, and I sincerely feel there is something there that I can't put my finger on. . .but I can't prove it to you."

"Well, you see, doctor," administrative law judge Buldain interrupted, "this is my dilemma—I follow your rationale and in many respects it's quite sensible. On the other hand, I've got the proposition—the law states that there be a medically determinable impairment. We have to have something on which we come up with a conclusion this man is hurting." "If you're going to have to depend only on what your eyes can see," Dr. Morales replied, "then you are going to come up many, many times with erroneous conclusions because I would be in that position frequently today, right now, at the hospital, if I didn't just follow what I feel is the correct diagnosis and your studies do not always indicate everything."

Dr. Morales also attempted to explain the negative findings of the doctors whose medical reports were in evidence, pointing out that the reports were perhaps influenced by Perales's distrust of Anglos:

[Dr. Morales]: Pedro has an intense distrust of Anglos and his whole attitude reflects it immediately. I pursued this one day and I asked him one day about his childhood and he told me a story that's very significant. I'm sure he won't mind my relating it now, but at one time he was asked by a bunch of Anglos...what his religion was. Well, he was limited in his vocabulary and he knew the word he wanted to use but he was unsure about the word, and in the confusion he used the wrong word, so he blurted out "cadillac," and everybody had a big laugh and said, "No, stupid, the word is Catholic, not cadillac." This hurt him deeply, you know, and ever since then he has disliked the English language and he does not trust Anglos too well. Besides, other things that have happened to him in the past [and] in this person here you have a problem [because of the] great many economic injustices which he feels, and other things, have caused him to be extremely doubtful about Anglos that he comes into contact with, especially as it relates to his illness and almost from the instant he walks in, he walks in with an attitude that is bound to be misinterpreted by the person who sees him.
[Administrative law judge]: In other words, you think his behavior and attitude when he talks to people, that his reaction is such that they have misinterpreted?
A. Misinterpreted and I don't know what value you want to put on that, but I [don't] think he's been evaluated properly. Probably even Munslow even rubbed him the wrong way.

Pedro Perales also testified and described the life he had been living since his injury. He lived with his wife and three children in a four-room house which he rented for $45 per month. After his injury, he said, he had received $75 a week in insurance payments, but those payments had stopped after six months. The only source of income for the Perales family at the time of the hearing was the $35 per week Mrs. Perales earned working at a drugstore. Perales also testified that he had been offered a job as a salesman for the Jim Walters Corporation, but had discovered that he could not drive his car for any significant distance without severe pain to his back and swelling of his arms and legs. Since being a salesman required both driving and walking, he had concluded that he would be unable to do the job.

Perales further testified that his daily routine since his injury was to wake up about 6:30 A.M. and see his wife off to work and his children off to school. He drank only a cup of coffee for breakfast and ate nothing else until his wife prepared him a meal in the evening. Perales said that he slept three or four hours during the day because, although he went to bed at eleven P.M., he rarely got to sleep until three or four in the morning because of the pain in his back. "I have to lay in bed most of the time because I can't sit for too long. . . ," he said. "I can't sit on the chair too long. I have to be in bed." The only exercise he got, Perales continued, was to occasionally walk a four-block distance around his house.

At the close of Perales's testimony, administrative law judge Buldain indicated that, given the obvious contradiction between the testimony of Dr. Morales and Pedro Perales and the medical reports of the doctors who had examined and treated Perales, he would consider holding a supplementary hearing at which a medical adviser would appear and give him an expert interpretation of the medical evidence in the case. Such a supplementary hearing was called by Buldain and was held on March 31, 1967. At this second hearing, Dr. Lewis A. Leavitt, a Houston specialist in physical medicine and rehabilitation, appeared as a medical adviser to interpret the medical evidence regarding the injury to Perales's back. Richard Tinsman again objected to the use of the hearsay written medical reports as evidence, and he objected to Dr. Leavitt's testimony on the ground that he had not personally examined Perales. Buldain again overruled Tinsman's objections.

Under close questioning by Buldain and cross-examination by Tinsman, Dr. Leavitt interpreted the various medical examinations Perales had undergone and the findings that had resulted. In response to questions by Buldain, Leavitt testified that in light of all of the medical evidence it was his opinion that Perales was suffering from "low back syndrome" of only mild severity. In his professional opinion, Leavitt said, "a person relatively able bodied with an impression—diagnostic impression of low back syndrome, mild, should be able over a relatively short period of time—by that I mean a month or so—to resume activity that should be commensurate with an eight hour day that would not have severe lifting or stress to the back, so one would not have an exacerbation of the previous condition. In general, one might say the person is 'ten percent disabled.'"

Under cross-examination by Richard Tinsman, Dr. Leavitt refused to alter his opinion of the nature and extent of the injury to Perales's back. Indeed, he asserted that he was familiar with individuals with much greater physical disabilities than Perales who were gainfully employed. He was aware of a quadraplegic confined to a wheel chair, Leavitt told Tinsman, who was gainfully employed. Tinsman responded that Leavitt appeared to believe that no one was totally disabled, even a person who had had both arms and both legs amputated, and Leavitt said that given proper care and rehabilitation such a person could be gainfully employed.

At the request of Buldain, a vocational expert, Professor J. C. Pool, also testified at the supplementary hearing. According to Pool, there were numerous jobs in the San Antonio area that Pedro Perales could adequately perform, assuming he had a mild low back syndrome. The best job for Perales, Pool said, would have been selling houses for the Jim Walters Corporation, but he could also work as a ticket taker, security guard, or at a garage, pumping gas. The point of Pool's testimony was of course that substantial gainful employment was available that Perales could perform, and that therefore Perales was not totally disabled within the meaning of the Social Security Act.

A month and a half after the completion of the supplemental hearing, administrative law judge Buldain issued his decision in the Perales case. In his "findings of fact," Buldain ruled that Perales was "suffering from low back syndrome of musculoligamentous origin, and of mild severity," while also suffering an "emotional overlay" to his medical impairment. Neither this emotional nor medical condition, Buldain found, had rendered Perales disabled within the meaning of the Social Security Act. Perales, Buldain said, was "capable of engaging as a salesman of predesigned and fabricated materials for the construction of individual homes" or working as a "watchman and security guard in establishments which do not require strenuous physical activity, and similarly as a ticket taker and janitor." "Accordingly," Buldain concluded, "it is the decision of the [administrative law judge] that, based on his application filed November 15, 1966, the claimant is not entitled to a period of disability or disability insurance benefits under the provisions of Sections 216(i) and 223(c). . .of the Social Security Act, as amended."

## THE EXHAUSTION OF ADMINISTRATIVE REMEDIES

Pedro Perales had thus lost again, but within the Social Security bureaucracy the decision of an administrative law judge is not final, since it may be appealed to the Appeals Council of the Social Security Administration. The Appeals Council consists of eight members possessing the final authority over the decision of Social Security claims. Unlike the administrative law judges, however, the members of the Appeals Council are employees of the Social Security Administration and are not insulated from agency influence under the provisions of the Administrative Procedure Act.

On June 16, 1967, Richard Tinsman submitted a letter on behalf of Pedro Perales requesting that the Appeals Council review and reverse Buldain's decision. Tinsman submitted an additional medical report, which had not been considered at the hearing before Buldain, indicating that Perales was suffering from a postoperative herniated disc.

Ironically, only two weeks after Buldain's decision denying him disability benefits under the Social Security Act, Pedro Perales was found to be totally disabled by a jury after a trial in the District Court for the 131st Judicial District of Bexar County, Texas. The suit had been initiated by Tinsman on behalf of Perales for workmen's compensation against the Continental Casualty Company, the carrier of workmen's compensation insurance for the Jim Walters Corporation. After the trial, the jury found Perales totally disabled and awarded him almost two thousand dollars in medical expenses and over eleven thousand dollars in compensation. The judgment in this case was of course submitted to the Appeals Council by Tinsman as further justification for the reversal of Buldain's decision.

On July 20, 1967, the Appeals Council nevertheless notified Perales of its decision affirming Buldain's decision. The Council, Perales was informed, had considered "all the evidence in your case, the law and regulations applicable to your claim, the [administrative law judge's] evaluation of the facts and the reasoning in his decision, and your reasons for believing your claim should be allowed." "The Appeals Council," the notice concluded, "has decided that the decision of the [administrative law judge] is correct. Further action by the Council would not, therefore, result in any change which would benefit you. Accordingly, the [administrative law judge's] decision stands as the final decision of the Secretary [of Health and Human Services] in your case."

Richard Tinsman and Pedro Perales had now exhausted the administrative remedies available to them in pursuing the disability claim, and, as the Appeals Council informed Perales, if further review of the disposition of his claim were desired, a civil action would have to be filed in the U.S. district court within sixty days. Since Tinsman was aware that Chief Judge Adrian Spears of the U.S. District Court for the Western District of Texas strongly objected to disability claims being decided on the basis of written medical reports, it came as no surprise that on August 17 Tinsman filed a complaint to set aside the Perales decision. The decision of the Social Security Administration, Tinsman alleged in the complaint, was contrary to the facts and was not supported by "substantial evidence."

## THE DISTRICT COURT REVERSES

The U.S. attorney's office responded with a motion to dismiss the complaint on the ground that the denial of Perales's claim was supported by substantial evidence, and a hearing on both the government's motion to dismiss and Tinsman's complaint was held before Judge Spears on February 13, 1968. At the hearing, neither government counsel nor counsel for Perales had much to say, since Judge Spears immediately began a long monologue denouncing the Social Security Administration's procedures for processing disability benefits claims.

Pedro Perales had not had a fair hearing, Judge Spears declared, because the administrative law judge had called in a medical adviser, who had never examined Perales, to interpret medical reports of doctors who were not present to be cross-examined, and then the administrative law judge had merely "parroted" the medical adviser's testimony in his decision. The medical adviser, Dr. Leavitt, Judge Spears noted, "admittedly did not examine the plaintiff, had never seen him professionally or at all before he went to the hearing, and the reaction I get from that sort of thing is nausea, because, in the first place, I think that hearsay evidence in the nature of *ex parte* statements of doctors on the critical issue of a man's present physical condition is just a violation of the concept with which I am familiar and which bears upon the issue of fundamental fair play in a hearing. Then, when you pyramid hearsay from a so-called medical adviser, who, himself, has never examined the man who claims benefits, then you just compound it—compound a situation that I simply cannot tolerate in my own mind. . . ."

Judge Spears proceeded to denounce the Social Security Administration's procedures in disability cases in general and in Pedro Perales's case in particular:

Now, I think that if a doctor is going to testify, his testimony is going to be relied upon by either side, and if both sides don't agree that his *ex parte* statement may be received in evidence, then I think the duty devolves upon which ever side wants him to get him there and let him be subjected to cross-examination, which, to me, is the greatest single thing in the adversary procedure. . . . Now, this concept is not new. This is not something that I am imposing upon the Secretary of Health [and Human Services]. This has been a part of our system and a part of our jurisprudence for many, many years. . . .

I noticed in this record that Mr. Tinsman, who represented this man, objected from the very beginning. He objected and he told the [administrative law judge] that it was this Court's attitude—and he used the name of the Court—that objections should be made. I think—although I can't assume this, but it seems to me apparent from reading the record—that the [administrative law judge] was perfectly well acquainted with this Court's attitude. . . .

Now, gentlemen, as I say, this is all so completely contrary to every concept that this Court has of a fair hearing that I can't possibly let a situation like this stand without sending it back for a review or a new hearing. I think the substantial evidence rule is a vicious thing anyway. I am not prepared to say that it should not be a part of our system; I have my doubts about it, but whether I like it or not I have to recognize that it's the law and I am prepared to follow it, even though I may have reservations about it. . .but before I am going to apply the substantial evidence rule to a case, I want to be sure that the initial hearing has been conducted in an atmosphere of fairness. . . .

I recognize those basic provisions of our law; as I say, whether I agree with it or not, I just have to follow them. . .[but] there are certain basic concepts of fundamental fair play that have to be observed, otherwise our government can very easily fall into the pattern of government by men rather than government by law. . . .

[Dr. Leavitt's testimony] compounded hearsay because it was hearsay on hearsay. I don't know where that could end. We'd probably have somebody coming in and interpreting by hearsay what Dr. Leavitt testified to on the basis of the *ex parte* reports he had read, and maybe somebody else coming in and testifying what he thinks about the testimony of the doctor who interpreted Dr. Leavitt's testimony on the basis of *ex parte* statements made by the doctor. Where would it end?. . .

If the practice in the past has been to do this, I think it is time for them to sit back and take another look because right is right, and I think that hearings ought to be conducted properly. . . .As I say, I don't think that is original with me at all. I don't think this represents any departure from long standing concepts, and it is just the way that I feel that it ought to be done. Until some appellate court tells me that I am wrong and I can't do it—I say some appellate court; I am talking about the Court of Appeals for the Fifth Circuit and the Supreme Court of the United States, those are the only two that can change it—until they do it, I am going to keep sending [disability benefits cases back to the Social Security Administration for rehearing] until. . .somebody with a little more authority than I have tells me that I am wrong. . . .

The reason I am spending so much time talking about this is that I would hope that. . .someone with the United States Attorney's Office or representing the Government would be able to get across to the [administrative law judges] or to the Secretary of Health [and Human Services] that. . .doctors' statements, as fine as doctors are, they are just not gospel and they are subject to all of the human frailties that all of the rest of us are subject. The mere fact that they have a degree doesn't put a halo around their heads, and they can make mistakes, and that this right to cross-examination—the longer I am in the law business, the more important I see how it is or that it is. . . .

[To counsel for Perales]: Well, do you have anything you want to say?
A. No, sir.

The Court: You guess from what the judge said it looked like the best thing to do was to keep quiet?

Gentlemen, I am going to send this back to the Secretary. I am going to ask that a new [administrative law judge] be supplied. I am going to provide that a new hearing be conducted and that the medical—that he be given a current medical examination and that the doctors who conduct these examinations be made available for testimony and for cross-examination. . . . I think a new [administrative law judge] is in order, because this [one] was told ahead of time what this Court's attitude was about it. He chose not to follow it. I think we ought to get one that is going to follow the Court's order. The order that I enter in this case is going to be the law of this case until some other court says it isn't.

I have a duty to perform as well as they do. I am going to do it to the best of my ability, and if, after a hearing, they come to the same conclusion, then I will be glad to hear you gentlemen on the substantial evidence rule, but right now I just don't think we have got a hearing, got a record that we can either apply or not apply the substantial evidence rule to. As a matter of fact, if I entered an order on the basis of this record I would reverse the Secretary and order that the benefits be given to the plaintiff. . . .

In his order remanding the *Perales* case for a rehearing by the Social Security Administration and in an opinion in the case filed subsequently, Judge Spears again emphasized his view that written medical reports which were not subject to cross-examination could not constitute "substantial evidence" supporting a disability benefits decision. Where "unsworn medical reports of examining physicians are received as original evidence on the critical issue of the plaintiff's physical condition," Spears said, "a non-examining medical expert is then allowed to 'interpret' those *ex parte* reports, and that 'interpretation' forms the basis for the decision by the [administrative law judge] , we have what amounts to pyramiding hearsay upon hearsay, which under the circumstances of this case, violates the fundamental rule of fair play and cannot be permited to stand."

## THE GOVERNMENT APPEALS

Richard Tinsman and Pedro Perales had finally won a round in the battle over the nature of the injury to Perales's back, but the government soon appealed Judge Spears's decision to the U.S. Court of Appeals for the Fifth Circuit. Although written medical reports were admittedly hearsay, the government argued before the court of appeals, such reports were highly reliable and probative and could constitute substantial evidence in an administrative hearing to determine disability. Defending Judge Spears's decision, Richard Tinsman argued that hearsay should be inadmissible as evidence in an administrative hearing and certainly could not constitute substantial evidence when contradicted by legally competent evidence and testimony produced at the hearing.

Supported by an amicus curiae brief filed by the Bexar County Legal Aid Society, Tinsman also urged the court of appeals to hold that the Administrative Procedure Act applied to disability benefits hearings and guaranteed the right of the claimant in such hearings to cross-examine witnesses. This argument was based on a provision of the APA that parties in administrative hearings have the right to present their cases "or defense by oral or documentary evidence, to submit rebuttal evidence, and to conduct such cross-examination as may be required for a full and true disclosure of the facts." By failing to have the doctors upon whose reports it relied to appear personally and testify, Tinsman argued, the Social Security Administration had denied Perales the right of cross-examination guaranteed in the APA.

The Fifth Circuit Court of Appeals decided the *Perales* case on May 1, 1969, and it affirmed Judge Spears's decision in the district court. The court of appeals, however, rejected Tinsman's argument that hearsay evidence was inadmissible in disability benefit hearings, pointing out that Congress had clearly provided for the admissibility of hearsay by exempting Social Security hearings from the "rules of evidence applicable to court procedure." The court also noted that Congress had delegated to the HHS secretary the power to prescribe rules governing disability hearings, and the secretary's rules also permitted the admission of hearsay evidence in such hearings.

The court additionally held that the guarantee of the right of cross-examination in the Administrative Procedure Act did not apply to hearings conducted under the Social Security Act. In any case, the court said, Tinsman could have requested that subpoenas be issued to compel the appearance of the doctors who had authored the disputed medical reports, but he had not done so. "The cases are clear," the court said, "that where a party has the right to subpoena witnesses by requesting the agency representative to issue them, and he does not make the request, he cannot later complain of the fact that he has been denied the right of confrontation of adverse witnesses and the right of cross-examination."

Having ruled that Tinsman could not legitimately claim a denial of the right of cross-examination in regard to the medical reports, and having also held that the hearsay medical reports were admissible as evidence, the court then turned to the question of whether or not the decision of the Social Security Administration denying disability benefits to Pedro Perales was supported by substantial evidence. Citing several decisions of the U.S. Supreme Court, the court noted that the Supreme Court had stated that "mere uncorroborated hearsay or rumor does not constitute substantial evidence," and the Court had additionally held that the administrative record as a whole must be evaluated by a reviewing court in applying the substantial evidence test.

"Applying these principles to the case before us," the court of appeals said,

. . .it is clear that the hearsay reports of the absent doctors were admissible in evidence before the [administrative law judge]. This is also true with respect to the testimony of the so-called "expert" Dr. Leavitt. However, this leaves the Secretary with nothing but uncorroborated hearsay, which the claimant has objected to, on which to base his decision. Under the decisions, such evidence is not substantial evidence. This is especially true in view of the fact that on the other side of the case we have the live and direct legal testimony of the claimant and his doctor which supports his claim. The trial court was correct in his remarks in the record that if he was called upon to render a final judgment in the case, he would render it for the claimant and against the Secretary, because the only probative evidence in the case that was not hearsay and that was substantial was in favor of the claimant. We agree that he would have been justified in entering judgment for the claimant for disability benefits in view of the foregoing and based on the law announced by the courts in similar cases. . . .

The court of appeals also noted Judge Spears's condemnation of the use of "medical experts" by administrative law judges in disability benefits hearings. Such experts, the court said, appeared to be "riding circuit" with the administrative law judges for the purpose of interpreting medical evidence without examining the claimants. "This procedure," the court held, "should be frowned upon, if not eliminated altogether." The testimony of such experts was not substantial evidence, the court concluded, especially when contradicted by the testimony of a claimant and the personal testimony of the claimant's doctor.

The court of appeals thus not only held that the Social Security Administration's decision in the *Perales* case was not supported by substantial evidence, but also joined Judge Spears in attacking the procedures being followed by the bureaucracy in disability cases. The government nevertheless petitioned the court for a rehearing *en banc,* arguing that, under the court's decision, all medical evidence at disability hearings would have to be supplied by doctors appearing personally and testifying at the hearings. This would seriously impede the expeditious conduct of disability hearings, the government argued, as well as discouraging doctors from cooperating with the Social Security Administration in determining disability claims.

On October 10, 1969, the court of appeals denied the government's petition for a rehearing but also clarified its opinion in the *Perales* case. It had not held, the court said, that medical reports could never be substantial evidence supporting a disability decision. What it had held, the court continued, was that hearsay medical reports did not constitute substantial evidence if the claimant "objects to the hearsay evidence and if the hearsay evidence is directly contradicted by the testimony of live medical witnesses and by the claimant who testify in person before the [administrative law judge] , as was done in the case at bar."

The court recognized that HHS "is required to handle thousands of these cases each year and is no doubt anxious to simplify the procedure for disposing of them," but, the court noted, a "social security disability claimant and his employer have paid for his coverage under the social security law whether they wanted it or not. He should not be denied the benefits of this law solely by hearsay evidence under the conditions outlined in our opinion."

The court was also unimpressed with the government's argument that its decision would increase hearing costs and discourage doctors from participating in disability cases. Any increased costs, the court said, would be paid out of the Social Security trust fund, since "this is one of the purposes of the fund." If a doctor refuses to serve in a disability case, the court continued, "another can be obtained. Litigants in other types of personal injury and disability cases manage to acquire the evidence of medical witnesses. There is no reason to excuse [HHS] from this requirement in a proper case. These arguments involve details that have little if anything to do with the merits of the case before us."

The district court and the court of appeals had, in effect, applied the "residuum rule" as a part of the substantial evidence test in reviewing the Social Security Administration's decision in the *Perales* case. That is, under the court of appeals decision, a disability benefits decision by the Social Security Administration could not be based entirely upon hearsay written medical reports, if the introduction of such reports was objected to by the claimant, and if the reports were contradicted by legally competent evidence or testimony supplied by the claimant. Since the admission of medical reports in disability benefits hearings would be almost uniformly objected to by counsel for claimants, the effect of the court of appeals decision would be to require the Social Security Administration to produce at least some of the authors of the medical reports at disability benefits hearings, where they could be cross-examined by counsel for claimants.

### THE PROCEEDINGS IN THE SUPREME COURT

From the government's standpoint, the decision of the court of appeals would have a serious impact on the disposition of disability benefits claims, as well as other similar claims under other federal programs, and the government consequently filed a petition for a writ of certiorari in the U.S. Supreme Court on March 9, 1970, seeking a reversal of the court of appeals decision in the *Perales* case. Although it is rare for the Supreme Court to review a Social Security Administration decision of any kind, the Court granted the petition for a writ of certiorari on April 20. Since Pedro Perales could not afford the costs of defending his victory in the lower federal courts before the Supreme Court, Richard Tinsman filed a motion to proceed *in forma pauperis* with the Court, and the Court granted the motion. Tinsman was appointed by the Court to continue serving as Perales's counsel in the proceedings before the Court.

In its argument before the Court, the government pointed out that the Social Security system "must deal with more than one hundred million individuals, and with millions of determinations and adjudications. Such a system must be fair—and it must work." The workability of the Social Security disability benefits program, with its more than twenty thousand hearings per year, would be threatened, the government argued, if the decision of the Fifth Circuit Court of Appeals were affirmed. If doctors cooperating with the Social Security system by examining claimants were compelled to appear personally and testify at disability hearings, the government contended, many if not most doctors would refuse further cooperation. This would both damage the workability of the disability benefits program and hurt the interests of claimants, since over two-thirds of the claimants were granted disability benefits on the basis of medical reports filed by examining physicians.

In the Social Security Act, the government noted, Congress had clearly provided for the admission of hearsay in disability benefits hearings, and the rules promulgated by the secretary of HHS to govern disability hearings legitimately provided for the admission of hearsay. The only question in the *Perales* case, the government argued, was whether written medical reports, based upon examinations of a claimant by competent doctors, constituted substantial evidence to support a decision denying disability benefits by the Social Security Administration. While the medical reports were admittedly hearsay, the government conceded, they nevertheless had "inherent reliability and are of obvious probative value in ascertaining a claimant's condition. They are customarily prepared by highly qualified physicians who have either treated the claimant or examined him as [consultants] ."

Under the decisions of the Court, the government pointed out, substantial evidence was "such relevant evidence as a reasonable mind might accept as adequate to support a conclusion." Other courts of appeals "and leading commentators," the government continued, had concluded contrary to the Fifth Circuit Court of Appeals "that this Court's opinions do not, and should not, require reviewing courts to set aside administrative findings merely because they are not supported by at least a 'residuum' of legally competent evidence." Rather, the government argued, the substantial evidence rule required a common-sense standard of evaluating evidence, and common sense indicated that the personal testimony of one doctor should not necessarily be always accepted over the written reports of other doctors. In the *Perales* case, it was therefore "entirely reasonable for the [administrative law judge] to rely on the [medical] reports at issue, which were not themselves specifically contradicted and which reflected scientific tests performed by highly qualified consultant physicians and surgical procedures performed by a former treating physician."

Finally, the government defended the use of medical advisers as expert witnesses in disability hearings, arguing that their role was to interpret the medical evidence for the administrative law judge. The lower courts should not have criticized the use of medical advisers, the government concluded, since they performed an "extremely useful and informative function in the adjudication of disability claims," and it was "entirely proper for [an administrative law judge] to elicit, and to rely upon, expert testimony from a qualified medical adviser in those cases in which he believes such testimony to be needed."

In defending the decision of the court of appeals and the victory he had won for Pedro Perales in that court, Richard Tinsman based his principal argument on the Supreme Court's decision in *Goldberg* v. *Kelly.* In *Goldberg,* the Court held that due process required a hearing before a welfare recipient's benefits could be terminated. And, the Court had said, in "almost every setting where important decisions turn on questions of fact, due process requires an opportunity to confront and cross-examine adverse witnesses."

Relying on the *Goldberg* case, Tinsman therefore argued that in Social Security disability hearings, on the crucial issue of the claimant's condition, "due process demands that either side should have the right to cross-examine witnesses as to that crucial issue, and, in that event, admission of written statements and reports concerning the crucial issue which are disputed by other live witnesses, cannot be substantial evidence to support the decision of the administrator." He was not contending that hearsay evidence was inadmissible in an administrative hearing, Tinsman told the Court, only that "even though admissible, where such hearsay is objected to and contradicted by direct, competent testimony, then hearsay. . .cannot be substantial evidence."

Although at the oral argument of the *Perales* case on January 13, 1971, the Court's questioning of Deputy Solicitor General Daniel M. Friedman, who argued the case for the government, was generally for informational purposes, the Court's questions of Richard Tinsman were more skeptical and antagonistic. This was especially true in regard to Tinsman's contention that the lack of opportunity to cross-examine the authors of the disputed medical reports had denied Perales due process of law. Justice White especially questioned Tinsman on this point, asking, if cross-examination was so important, why hadn't Tinsman subpoenaed the absent doctors and required their appearance at the hearing? Tinsman replied that he was only required to prove at the hearing that Perales was disabled and was not required to disprove the government's case. But under White's questioning,

Tinsman was forced to admit that, had he subpoenaed the doctors, their testimony would have been adverse to his case.

In regard to proving that Perales was disabled, Justice Blackmun asked why Tinsman had not produced his own specialists to rebut the medical reports of the government's specialists. Tinsman replied that he had produced a specialist, Dr. Morales, whom he regarded as a specialist in medicine generally. "You feel you made your case with a general practitioner's testimony on as elusive a subject as back injury?" Blackmun skeptically asked. "Yes, sir," Tinsman replied.

In addition to arguing that hearsay medical reports alone could not constitute substantial evidence in an administrative proceeding, Tinsman also attacked the role of the administrative law judge in disability hearings. The administrative law judge served as both the prosecutor for the government and as judge, Tinsman charged, and this was an additional violation of the right to a fair hearing required by due process. The administrative law judge, Tinsman said, gathered the evidence for the government, then put on his "judge's hat" and ruled on the admissibility of the evidence he himself had gathered as well as evaluating the claimant's evidence. "I mean, if you say that a lawyer can be basically fair in this context," Tinsman told the Court, "you could say, well, the plaintiff's lawyer should be the [administrative law judge], he's a lawyer, he's gathered the evidence for his claimant, he can listen to the government's evidence, but that's ridiculous, and we all agree with that, but it's not any more ridiculous than allowing the government's lawyer, who has gathered the government's evidence, to be the [administrative law judge] . . . ."

Tinsman's objections to the role of the administrative law judge in disability hearings was sharply questioned by Justice Marshall, who indicated substantial doubt that the administrative law judge's role resulted in an unfair hearing. And Deputy Solicitor General Friedman assured the Court that the administrative law judges in disability benefits hearings were protected by the Administrative Procedure Act and were independent of the Social Security Administration.

In addition to the arguments of Tinsman and the government, the *Perales* case attracted the attention of several interested groups which presented their views in amicus curiae briefs filed with the Court. The Administrative Law Section of the American Bar Association had intervened as amicus in the court of appeals on the issue of whether the Administrative Procedure Act applied to Social Security disability benefits hearings, and the ABA also filed a brief in the Supreme Court on this point. Since the ABA was perhaps the principal group responsible for the passage of the APA, it argued in its amicus brief that the APA should apply to Social Security disability benefits hearings in spite of the ruling to the contrary in the court of appeals. The ABA, however, took no position on the merits of the *Perales* case.

The Bexar County, Texas, Legal Aid Association had also intervened in the *Perales* case as amicus curiae in the court of appeals, and it filed a similar amicus brief in the Supreme Court, strongly backing Tinsman's argument that hearsay written medical reports, when contradicted by legally competent evidence, should not be considered as substantial evidence. The Legal Aid Association also strongly defended the traditional rule excluding hearsay and argued that the "abandonment of the lessons learned from centuries of experience does not commend itself to thinking men. . . . Under the guise of the 'substantial evidence' rule [the government] would have this Court abandon the traditional concepts of the law of evidence." The government, the Legal Aid Association told the Court, was attempting to "place uncorroborated, hearsay evidence on an equal footing with direct, competent evidence."

The Appalachian Research and Defense Fund, Legal Research for the Appalachian Elderly, and the Center on Social Welfare Policy and Law also filed a joint amicus curiae brief in the *Perales* case. These organizations were funded by the federal Office of Economic Opportunity for the purpose of advancing ways by which the legal system could more effectively respond to the needs of the low income elderly. Their argument as amicus curiae attacked the use of so-called objective tests to determine disability under the Social Security system. Such tests were often unreliable and were not required by the Social Security Act, and, in any case, the best evidence of disability was the testimony of the physician treating a claimant. The continued use of the so-called objective tests by the Social Security Administration in disability cases, it was argued, made it extremely difficult for the poor to obtain disability benefits, since they could not afford to hire their own specialists to refute the government's evidence in disability hearings. Consequently, the Court was urged to affirm the decision of the court of appeals in the *Perales* case.

The question of what constituted substantial evidence as to the nature of the injury to Pedro Perales's back was now in the hands of the Supreme Court. The Court gave its answer on May 3, 1971, reversing the decision of the court of appeals and handing yet another defeat to Richard Tinsman and Pedro Perales.

*Richardson* v. *Perales*
402 U.S. 389. Argued January 13, 1971. Decided May 3, 1971
Mr. Justice Blackmun delivered the opinion of the Court.

[Justice Blackmun reviewed the facts in the case, the administrative proceedings regarding the case, and the decisions of the lower courts.]

We therefore are presented with the not uncommon situation of conflicting medical evidence. The trier of fact has the duty to resolve that conflict. We have, on the one hand, an absence of objective findings, an expressed suspicion of only functional complaints, of malingering, and of the patient's unwillingness to do anything about remedying an unprovable situation. We have, on the other hand, the claimant's and his personal physician's earnest pleas that significant and disabling residuals from the mishap of September 1965 are indeed present.

The issue revolves, however, around a system which produces a mass of medical evidence in report form. May material of that kind ever be "substantial evidence" when it stands alone and is opposed by live medical evidence and the client's own contrary personal testimony? The courts below have held that it may not. . . .

The Social Security Act has been with us since 1935. . . . It affects nearly all of us. The system's administrative structure and procedures, with essential determinations numbering into the millions, are of a size and extent difficult to comprehend. But, as the Government's brief here accurately pronounces, "Such a system must be fair—and it must work."

Congress has provided that the Secretary "shall have full power and authority to make rules and regulations and to establish procedures. . . necessary or appropriate to carry out such provisions, and shall adopt reasonable and proper rules and regulations to regulate and provide for the nature and extent of the proofs and evidence and the method of taking and furnishing the same in order to establish the right to benefits [under the disability benefits provisions of the Social Security Act]. . . ."

Section 205(b) directs the Secretary to make findings and decisions; on request to give reasonable notice and opportunity for a hearing; and in the course of any hearing to receive evidence. It then provides: "Evidence may be received at any hearing before the Secretary even though inadmissible under rules of evidence applicable to court procedure." In carrying out these statutory duties the Secretary has adopted regulations that state, among other things: "The [administrative law judge] shall inquire fully into the matters at issue and shall receive in evidence the testimony of witnesses and any documents which are relevant and material to such matters. . . . The. . .procedure at the hearing generally. . .shall be in the discretion of the [administrative law judge] and of such nature as to afford the parties a reasonable opportunity for a fair hearing. . . ."

From this it is apparent that (a) the Congress granted the Secretary the power by regulation to establish hearing procedures; (b) strict rules of evidence, applicable in the courtroom, are not to operate at social security hearings so as to bar the admission of evidence otherwise pertinent; and (c) the conduct of the hearing rests generally in the [administrative law judge's] discretion. There emerges an emphasis upon the informal rather than the formal. This, we think, is as it should be, for this administrative procedure, and these hearings, should be understandable to the layman claimant, should not necessarily be stiff and comfortable only for the trained attorney, and should be liberal and not strict in tone and operation. This is the obvious intent of Congress so long as the procedures are fundamentally fair.

With this background and this atmosphere in mind, we turn to the statutory standard of "substantial evidence" prescribed by [the Social Security Act]. The Court has considered this very concept in other, yet similar, contexts. The National Labor Relations Act. . .provided that the NLRB's findings of fact "if supported by evidence, shall be conclusive. . . ." The Court said this meant "supported by substantial evidence" and that this was "more than a mere scintilla. It means such relevant evidence as a reasonable mind might accept as adequate to support a conclusion." Consolidated Edison Co. v. NLRB. . . .

The Court has adhered to that definition in varying statutory situations. . . .

We may accept the propositions advanced by the claimant, some of them long established, that procedural due process is applicable to the adjudicative administrative proceeding involving "the differing rules of fair play, which through the years, have become associated with differing types of proceedings. . . ;" that "the 'right' to Social Security benefits is in one sense 'earned' ". . .and that the "extent to which procedural due process must be afforded the recipient is influenced by the extent to which he may be 'condemned to suffer grievous loss'. . . .Accordingly. . . 'consideration of what procedures due process may require under any given set of circumstances must begin with a determination of the precise nature of the government function involved as well as of the private interest that has been affected by governmental action.' " Goldberg v. Kelly. . . .

The question, then, is as to what procedural due process requires with respect to examining physicians' reports in a social security disability claim hearing.

We conclude that a written report by a licensed physician who has examined the claimant and who sets forth in his report his medical findings in his area of competence may be received as evidence in a disability hearing and, despite its hearsay character and an absence of cross-examination, and despite the presence of opposing direct medical testimony and testimony by the claimant himself, may constitute substantial evidence supportive of a finding by the [administrative law judge] adverse to the claimant, when the claimant has not exercised his right to subpoena the reporting physician and thereby provide himself with the opportunity for cross-examination of the physician.

We are prompted to this conclusion by a number of factors that, we feel, assure underlying reliability and probative value:

1. The identity of the five reporting physicians is significant. Each report presented here was prepared by a practicing physician who had examined the claimant. A majority (Drs. Langston, Bailey, and Mattson) were called into the case by the state agency. Although each received a fee, that fee is recompense for his time and talent otherwise devoted to private practice or other professional assignment. We cannot, and do not, ascribe

bias to the work of these independent physicians, or any interest on their part in the outcome of the administrative proceeding beyond the professional curiosity a dedicated medical man possesses.

2. The vast workings of the social security administrative system make for reliability and impartiality in the consultant reports. We bear in mind that the agency operates essentially, and is intended so to do, as an adjudicator and not as an advocate or adversary. This is the congressional plan. We do not presume on this record to say that it works unfairly.

3. One familiar with medical reports and the routine of the medical examination, general or specific, will recognize their elements of detail and of value. The particular reports of the physicians who examined claimant Perales were based on personal consultation and personal examination and rested on accepted medical procedures and tests. . . . These are routine, standard, and unbiased medical reports by physician specialists concerning a subject whom they had seen. That the reports were adverse to Perales' claim is not in itself bias or an indication of nonprobative character.

4. The reports present the impressive range of examination to which Perales was subjected. . . . It is fair to say that the claimant received professional examination and opinion on a scale beyond the reach of most persons and that this case reveals a patient and careful endeavor by the state agency and the [administrative law judge] to ascertain the truth.

5. So far as we can detect, there is no inconsistency whatsoever in the reports of the five specialists. Yet each result was reached by independent examination in the writer's field of specialized training.

6. Although the claimant complains of the lack of opportunity to cross-examine the reporting physicians, he did not take advantage of the opportunity afforded him under [the Secretary of HHS's regulations] to request subpoenas for the physicians. The five-day period specified by the regulation for the issuance of the subpoenas surely afforded no real obstacle to this, for he was notified that the documentary evidence on file was available for examination before the hearing and, further, a supplemental hearing could be requested. In fact, in this very case there was a supplemental hearing more than two and a half months after the initial hearings. This inaction on the claimant's part supports the Court of Appeals' view. . .that the claimant as a consequence is to be precluded from now complaining that he was denied the rights of confrontation and cross-examination.

7. Courts have recognized the reliability and probative worth of written medical reports even in formal trials and, while acknowledging their hearsay character, have admitted them as an exception to the hearsay rule. . . .

8. Past treatment by reviewing courts of written medical reports in social security disability cases is revealing. Until the decision in this case, the courts of appeals, including the Fifth Circuit, with only an occasional criticism of the medical report practice, uniformly recognized reliability and probative value in such reports. . . . [The] decisions do demonstrate traditional and ready acceptance of the written medical report in social security disability cases.

9. There is an additional and pragmatic factor which, although not controlling, deserves mention. This is. . ."[t]he sheer magnitude of that

administrative burden," and the resulting necessity for written reports without "elaboration through the traditional facility of oral testimony. . . ." With over 20,000 disability claim hearings annually, the cost of providing live medical testimony at those hearings, where need has not been demonstrated by a request for a subpoena, over and above the cost of the examinations requested by the [administrative law judges], would be a substantial drain on the trust fund and on the energy of physicians already in short supply.

1. Perales relies heavily on the Court's holding and statements in Goldberg v. Kelly. . . , particularly the comment that due process requires notice "and an effective opportunity to defend by confronting adverse witnesses. . . ." Kelly, however, had to do with termination of [Aid to Families with Dependent Children] benefits without prior notice. It also concerned a situation, the Court said, "where credibility and veracity are at issue, as they must be in many termination proceedings. . . ."

The Perales proceeding is not the same. We are not concerned with termination of disability benefits once granted. Neither are we concerned with a change of status without notice. Notice was given to claimant Perales. The physicians' reports were on file and available for inspection by the claimant and his counsel. And the authors of those reports were known and were subject to subpoena and to the very cross-examination that the claimant asserts he has not enjoyed. Further, the specter of questionable credibility and veracity is not present; there is professional disagreement with the medical conclusions, to be sure, but there is no attack here upon the doctors' credibility or veracity. Kelly affords little comfort to the claimant.

2. Perales also, as the Court of Appeals stated, . . .would describe the medical reports in question as "mere uncorroborated hearsay" and would relate this to Mr. Chief Justice Hughes' sentence in Consolidated Edison Co. v. NLRB. . . : "Mere uncorroborated hearsay or rumor does not constitute substantial evidence."

Although the reports are hearsay in the technical sense, because their content is not produced live before the [administrative law judge], we feel that the claimant and the Court of Appeals read too much into the single sentence from Consolidated Edison. The contrast the Chief Justice was drawing, at the very page cited, was not with material that would be deemed formally inadmissible in judicial proceedings but with material "without a basis in evidence having rational probative force." This was not a blanket rejection by the Court of administrative reliance on hearsay irrespective of reliability and probative value. The opposite was the case.

3. The claimant, the District Court, and the Court of Appeals also criticize the use of Dr. Leavitt as a medical adviser. . . . Inasmuch as medical advisers are used in approximately 13% of disability claim hearings, comment as to this practice is indicated. We see nothing "reprehensible" in the practice, as the claimant would describe it. The [administrative law judge] is a layman; the medical adviser is a board-certified specialist. He is used primarily in complex cases for explanation of medical problems in terms understandable to the layman-[administrative law judge]. . . .We see nothing unconstitutional or improper in the medical adviser concept and in the presence of Dr. Leavitt in this administrative hearing.

4. Finally, the claimant complains of the system of processing disability claims. He suggests, and is joined in this by the briefs of amici, that the Administrative Procedure Act, rather than the Social Security Act, governs the processing of claims and specifically provides for cross-examination. . . . The claimant goes on to assert that in any event the hearing procedure is invalid on due process grounds. He says that the [administrative law judge] has the responsibility for gathering the evidence and "to make the government's case as strong as possible"; that naturally he leans toward a decision in favor of the evidence he has gathered; that justice must satisfy the appearance of justice. . .; and that an "independent [administrative law judge]. . .should be provided."

We need not decide whether the APA has general application to social security disability claims, for the social security administrative procedure does not vary from that prescribed by the APA. Indeed, the latter is modeled upon the Social Security Act. . . .

The matter comes down to the question of the procedure's integrity and fundamental fairness. We see nothing that works in derogation of that integrity and of that fairness in the admission of consultants' reports, subject as they are to being material and to the use of the subpoena and consequent cross-examination. This precisely fits the statutorily prescribed "cross-examination as may be required for a full and true disclosure of the facts." That is the standard. It is clear and workable and does not fall short of procedural due process.

Neither are we persuaded by the advocate-judge-multiple-hat suggestion. It assumes too much and would bring down too many procedures designed, and working well, for a governmental structure of great and growing complexity. The social security [administrative law judge], furthermore, does not act as counsel. He acts as an examiner charged with developing the facts. The 44.2% reversal rate for all federal disability hearings in cases where the state agency does not grant benefits. . .attests to the fairness of the system and refutes the implication of impropriety.

We therefore reverse and remand for further proceedings. We intimate no view as to the merits. It is for the District Court now to determine whether the Secretary's findings, in the light of all material proffered and admissible, are supported by "substantial evidence" within the command of [the Social Security Act].

It is so ordered.

[Justice Douglas, joined by Justices Black and Brennan, dissented, arguing that both the Social Security Act and the Administrative Procedure Act required substantial evidence to support a denial of disability benefits, and that medical reports of doctors who were not subject to cross-examination did not constitute substantial evidence.]

## THE SUBSTANTIAL EVIDENCE TEST AND THE PERALES CASE

The Supreme Court's holding in *Richardson* v. *Perales* that hearsay written medical reports may constitute substantial evidence supportive of a denial of Social Security disability benefits, even when contradicted by legally competent evidence in the record, has been widely interpreted as constituting a rejection of the incorporation of the residuum rule into the substantial evidence test. Under the Court's ruling in the *Perales* case, therefore, uncorroborated hearsay may be sufficiently reliable and probative to satisfy a reviewing court that an administrative decision is supported by substantial evidence.

The Court of course additionally held in the *Perales* case that if the right to subpoena and cross-examine adverse witnesses is not exercised by a party in an administrative hearing, it cannot be later validly argued that the party was denied the right of confrontation and cross-examination. At least in Social Security disability benefits hearings, the burden is not upon the government to present the doctors whose reports are relied upon to deny benefits, but rather the burden is upon the claimant, if he so desires, to subpoena the authors of the medical reports in evidence for purposes of cross-examination.

## THE PERALES CASE ON REMAND

By 1978, the Social Security disability benefits program was beset by criticism from a variety of sources and had encountered serious financial problems. Decisions to award or deny benefits, critics charged, were frequently arbitrary, with similarly situated applicants treated differently under the Social Security decision-making process. Perhaps as a consequence, cases involving challenges to the Social Security Administration's determinations of disability or nondisability doubled between 1974 and 1978, and the caseload of the federal courts involving the disability benefits program was expected to grow at a yearly rate of 25 percent thereafter.

Government actuaries also greatly underestimated the cost of the disability benefits program, which, along with the Social Security retirement system, was in serious financial difficulty by the late 1970s. While the number of recipients of retirement and survivor benefits under Social Security doubled between 1960 and 1978, the number of persons receiving disability benefits increased seven times during the same period, and the cost of the disability benefits program rose to $13.7 billion in 1978. Approximately five million workers or their dependents were drawing disability benefits in 1978, and, interestingly enough, that number included Pedro Perales.

In its decision, the Supreme Court had held only that hearsay medical reports might constitute substantial evidence supportive of a denial of disability benefits, but it had remanded the *Perales* case for a determination whether the evidence in the case actually did constitute substantial evidence. During the litigation in his case, Perales and his family went on welfare, since he continued to be unable to work. He additionally underwent further surgery, this time a spinal fusion, as a result of the injury to his back. Following the Supreme Court's decision, Perales was given yet another adjudicative hearing before an administrative law judge. Again, however, the administrative law judge ruled against Perales's claim for disability benefits, but Richard Tinsman once more sought judicial review of the administrative decision against Perales's claim. In the proceedings in the district court, it was ordered that Perales should undergo a psychiatric examination, and the examining psychiatrist reported to the court that Perales had suffered a conversion reaction. The court therefore held that Perales was disabled within the meaning of the Social Security Act, and it not only ordered that he be given disability benefits but it also ordered that the benefits be granted retroactively to the date of his initial claim in 1966, a ruling that resulted in an immediate payment to Perales of $11,000 in retroactive benefits.

# 3

## THE ADMINISTRATIVE EXERCISE
## OF LEGISLATIVE POWER
### Rule Making

The power of administrative agencies to promulgate rules and regulations having the force of law involves the exercise of legislative power by the agencies. Although administrative agencies have exercised such legislative, rule-making power from the earliest days of the Republic, the validity of the possession of legislative power by administrative agencies was at one time a hotly debated and contested issue in administrative law. The fact is, however, that the possession of legislative, rule-making power is a principal characteristic of modern administrative agencies. Given the complexities of modern industrial society, legislatures at both the state and federal levels discovered their inability to legislate with sufficient prescience and in sufficient detail to carry out the tasks of governmental regulation. They thus increasingly turned to the creation of administrative agencies, to the description of the jurisdiction and tasks of such agencies in broad terms, and to the delegation to the agencies of legislative, rule-making power to "fill up the details" of broad policy declarations enacted by the legislatures.

Those who opposed the growth of administrative power frequently charged that the delegation by Congress of its legislative power to administrative agencies was a violation of the fundamental principle of the separation of powers embodied in the Constitution. The Constitution ordained, it was argued, that legislative, judicial, and executive powers be exercised by separate branches of the government, and therefore the delegation of legislative powers to administrative agencies, particularly when executive and judicial powers were also possessed by the agencies, constituted a dangerous combination of all forms of governmental power in the agencies in violation of the principle of the separation of powers. The separation of powers principle, it was also argued, was an important guarantee of liberty in the Constitution, since it provided for each of the three branches to check the exercise of power by the others. Combining legislative along with executive and judicial power in administrative agencies thus not only violated a fundamental constitutional principle but also jeopardized the liberties of citizens.

## THE DEMISE OF THE NONDELEGATION DOCTRINE

For much of the nineteenth century, the courts in the United States paid at least lip service to the nondelegation doctrine—that legislative power could not be delegated to executive or administrative officials. As late as 1892, for example, the Supreme Court declared in *Field* v. *Clark* that it adhered to the nondelegation doctrine. "That Congress cannot delegate legislative power. . . ," the Court said, "is a principle universally recognized as vital to the integrity and maintenance of the system of government ordained by the Constitution."

The nondelegation doctrine rested upon two principal bases in the decisions of the courts. First was of course the principle of separation of powers embodied in the Constitution. An additional basis for the nondelegation doctrine was the maxim, drawn from the common law of agency, *Delegata potestas non potest delegari*—"One to whom power is delegated may not in turn delegate power." This concept was applied in the field of constitutional law to mean that, since the power of Congress was delegated to it by the people, Congress therefore could not delegate its powers to others, including administrative or executive officials.

Despite the lip service paid to the nondelegation doctrine, the Supreme Court in fact did not invalidate any act of Congress as involving an unconstitutional delegation of legislative power until the 1930s. And as administrative agencies proliferated and more and more delegations of legislative power to the agencies occurred, the nondelegation doctrine was increasingly viewed as unrealistic. In an oft-quoted presidential address to the American Bar Association in 1916, Elihu Root thus declared to his colleagues that the nation was "entering upon the creation of a body of administrative law quite different in its machinery, its remedies, and its necessary safeguards from the old methods of regulation by specific statutes enforced by the courts." With the rise of modern administrative agencies, Root continued, "the old doctrine prohibiting the delegation of legislative power has virtually retired from the field and given up the fight."

In the face of the realities of modern governmental regulation through administrative agencies, as recognized by Root, the courts began to modify the nondelegation doctrine. Rather than denying that legislative power could be delegated at all, the modified standard imposed by the courts regarding the delegation of legislative power required that such delegations were valid if Congress provided "intelligible," "recognizable," or "ascertainable" standards to guide the exercise by administrative agencies of the power being delegated. As the Supreme Court said in 1928 in *J.W. Hampton, Jr., & Co.* v. *United States,* "If Congress shall lay down by legislative act an intelligible principle to which the [administrative agency] . . .is directed to conform [in the exercise of its rule-making power] , such legislative action is not a forbidden delegation of legislative power."

### THE "HOT OIL" AND "SICK CHICKEN" CASES

By the time the Supreme Court confronted the New Deal legislation of the 1930s, therefore, the nondelegation doctrine had been substantially modified. By insisting on "intelligible" or "ascertainable" standards to guide and channel the exercise of delegated legislative power, however, the courts were still imposing important restrictions upon the ability of Congress to delegate its powers. And when the massive delegation of legislative power by Congress in the National Industrial Recovery Act of 1933 (NIRA) was reviewed by the Supreme Court, the Court for the first time invalidated a congressional enactment on the ground that it involved an unconstitutional delegation of legislative power.

In *Panama Refining Co.* v. *Ryan,* popularly known as the Hot Oil case, the Court in January of 1935 invalidated a relatively minor provision of the NIRA authorizing the president in his discretion to prohibit the transportation in interstate and foreign commerce of oil produced in violation of limits imposed by state laws—that is, hot, illegally produced, oil. In authorizing the president to take such action, however, the Court held that "the Congress has declared no policy, has established no standard, has laid down no rule. There is no requirement, no definition of circumstances and conditions in which the transportation is to be allowed or prohibited." Rather than establishing an ascertainable legislative standard to guide the president's exercise of the power Congress had delegated to him, the Court found, the hot oil provision of the NIRA simply gave "to the President an unlimited authority to determine the policy and to lay down the prohibition, or not to lay it down, as he may see fit." Such unlimited delegations of legislative power, unrestrained by standards established by Congress to guide the exercise of such power, the Court concluded, constituted unconstitutional delegations of legislative power and were invalid.

In addition to being the first case in which the Court had invalidated an act of Congress on the ground that it involved an unconstitutional delegation of legislative power, the Hot Oil case was important for another reason. During the litigation of the case, the government had charged the Panama Refining Company with violating rules and regulations issued under the NIRA, but when the case reached the Supreme Court, the government discovered that the rules and regulations the company had been charged with violating had been repealed. Throughout the litigation in the lower federal courts, therefore, the oil company had been attacking and the government defending nonexistent rules and regulations. Not only was this embarrassing to the government, but it also highlighted the fact that there was no publication at the time that contained administrative rules and regulations. Congress reacted by enacting the Federal Register Act of 1935, creating the *Federal Register* and requiring the publication in the *Register* of all rules and regulations "of general applicability and legal effect." The *Federal Register* is presently published almost daily in newspaper format, while administrative rules and regulations are published also in bound volumes in the *Code of Federal Regulations* (C.F.R.). The Hot Oil case thus introduced a significant reform in the administrative process, since the Federal Register Act provided for the first time for the systematic publication of the rules and regulations promulgated by the administrative agencies of the federal government.

The Hot Oil case, however, did not end the Supreme Court's examination of the validity of the NIRA, since the entire regulatory scheme under the act was attacked before the Court in *Schechter Poultry Corp.* v. *United States* (popularly called the Sick Chicken case), which was also decided in 1935. In the NIRA, Congress provided that codes of fair competition could be formulated for each industry. The codes included provisions regulating minimum wages, maximum hours, and child labor and guaranteeing the right of workers to organize into unions. In addition to these provisions relating to labor and working conditions, the codes contained provisions outlawing "unfair competitive practices" and regulating various trade practices in the industries covered. While technically the NIRA involved a delegation of legislative power to the president, whose approval of the codes of fair competition was necessary for them to have the force of law, the NIRA in its practical operation involved a massive delegation of legislative power to trade associations and industrial groups, which in fact formulated most of the codes for their industries.

In the Sick Chicken case, the Schechter Poultry Corporation attacked various provisions of the Live Poultry Code on the ground, among others, that the provisions of the NIRA authorizing the code involved an unconstitutional delegation of legislative power by Congress. As in the Hot Oil case, the Supreme Court examined the NIRA to determine if Congress had provided standards to guide and control the exercise of the legislative power to formulate codes of fair competition that it was delegating. And the Court again concluded that nowhere in the NIRA had Congress defined what "fair competition" was, thus leaving the formulators of codes of fair competition without any standards to guide their exercise of the legislative power delegated by the act.

Because of this lack of "ascertainable" or "intelligible" standards in the NIRA, the Court concluded, the "discretion of the President in approving or prescribing codes, and thus enacting laws for the government of trade and industry throughout the country, is virtually unlimited. We think that the code-making authority thus conferred is an unconstitutional delegation of legislative power." And Justice Cardozo, in a concurring opinion, characterized the code-making authority delegated by Congress in the NIRA as "delegation running riot."

## THE CURRENT LAW OF DELEGATION

Despite the forcefulness of the Supreme Court's condemnation of Congress's delegation of legislative power in the Hot Oil and Sick Chicken cases, subsequent decisions of the Court involving the delegation of legislative power have largely ignored the principles enunciated in those cases. The Court has thus subsequently upheld delegations of legislative power to administrative agencies to be exercised under such vague and indefinite standards as "the public interest," or "the public convenience, interest, or necessity," or in a "just and reasonable" fashion. As a consequence, most students of administrative law have concluded that the Court has in effect abandoned its insistence that delegated legislative power must be limited by "ascertainable" or "intelligible" standards which guide its exercise by administrative agencies.

This is borne out by the fact that the Supreme Court has not declared a congressional delegation of legislative power unconstitutional since the Hot Oil and Sick Chicken cases in the 1930s. More reflective of the modern law of delegation, and in contrast to the condemnatory language of the Hot Oil and Sick Chicken cases, is the Court's language in 1940 upholding in *F.C.C.* v. *Pottsville Broadcasting Co.* a congressional grant to the Federal Communications Commission of the power to license broadcasting stations when it served the "public convenience, interest, or necessity." Rather than condemning the congressional grant of legislative power to the FCC under such a vague standard, the Court unanimously held that the public convenience, interest, or necessity "criterion is as concrete as the complicated factors for judgment in such a field of delegated authority permits, [and] it serves as a supple instrument for the exercise of discretion by the expert body which Congress has charged to carry out its legislative policy."

## THE SCOPE OF JUDICIAL REVIEW OF ADMINISTRATIVE RULE MAKING

Given the demise of the nondelegation doctrine, and the fact that the courts now will sustain delegations of legislative power to administrative agencies under the vaguest of standards, it is evident that challenges to administrative rules and regulations on the ground that they are the products of unconstitutional delegations of legislative power have only the slightest chances for a favorable reception in the courts. Administrative rules, however, are still susceptible to challenge in the courts on other grounds. Administrative rules may thus be challenged in the courts on the grounds that (1) they violate a provision of the Constitution, such as freedom of speech or the Due Process Clauses; (2) they constitute an exercise of power by the administrative agency beyond that delegated to the agency by Congress; (3) they are arbitrary, capricious, an abuse of discretion, or otherwise not in accordance with law; and (4) they were not adopted according to the procedures Congress has specified for the adoption of such rules and regulations.

Administrative rules and regulations, like acts of Congress, are of course subject to those limitations imposed on the exercise of governmental power embodied in the Constitution, and administrative rules, like other governmental actions, are thus subject to invalidation for violation of the Constitution upon judicial review. The basic charters of administrative agencies are also set down in congressional statutes, which prescribe the purposes and jurisdiction of the agencies. If an agency exercises power beyond that which Congress has granted to it, such as exercising rule-making power not delegated to it or issuing rules not authorized by statute, the agency action is illegal and will be invalidated by the courts upon judicial review.

Agency rules may also be declared by the courts upon review to be "arbitrary, capricious, an abuse of discretion, or otherwise not in accordance with law." The courts are explicitly authorized to apply this standard upon judicial review of administrative rules by the Administrative Procedure Act. Finally, the procedures by which administrative agencies may promulgate rules and regulations are also frequently prescribed by statute. The statutes creating many federal agencies thus prescribe the particular procedures the agencies must follow before they may issue rules and regulations. Again, if an agency fails to follow the congressionally pre-scribed procedure for the adoption and issuance of rules and regulations, its rules and regulations are subject to challenge and invalidation in the courts.

The congressionally prescribed procedure for particular agencies may vary from a requirement that almost no formal procedure at all be fol-lowed by an agency before rules are adopted, to an extreme of a require-ment that an agency hold formal, trial-type hearings before the issuance of rules and regulations. In the latter case, it should be noted, agency rules are subject to the substantial evidence test upon judicial review of their validity, in addition to the other elements governing judicial review of agency rules.

An intermediate requirement imposed by Congress, and one that is often encountered in the administrative process, involves the rule-making provisions of the Administrative Procedure Act, provisions that are fol-lowed by many federal agencies in the rule-making process. The APA's pro-visions require agencies to follow three steps in rule making. First, notice of the proposed rule making must be published in the *Federal Register,* accompanied by a statement of the time, place, and nature of any public rule-making proceedings contemplated by the agency, a reference to the legal authority under which the rule is proposed, and a description of the proposed rule or of the subjects or issues involved. Secondly, the agency must allow interested persons an opportunity to submit written data, views, or arguments regarding the proposed rule. And finally, after consid-eration of the materials submitted, the agency publishes its rule or rules along with a concise statement of the basis and purpose of the rules, with the rules usually not being effective until thirty days after their publication.

When these informal rule-making provisions of the APA are applicable to particular agencies, the Supreme Court has strongly discouraged the lower federal courts from imposing any additional, judicially created procedural requirements upon the agencies for the adoption of rules. The APA's informal rule-making procedures, the Court held in *Vermont Yankee Power Corp.* v. *Natural Resources Defense Council* in 1978, "generally speaking. . .established the maximum procedural requirements which Congress was willing to have the courts impose upon agencies in conducting rulemaking proceedings. Agencies are free to grant additional procedural rights in the exercise of their discretion, but reviewing courts are generally not free to impose them if the agencies have not chosen to grant them. This is not to say necessarily that there are no circumstances which would ever justify a court in overturning agency action because of a failure to employ procedures beyond those required by the [APA]. But such circumstances, if they exist, are extremely rare."

We shall now examine an agency, the Federal Communications Commission, which possesses a delegation of legislative, rule-making power from Congress under one of the vague standards sanctioned by the courts since the 1930s—a mandate to regulate the broadcasting media to serve the "public convenience, interest, or necessity." After almost thirty years of defining what the "public convenience, interest, or necessity" meant in relation to the responsibility of broadcast licensees to be "fair" in the presentation of controversial issues of public importance, the FCC resorted to the rule-making process as prescribed in the Administrative Procedure Act. And the result was a monumental battle between the commission and the broadcasting industry that involved a basic challenge to the premises upon which public regulation of the broadcast media and the commission's authority rested.

### CASE STUDY
### BROADCASTING AND THE BUREAUCRACY
#### The FCC and The Red Lion Case

The Federal Communications Commission (FCC) was preceded as an agency by the Federal Radio Commission, which was created by Congress in the Federal Radio Act of 1927 and empowered to regulate the licensing of radio broadcasting stations. Congressional enactment of the Radio Act had proven necessary during the 1920s because of the proliferation of radio stations which, without regulation, frequently broadcast on the same wavelengths. The Federal Radio Commission was therefore authorized to license radio stations if the licensing of such stations would serve the "public interest, convenience, or necessity" in order to prevent broadcasting chaos.

The Federal Radio Commission was supplanted by the Federal Communications Commission, which was created by the Federal Communications Act of 1934. The FCC was given the status of an independent regulatory agency similar to the Federal Trade Commission, and the regulation of facilities of communication was centralized under the FCC's control, including interstate telephone and telegraph communication as well as radio (and later television) broadcasting. The Federal Radio Commission's broad mandate to license broadcasters when justified by the "public interest, convenience, or necessity" was transferred to the FCC. The Federal Communications Act, like the earlier Radio Act, also embodied the premise that the airwaves belonged to the public and therefore could not be "owned" by individual broadcasters. A broadcasting license was therefore a temporary permit, allowing a broadcaster to use the public airwaves when the "public interest, convenience, or necessity" would be served thereby. The Communications Act additionally recognized that the public airwaves were a scarce resource because of the limited number of broadcast frequencies available. Not everyone could therefore have access to the airwaves, but rather through the broadcast licensing system, only broadcasters serving the public interest, convenience, or necessity would be licensed to use the public airwaves.

## THE ESTABLISHMENT OF THE FAIRNESS AND RELATED DOCTRINES

Congress provided in the Radio Act of 1927 that if a broadcaster permitted a "legally qualified candidate" for public office to air his views, the station was required to afford equal opportunities to all other legally qualified candidates for the same office to use its broadcasting facilities for the airing of their views. In interpreting this provision, the Federal Radio Commission went even further by adopting what would come to be called the fairness doctrine, which provided that if a program were broadcast that involved the discussion of public questions, the "public interest requires ample play for the free and fair competition of opposing views." Under this interpretation of the Radio Act, a broadcast licensee was thus required not only to grant equal time to opposing political candidates but also to air opposing views on issues of importance to the public.

The Federal Communications Act of 1934, which created the FCC, embodied the same provisions relating to equal time for political candidates as had the Radio Act, and the FCC continued the fairness doctrine that it inherited from the Federal Radio Commission. Indeed, the FCC expanded the doctrine to prohibit editorializing by broadcast licensees in 1940, but this policy was reconsidered by the FCC in the late 1940s. In its *Report on Editorializing by Broadcast Licensees,* issued in 1949, the FCC reversed itself and lifted the ban on editorializing by licensees, but it continued to emphasize the importance of "the maintenance of radio and television as a medium of freedom of speech and freedom of expression for the people of the Nation as a whole." Consequently, the FCC said, in the "presentation of news and comment the public interest requires that the licensee must operate on a basis of overall fairness, making his facilities available for the expression of the contrasting views of all responsible elements in the community on the various issues which arise."

In imposing the requirement that radio and television broadcasters afford time for the presentation of differing views of individuals and groups in the community, the FCC rejected the argument that such a requirement violated the broadcasters' right of free expression under the First Amendment. "We believe, on the contrary," the FCC said, "that a requirement that broadcast licensees utilize their franchises in a manner in which the listening public may be assured of hearing varying opinions on the paramount issues facing the American people is within both the spirit and letter of the First Amendment."

In the late 1950s, the FCC ruled that if a political candidate appeared on a newscast, all other opposing candidates had to be afforded an equal opportunity to reply on a licensee's facilities. Congress, however, reversed this policy by amending the Communications Act in 1959 to provide that the appearance of a political candidate on a bona fide newcast, news interview, news documentary, or on-the-spot coverage of news events (such as political conventions) would not entitle opposing candidates to equal time for reply. In passing these provisions, Congress nevertheless emphasized that it did not intend to relieve broadcasters of their obligation "to afford reasonable opportunity for the discussion of conflicting views on issues of public importance."

Despite this congressional rebuke, the FCC continued to tighten the requirements under the fairness and equal time policies by ruling in the early 1960s that any person whose character was criticized in any discussion of a controversial public question must be afforded a right to reply without charge, and that if a licensee's facilities were used to take a partisan position on the issues in an election, or to support or oppose candidates, the licensee was required to notify opposing individuals and candidates and offer free time for responses. By the 1960s, therefore, the fairness doctrine through administrative interpretation had become a general requirement of "fairness" of coverage of issues of public importance by broadcasters and also a specific requirement that equal time and the right of reply must be provided by broadcasters not only to political candidates but also to any person whose character was attacked in the discussion of any issue of public importance.

As the requirements of the fairness doctrine broadened, the filing of complaints with the FCC against broadcasters for failure to comply with these broadened requirements also increased. Responding to the failure of many broadcasters to comply with the fairness doctrine, the FCC issued a *Fairness Primer* in 1964, in which it compiled its rulings under the fairness doctrine and emphasized the responsibilities of broadcasters in complying with the right of reply, equal time, and fairness doctrines. With reference to the right of reply doctrine, the *Fairness Primer* thus specified that when "an attack is made on an individual's or group's integrity, character, honesty, or like personal qualities, in connection with a controversial issue of public importance, the licensee has an affirmative duty to take all appropriate steps to see to it that the person or persons attacked are afforded the fullest opportunity to respond." The broadcast licensee, the FCC emphasized, was "fully responsible for all matter which is broadcast over his station."

## THE GENESIS OF THE RED LION CASE

The FCC's publication of the *Fairness Primer* was to an extent an admission by the commission that its enforcement of the fairness, equal time, and right of reply doctrines had not been effective. The fairness and related doctrines had been the product of an evolutionary process of statutory interpretation by both the Federal Radio Commission and the FCC over a period of some thirty years, and the doctrines were embodied in a series of ad hoc rulings in specific cases as well as administrative responses to complaints against particular broadcasters alleging noncompliance with the doctrines. The FCC's approach to the enforcement of these doctrines in the early 1960s was essentially one of responding with letters of admonition to complaints charging noncompliance by licensees. The ultimate weapon of enforcement was of course a decision by the FCC to deny renewal of a broadcaster's license. License nonrenewal, however, appeared to be a drastic, meataxe approach to administrative enforcement problems requiring intermediate remedies. Until the mid-1960s, the FCC had nonetheless not devised other methods of enforcing the fairness, equal time, and right of reply doctrines.

It was within this context of administrative enforcement (or lack thereof) of the fairness and related doctrines that the *Red Lion* case arose. And the *Red Lion* case would not only induce a major shift in the FCC's enforcement approach to the fairness and related doctrines but also would generate a major challenge to the FCC's exercise of its rule-making power in regard to the broadcasting industry as a whole.

The Red Lion Broadcasting Company operated radio stations WGCB AM/FM at Red Lion, Pennsylvania. The principal stockholder and president of the Red Lion Broadcasting Company was the Reverend John M. Norris. On November 25, 1964, station WGCB carried a fifteen-minute "Christian Crusade" broadcast by the Reverend Billy James Hargis, who during the course of the broadcast commented on a recently published paperback book by Fred J. Cook titled *Goldwater–Extremist of the Right.* Regarding Fred Cook, Hargis said:

Who is Cook? Cook was fired from the New York *World Telegram* after he made a false charge publicly on television against an unnamed official of the New York City government. New York publishers and *Newsweek* magazine for December 7, 1959, showed that Fred Cook and his pal, Eugene Gleason, had made up the whole story and this confession was made to New York District Attorney, Frank Hogan. After losing his job, Cook went to work for the left-wing publication, *The Nation,* one of the most scurrilous publications of the left which has championed many communist causes over many years. Its editor, Carry McWilliams, has been affiliated with many communist enterprises, scores of which have been cited as subversive by the Attorney General of the U.S. or by other government agencies. . . . Now, among other things Fred Cook wrote for *The Nation,* was an article absolving Alger Hiss of any wrong doing. . .there was a 208 page attack on the FBI and J. Edgar Hoover; another attack by Mr. Cook on the Central Intelligence Agency. . .now this is the man who wrote the book to smear and destroy Barry Goldwater called "Barry Goldwater—Extremist of the Right"!

In 1959, Fred Cook had indeed been dismissed as a reporter for the New York *World-Telegram and Sun* after having falsely charged an un-named New York City official with attempting to bribe his partner, Eugene Gleason, to stop investigative reporting on corruption involving slum clearance projects in the city. Cook made the charge on David Susskind's "Open End" program on WNTA-TV, basing the charge on Gleason's statement to him. When both Cook and Gleason were questioned later by New York District Attorney Frank Hogan, however, Gleason admitted he had fabricated the story. Gleason took full blame for the false charge, admitting that Cook had only repeated on the Susskind show what Gleason had told him. The *World-Telegram and Sun* nevertheless dismissed both Cook and Gleason as reporters.

Working subsequently as a reporter for *The Nation,* Cook ironically published in the spring of 1964 an article exposing the proliferation of extreme conservative radio programs which were being broadcast throughout the nation. In the article, titled "Radio Right: Hate Clubs of the Air," Cook charged that "[r]ight wing fanatics, casting doubt on the loyalty of every President of the United States since Herbert Hoover, are pounding the American people, this Presidential election year, with an unprecedented flood of radio and television propaganda." "The hate clubs of the air," Cook continued, "are spewing out a minimum of 6,600 broadcasts a week, carried by more than 1,300 radio and television stations—nearly one out of every five in the nation—in a blitz that saturates every one of the fifty states with the exception of Maine." Cook listed the leading extreme conservative broadcasts in his article, including the Reverend Mr. Hargis's "Christian Crusade," and charged that throughout the extreme conservative movement, "the tie that binds seems to be that of the John Birch Society."

Cook's article was indicative of the mounting concern in liberal circles over the rising tide of extreme conservative propaganda on both radio and television during the 1960s. Indeed, in the spring of 1964, the Democratic National Committee warned radio and television stations that many of the extreme conservative programs being broadcast on those stations repeatedly attacked the candidates, programs, and policies of the party and that the Democratic party intended to demand equal time to answer the broadcasts. Concern over the extreme conservative broadcasts was also reflected in increased criticism of the FCC for its failure to enforce effectively the fairness and right of reply doctrines. *Newsweek* magazine thus reported that there "has so far been no rein whatsoever on the radio of the right. The FCC's 'fairness doctrine' declares that broadcasters must give equal time for reply to any subject or individual attacked, but it has no control over the virulence of the attack. Besides, the doctrine is seldom invoked. 'FCC enforcement in this area is terrible,' says one Senate staffer." In the same vein, *The Atlantic* published an article in 1967 entitled, "Is the FCC Dead?"

Fred Cook discovered the lack of compliance by broadcasters with the right of reply requirement when he sought to reply to the attack on him by Mr. Hargis. Cook recorded a reply to the Hargis broadcast, pointing out that he had not consciously stated a falsehood on the Susskind show and that District Attorney Frank Hogan had stated that Eugene Gleason had "completely exonerated [Cook] of all responsibility for the false accusation made on the television program." He was making his reply to Hargis, Cook said in his tape, because the issue was "very simply facts and truth versus the technique of smear, innuendo, the discrediting of a man by a label." Public decisions, he said, should be made on the "basis of facts and reason, not on the basis of labels designed to blot out facts and reason and not on the basis of the distortions of a demagogue." When Cook contacted the numerous radio stations that had broadcast the Hargis attack, requesting free air time for broadcasting his taped reply, many of the stations replied that Cook would have to pay for the air time required for his reply.

When Cook requested free time to reply to the Hargis attack from station WGCB in Red Lion, Pennsylvania, for example, the Reverend John M. Norris, owner of the station, responded by sending Cook the station's rate card and offering time for Cook to reply if he were willing to pay the station's prevailing rates. Cook replied on December 28, 1964, and pointed out to Norris that station WGCB was required, under FCC requirements, to furnish him free time to air his reply to Hargis. If payment were required of those wishing to reply to broadcast attacks on them, Cook noted, "it is conceivable that radio stations might be able to drum up a fairly good business by selling time to persons who have been slandered."

Mr. Norris responded to Cook in January of 1965 and professed to be "at a loss to understand your statement that may imply we ought *not* to 'drum up business'—we could ask, 'How else may we be expected to stay in business?'" Cook's request for free time to reply to the Hargis attack, Norris continued, "prompts me to ask what would happen if General Motors advertised the 'best car' and Ford then demanded 'free time' to inform our listeners that they had been slandered. This would soon remove all broadcasting from the realm of free enterprise, leaving only government subsidized and controlled radio." "For your information," Norris concluded, "it was your article on 'Hate Clubs of the Air' which alerted us to several of these broadcasts which we later acquired, so that now we carry them all. Your article has resulted in cutting our deficit spending by almost one half, thus the harm that was intended has greatly benefited us."

Norris's impression, that the FCC's right of reply requirement permitted stations to charge those seeking to reply to personal attacks, was shared by many of the stations Cook contacted. This impression was perhaps fostered by a memorandum from Hargis which was sent to all the stations carrying his broadcasts in response to Cook's demands for equal time to reply. Hargis pointed out that many stations were responding to demands for equal time to reply by noting "that since Christian Crusade pays for its time, those people may have equal time also on a paying basis. This satisfies the Federal Communication Commission and stops the harasser." "I am sorry if Cook has harassed you," Hargis concluded. "You can now see just a little of what we go through in our defense of the Constitution and Christianity."

Having been largely frustrated in his attempts to obtain air time to reply to the Hargis attack, on February 7, 1965, Fred Cook filed a complaint with the FCC against sixteen radio stations, including station WGCB in Red Lion, Pennsylvania, for refusing him free air time. Cook pointed out to the FCC that under the right of reply requirement as enunciated by the commission, a station broadcasting a personal attack was required to notify the person attacked and offer free air time for a reply. Of all the stations carrying Hargis's "Christian Crusade" program, Cook said, only one had notified him of the Hargis attack, and the stations listed in his complaint were also insisting on being paid for the time required for his reply.

The FCC responded to Cook on March 12, stating that it was "the usual practice of the Commission to associate complaints with our files on the station involved and to afford such station the opportunity to comment on the complaint." The commission therefore informed all the stations listed by Cook of his complaint, and requested the stations to submit responses within twenty days. Mr. Norris of station WGCB in Red

Lion, Pennsylvania, replied to the FCC's letter on May 19 and said that it was his understanding that stations were required to provide free air time for replies to personal attacks only if sponsorship were unavailable. If Fred Cook would inform station WGCB that he was financially unable to sponsor his reply, Norris said, then the station would furnish him free time to reply to the Hargis broadcast.

On October 6, the commission replied to Norris by pointing out that under its right of reply requirements, when a personal attack was broadcast by a station "the licensee has an obligation to inform the person attacked of the attack, by sending a tape or transcript of the broadcast, or if these are unavailable, as accurate a summary as possible of the substance of the attack, and to offer him a comparable opportunity to respond." Station WGCB was free to obtain sponsorship for Cook's reply if it desired, the FCC said, but Cook was not obliged to pay for the time required for his reply. "Accordingly," the commission concluded, "you are requested to advise the Commission of your plans to comply with the 'fairness doctrine,' applicable to the situation."

Norris responded again to the FCC on November 8, and argued that since Fred Cook had attacked Hargis and the "Christian Crusade" in his "Hate Clubs of the Air" article in *The Nation,* Hargis was within his rights to attack Cook in his radio broadcast. "Under the circumstances, we are at a loss to see the 'fairness' in the Commission's letter to us of October 6, 1965. The Commission has directed that we give Mr. Cook free time to answer an alleged attack upon him made in a paid broadcast by one who had previously been the subject of a nationwide attack by Mr. Cook . . . ," Norris argued. "The Commission has given us no reason why the 'Fairness Doctrine' requires an offer of free time to Mr. Cook to be made without condition as to his inability to pay." Norris thus requested that the commission reconsider its position and advise WGCB "whether in good conscience and in 'fairness,' we should now be forced to give Mr. Cook free time to reply to an attack by one whom he has previously attacked. And, if Mr. Cook, in his reply, should personally attack Mr. Hargis and other 'Hate Clubs,' as he calls them, would we then be required to give free time to Mr. Hargis and others whom Mr. Cook may again attack? Or, if Mr. Hargis should then reply to Mr. Cook in his paid broadcast, would we then be required to give Mr. Cook more free time for further reply?"

On December 10, the FCC in a "Broadcast Action" again responded to Norris and ruled that compliance with the fairness and right of reply requirements had nothing to do with what might have been reported in other media of communications. Fred Cook's article in *The Nation,* the FCC therefore ruled, was irrelevant to station WGCB's obligation to furnish Cook with free air time to reply to the Hargis attack. The furnishing of free air time for replies by those attacked on the air, the FCC said, was essential to assure the public of its right to hear all sides of controversial issues of public importance. And any other policy, the commission continued, "would mean that in the case of a network or widely syndicated program containing a personal attack in a discussion of a controversial issue of public importance, the person attacked might be required to deplete or substantially cut into his assets, if he wished to inform the public of his side. . . ."

Its letter of October 6, the commission said, was a "final order" which could be contested in the courts if Norris and station WGCB so desired. "A broadcaster has sought the license to a valuable public frequency, and has taken it, subject to the obligation to operate in the public interest," the FCC concluded. "Valuable frequency space has been allocated to broadcasting in considerable part, so that it may contribute to an informed electorate. . . . Viewed against these reasonable precepts, our ruling is, we believe, reasonably related to the public interest. . . . Since that is so, it is a requirement fully consistent with the Constitution. . . ."

The FCC's action on Fred Cook's complaint against Norris and WGCB was not the only difficulty Norris was encountering from the commission. The licenses for station WGCB and also WINB, another station owned by Norris, were subject to renewal in the summer of 1966, but the FCC had not acted on the renewals of the licenses as late as June of 1967. Norris had also applied for television channel 49 in Red Lion, Pennsylvania, an application that also had been pending before the FCC since December of 1965. Station WGCB also was the subject of a complaint by the Democratic National Committee during the 1964 presidential campaign for violations of the fairness doctrine. When the FCC requested comments from Norris regarding the DNC complaint, he replied that he was "amazed." "Now well into my 82nd year," Norris told the FCC, "I have never before been subjected to such religious and political persecution. 'Blessed are ye, when men shall revile you, and persecute you and shall say all manner of evil against you falsely, for my sake.' Matthew 5:11."

The response of Norris to his difficulties with the commission was to file a suit in the U.S. District Court for the District of Columbia seeking a judgment that the fairness doctrine was unconstitutional and an injunction against the FCC to prevent its enforcement of the doctrine against station WGCB. Norris also sued the Democratic National Committee for five million dollars in damages. These cases were held in abeyance, however, when Norris filed on February 1, 1966, a petition for review in the U.S. Court of Appeals for the District of Columbia Circuit challenging the FCC's order that Fred Cook be given free time for a reply to the Hargis attack. The FCC's order, the petition for review alleged, violated the First

Amendment by restraining Norris's "expression of views, arguments and opinions" as well as "those who seek to pay for and use" his radio station. The commission's order also was invalid, the petition for review asserted, because the Federal Communications Act involved an unconstitutional delegation of legislative power and violated the "fundamental principle that Congress may not in the absence of clearly ascertainable criteria delegate its legislative function to an administrative agency or officer." Finally, the FCC's order, if it were enforced, the petition said, would deprive Red Lion Broadcasting Company of its property without due process of law in violation of the Due Process Clause of the Fifth Amendment. Norris and the Red Lion Broadcasting Company had thus launched the first constitutional challenge to the FCC's enforcement of the fairness and related doctrines.

## THE BATTLE BROADENS: THE FCC RESORTS TO RULE MAKING

The technique of informal adjudication used by the FCC in the *Red Lion* case was, until 1966, not only the method by which the commission had enforced the fairness and related doctrines, but it had also been the principal method by which the commission had developed those doctrines. In April of 1966, however, the FCC departed significantly from the method by which it had both formulated and enforced the fairness and related doctrines. On April 13, 1966, the commission filed a public notice of proposed rule making in the *Federal Register* and indicated in the notice that it proposed to embody the right of reply requirement and the standards governing political editorializing by broadcasters in its formal rules.

Under the provisions of the Administrative Procedure Act, an administrative agency which desires to promulgate new rules or regulations must publish a notice in the *Federal Register* stating the legal authority for the proposed rules and describing the nature of the proposed rules. The agency, the APA also provides, "shall give interested persons an opportunity to participate in the rule making [process] through submission of written data, views, or arguments with or without opportunity for oral presentation."

It was this rule-making procedure that the FCC initiated by its April 13 notice of proposed rule making in the *Federal Register*. The new rules were needed, the Commission said, because its requirement regarding the right of reply and political editorializing had "not always been followed even when flagrant personal attacks have occurred in the context of a program dealing with a controversial issue." By embodying the standards governing the right of reply and political editorializing in its formal rules, the commission said, it would "emphasize and make more precise licensees' obligation in the area" and assist its own procedures "in taking effective action in appropriate circumstances when the [requirements] are not followed." Indeed, once the right of reply and political editorializing requirements were embodied in its formal rules, the FCC could enforce the rules by imposing fines of $1,000 for each day the rules were violated, by criminal prosecutions, or by cease and desist orders. By the adoption of its proposed rules, therefore, the commission would have intermediate remedies to enforce the rules, rather than having to resort to the drastic action of revoking or not renewing a broadcast license or resorting to the slap on the wrist of a letter of reprimand.

During the period allowed for public comment on the FCC's proposed rules—the period from April 13 to July 5, 1966—the commission learned, however, that the broadcast industry was virtually unanimous in its opposition to the proposed rules. In written comments filed with the commission regarding the proposed rules, the National Association of Broadcasters, the National Broadcasting Company (NBC), Columbia Broadcasting System (CBS), and numerous broadcast organizations and individual stations denounced the proposed rules. Indeed, it was apparent from the written comments filed by the broadcast industry that it not only opposed the proposed rules but also was prepared to challenge the validity of the commission's power to impose the fairness and related doctrines on the industry.

In comments on the proposed rules that were typical of the broadcast industry as a whole, the National Association of Broadcasters thus argued that the FCC's imposition of the fairness and related doctrines on broadcasters was essentially illegitimate. The fairness doctrine, the NAB argued, was a violation of the First Amendment's guarantees of freedom of speech and freedom of the press, since it "discourages the use of broadcasting for the expression of opinion and thus abridges the right of the broadcaster as a communicator." And CBS offered a similar argument, contending that the "First Amendment is media blind," and that the guarantees of freedom of speech and freedom of the press were "as much violated by the Commission's directing a licensee to present an individual speaking on an issue the Commission finds 'controversial' as it would be if the United States Post Office Department demanded the publication by the *New York Times* of the same statement at the risk of losing its special mailing privileges."

The commission's proposed rules were, on the other hand, supported by the Laborers' International of North America, the International Typographical Union, and the United Steel Workers of America. The unions generally were concerned with fair coverage of labor disputes by the broadcast media which they felt the proposed rules would facilitate. The proposed rules were also endorsed by the American Civil Liberties Union, the National Rifle Association, and the Broadcasting and Film Commission of the National Council of Churches of Christ in the U.S.A.

Despite the overwhelming opposition of the broadcast industry, the FCC announced on July 10, 1967, that it was adopting its rules essentially as proposed. The commission defended its action on the ground that by adopting the rules, it would have a wider range of enforcement options and licensees would be more clearly informed as to what the commission demanded of them. Objections that the rules violated the right of free expression under the First Amendment, the commission argued, were "without merit." The rules did not "proscribe in any way the presentation by a licensee of personal attacks or editorials on political candidates," the commission said. "They simply provide that where [a licensee] chooses to make such presentations, he must take appropriate notification steps and make an offer for reasonable opportunity for response by those vitally affected and best able to inform the public of the contrasting viewpoint." That the rules it was adopting "are reasonably related to the public interest," the commission concluded, "is shown by consideration of the converse of the rules—namely operation by a licensee limited to informing the public of only one side of these issues, i.e., the personal attack or the licensee's editorial."

The following rules were thus adopted by the FCC, to become effective on August 14, 1967:

[Personal attack rule]: When, during the presentation of views on a controversial issue of public importance, an attack is made upon the honesty, character, integrity or like personal qualities of an identified person or group, the licensee shall, within a reasonable time and in no event later than one week after the attack, transmit to the person or group attacked (1) notification of the date, time and identification of the broadcast; (2) a script or tape (or an accurate summary if a script or tape is not available) of the attack; and (3) an offer of a reasonable opportunity to respond over the licensee's facilities.

[Political editorial rule]: Where a licensee, in an editorial, endorses or opposes a legally qualified candidate or candidates, the licensee shall, within 24 hours after the editorial, transmit to respectively the other qualified candidate or candidates for the same office or the candidate opposed in the editorial (1) notification of the date and the time of the editorial; (2) a script or tape of the editorial; and (3) an offer of a reasonable opportunity for a candidate or a spokesman for the candidate to respond over the licensee's facilities: *Provided, however,* that where such editorials are broadcast within 72 hours prior to the day of the election, the licensee shall comply with the provisions of this subsection sufficiently far in advance of the broadcast to enable the candidate or candidates to have a reasonable opportunity to prepare a response and to present it in a timely fashion.

Commissioner Lee Loevinger concurred in the adoption of these rules, although he suggested they they were unduly vague, while Commissioner Robert T. Bartley dissented from the FCC's decision adopting the rules. The commission's adoption of the rules was perceived by the broadcasting industry, on the other hand, as the second of two major blows delivered by the FCC against the industry's interests during 1967. For on June 2, 1967, the commission had ruled that cigarette advertisements on radio and television fell under the fairness doctrine and that broadcasters therefore were required to offer "significant" free time for antismoking advertisements. This ruling was in response to a complaint filed by John F. Banzhaf against station WCBS in New York for its refusal to furnish him free time to reply to cigarette commercials.

Although the National Association of Broadcasters had financially contributed to Norris and station WGCB's challenge to the fairness doctrine in the *Red Lion* case, lawyers in the broadcasting industry had viewed the *Red Lion* case as a poor vehicle for testing the constitutionality of the fairness doctrine because it involved the question of the right of reply of a specific individual (Fred Cook) who had been personally attacked and perhaps, because of the extreme right wing orientation of both Norris and the Hargis program. With the promulgation of the FCC's right of reply and political editorializing rules, however, the broadcasting industry could launch another attack on the fairness doctrine without the disadvantages some perceived in the *Red Lion* litigation. And, of course, given the FCC's application of the fairness doctrine to cigarette advertising, which contributed $201 million to broadcasters in 1967, the industry now had a powerful financial incentive to attack the fairness doctrine in the courts and seek a judicial invalidation of the doctrine.

Less than three weeks after their adoption, the FCC's new rules were thus challenged by the Radio Television News Directors Association (RTNDA) and several broadcasting interests in a petition for review filed in the U.S. Court of Appeals for the Seventh Circuit. The RTNDA is an association of over one thousand news directors, news executives, and other news personnel employed by radio and television stations or networks, and it was soon joined in its suit challenging the FCC's rules by the Columbia Broadcasting System (CBS) and the National Broadcasting Company (NBC).

On August 7, however, the FCC announced the first of its amendments to the rules it had adopted on July 10. The personal attack rule, the commission said, was inapplicable "to a bona fide newscast or on-the-spot coverage of a bona fide news event." If a personal attack occurred on a "bona fide" newscast or during coverage of an on-the-spot news event, the general fairness doctrine applied, the commission said, and in such an event, the broadcaster "usually turns, as part of the news coverage to be presented that day or in the very near future, to the other side and again makes the same good faith journalistic judgment as to its presentation and what fairness requires in the particular circumstances." To require notification of the person attacked and the extension of a right of reply to that person in such circumstances, the commission said, would be "impractical and might impede the effective execution of important news functions of licensees or networks. . . ." The exemption of personal attacks occurring on bona fide newscasts or on-the-spot news coverage from the personal attack rule, the commission added, did not apply to editorials or similar commentary embodying personal attacks, even if broadcast in the course of newscasts.

Despite this "clarification" of its rules, the commission was soon to discover that further amendment of its rules was necessary. Like most administrative agencies, the FCC of course has it own legal staff, but when federal agencies are challenged in the courts, the duty of defending the agencies falls on the Department of Justice, which possesses a virtual monopoly on handling government litigation. The defense of the FCC's rules in the Seventh Circuit Court of Appeals, therefore, had to be coordinated between the commission's legal staff and Justice Department lawyers.

On February 29, 1968, Assistant Attorney General Donald F. Turner notified the chairman of the FCC that in regard to the *RTNDA* case in the Seventh Circuit, "we are fully prepared to support the Commission's position that the 'fairness doctrine' is constitutional and within the Commission's statutory powers, and that, as a general proposition, some special rule with regard to personal attack is a valid facet of that doctrine." "However," Turner continued, "we have some concern that the rule, as drafted, raises possible problems that might be minimized by appropriate revisions in the rule without materially interfering with the public interest objectives that the rule is intending to serve." Turner thus suggested "that the Commission might wish to weigh the possibility of considering revisions of the rule before proceeding further with the [*RTNDA* case] now before the Seventh Circuit."

The misgivings of the Justice Department regarding the commission's personal attack rule were apparently prompted by an exhibit filed by CBS in the Seventh Circuit Court of Appeals. The CBS exhibit consisted of transcripts of Eric Sevareid's commentaries on the "CBS Evening News," extracts from news interviews on "Face the Nation," and excerpts from six CBS news documentaries. The FCC's personal attack rule, CBS argued, would apply to each of these facets of its news programming, making it almost impossible for such programming to continue.

In response to the Justice Department's misgivings and in light of the CBS exhibit, on March 1, 1968, the FCC and the Justice Department filed a motion to hold the *RTNDA* case in abeyance pending further revision of the commission's rules, and the courts of appeals granted the motion. The commission's action, however, prompted Commissioner Lee Loevinger to attack his colleagues' motives for delaying the *RTNDA* case. In a dissenting opinion opposing the commission's decision to ask for a delay in the *RTNDA* case, Loevinger accused his colleagues of obstructing judicial review of the commission's powers. Until the *Red Lion* and *RTNDA* cases, Loevinger asserted, the fairness and related doctrines had never been challenged in the courts, "because licensees have generally deemed it more prudent not to hazard their licenses or antagonize the bureaucracy which has such great discretionary power over their business." By the "endless tinkering" with its rules, Loevinger argued, the commission was attempting to delay legal challenges to its powers, which it professed to welcome, and the course the commission was following "serves only its own interest as a litigant, has no public purpose, and falls considerably short of the diligence, promptness and candor which the Commission demands of its own licensees."

Despite Loevinger's protest, the FCC reconsidered its personal attack rule, and on March 29, 1968, announced a further revision of the rule. The personal attack rule, the commission announced, was amended to exempt not only personal attacks that might occur during newscasts or on-the-spot coverage of news events (as the August 7, 1967, amendment provided) but also personal attacks that might occur during "bona fide news interviews" or "commentary or analysis contained in the foregoing programs." The commission's revision of the personal attack rule was thus clearly tailored to meet the objections to the rule CBS had offered in its exhibit in the court of appeals in the *RTNDA* case. Under the rule as amended, personal attacks occurring in such situations as Eric Sevareid's commentary on the "CBS Evening News" or interviews on programs like "Face the Nation" were exempt from the rule.

Commissioner Loevinger, however, again denounced his colleagues' action and condemned the "tortuous and changing course of the Commission with respect to the present rules [as] evidence of the inadequacy of research and consideration underlying the rules." "No more important issue has ever confronted this Commission," Loevinger declared, and he dissented from the commission's action because he felt the rules were unconstitutional. The FCC was merely reacting to the CBS exhibit filed in the Seventh Circuit Court of Appeals, he charged, and the amendment of the personal attack rule was prompted by "the great respect which the Commission, its lawyers and the public have for Eric Sevareid. It would not be inappropriate to call the present revision of the rules the 'Eric Sevareid rule.'"

Loevinger also contended that specialized administrative agencies like the FCC were inappropriate bodies to formulate rules such as those the commission was adopting. "Here, more than elsewhere, the creation or delegation of power and the formulation of rules should be by elected legislative bodies," he argued, "with only enforcement and application left to administrative agencies." "The Commission's course with respect to these rules argues strongly against the wisdom of their adoption," Loevinger concluded. "The rules as revised seem clearly to burden, and thus abridge, free expression through the broadcast media. In case of even arguable conflict between administrative action or power and First Amendment protections I will not hesitate to resolve my doubt in favor of maintaining the First Amendment freedoms."

*Broadcasting* magazine also blasted the FCC editorially, pointing out that "hard-line regulators on the FCC and its staff have often challenged broadcasters to court tests of the agency's powers of program regulation. Now the hard-liners want to cut and run from a meaningful showdown on the constitutionality of the fairness doctrine rules, and they have persuaded a majority of the commissioners to cut and run with them." "The performance is to be admired more for its legal slickness than its principle," *Broadcasting* continued. "If the FCC succeeds in ducking this fight, broadcasters can expect to be pecked into groveling submission by case-by-case applications of individual sanctions."

## THE COURTS OF APPEALS DECIDE: CONFLICT IN THE CIRCUITS

While the commission was, somewhat awkwardly, attempting to hammer out a defensible personal attack rule, it was handed a victory in the *Red Lion* case which had been pending in the Court of Appeals for the District of Columbia Circuit. On June 13, 1967, the court of appeals announced a decision upholding the FCC's order to Red Lion Broadcasting Company requiring it to furnish Fred Cook free time to reply to the Hargis attack. Addressing Red Lion's argument that the Communications Act unconstitutionally delegated legislative power to the FCC because Congress failed to provide adequate standards and ascertainable criteria to guide the commission's decision making, the court noted that the standard of the "public interest, convenience or necessity" under which Congress delegated power to the commission had been repeatedly upheld as a "valid basis for the legislative grant of administrative power. . . ."

And the court further held that the commission's application of the fairness doctrine to Red Lion and station WGCB did not deprive them of their freedom of expression or of property without due process of law. Because of the unique characteristics of the broadcasting industry, the court said, "the courts have consistently held that regulatory action by the Commission, acting within the framework and provisions of [the Communications Act], does not per se violate the First Amendment." Rather than limiting Red Lion's freedom of expression, the court continued, the fairness doctrine "recognizes and enforces the free speech right of the victims of any personal attack made during [a] broadcast," and "absent the remedial procedures afforded. . .[Fred] Cook," Red Lion's conduct "would, in fact, constitute a serious abridgment of his free speech rights." The court thus ordered and adjudged "that the action of the Federal Communications Commission on review in this case is affirmed."

Norris denounced the decision, saying that it was the "most ridiculous thing that could have happened for freedom of speech in this country." And both counsel for Red Lion Broadcasting Company and the general counsel for the National Association of Broadcasters, which had contributed financially to the *Red Lion* case, indicated that the case would be appealed to the Supreme Court. A petition for a writ of certiorari was therefore filed in the Supreme Court on September 11, and the Court granted the petition in December. As the *Red Lion* case proceeded to the Supreme Court, however, the *RTNDA* case, challenging the FCC's personal attack and political editorializing rules, was pending in the Seventh Circuit Court of Appeals, and this circumstance prompted considerable procedural maneuvering by the government and the RTNDA and other interests involved in the case.

On December 14, 1967, the government thus filed a motion with the Seventh Circuit Court of Appeals to hold in abeyance the petitions for review challenging the FCC's rules pending a decision by the Supreme Court in the *Red Lion* case. The issues in the *Red Lion* case were essentially the same as those in the *RTNDA* case, the government argued, and the Supreme Court's decision in the *Red Lion* case would undoubtedly be largely dispositive of the issues in the *RTNDA* case. Counsel for the RTNDA, on the other hand, opposed the government's motion, while requesting that the court of appeals delay hearing the *RTNDA* case for thirty days to allow time for a petition for a writ of certiorari before judgment to be filed and acted upon in the Supreme Court. If the Court granted such a writ, the *RTNDA* case would proceed directly to the Court and be heard together with the *Red Lion* case.

The court of appeals granted the RTNDA's request for a delay, but the Supreme Court refused to grant certiorari before judgment on January 19, 1968. The Court did, however, order that the oral argument in the *Red Lion* case be delayed pending the decision of the Seventh Circuit Court of Appeals in the *RTNDA* case and "pending this Court's action on any petition for certiorari which may be filed to review that decision." The Court thus indicated that it wished to hear the *Red Lion* and *RTNDA* cases argued together.

After further delay that the FCC's revision of its rules entailed, the *RTNDA* case was finally decided by the Seventh Circuit Court of Appeals on September 10, 1968. In contrast to the decision of the District of Columbia Court of Appeals in the *Red Lion* case, however, the Seventh Circuit Court of Appeals held that the FCC's personal attack and political editorializing rules infringed upon broadcasters' right of freedom of expression under the First Amendment.

"Despite the Commission's disclaimers to the contrary," the court of appeals said, "we agree with [the broadcasters] that the rules pose a substantial likelihood of inhibiting a broadcast licensee's dissemination of views on political candidates and controversial issues of public importance. This inhibition stems, in part, from the substantial economic and practical burdens which attend the mandatory requirements of notification, the provision of a tape, and the arrangement for a reply." Broadcasters would also be inhibited in exercising their First Amendment rights, the court continued, by the penalties the commission could impose for violations of the rules—penalties that included fines of $1,000 per day a violation existed, criminal penalties, cease and desist orders, or revocation of licenses. "When a licensee considers the vagueness of the rules, the mandatory and pervasive requirement of the rules, and the threat of suffering serious sanctions for non-compliance with them," the court held, "it is likely that he will become far more hesitant to engage in controversial issue programming or political editorializing."

In what was a significant victory for the broadcast media, the court of appeals also rejected the FCC's contention that while broadcasting was protected by the First Amendment, it was "entitled to a lower order of First Amendment protection than the printed press." This contention by the FCC was based on the traditional view that since the airwaves constituted a scarce, public resource, access to the airwaves and the conditions of such access could be subjected to greater governmental regulation than that which could be applied to the print media. But the court of appeals noted that there were more commercial radio and television stations than there were general circulation daily newspapers, that there were many broadcast frequencies that went unused, and that the recent development of ultrahigh television frequencies would further increase the number of broadcast frequencies. Entrance into the field of broadcasting was therefore not limited primarily by the technical factor of lack of frequencies, the court held, but was limited primarily by economics, just as economic considerations were the primary factor limiting entrance into the print media. While conceding the need for public regulation of the technical, financial, and ownership aspects of radio and television stations, the court concluded that the broadcast media deserved essentially the same First Amendment protection as the print media. Just as the government could not dictate the content of newspapers or magazines, consistent with the First Amendment, the FCC could not dictate program content to the broadcast media, the court concluded, and the FCC's rules therefore had to be set aside.

The decision of the Seventh Circuit Court of Appeals was thus directly in conflict with the decision of the District of Columbia Court of Appeals in the *Red Lion* case on the question of the constitutional validity of the FCC's power to impose the personal attack and political editorializing requirements on the broadcast industry. The government, however, filed a petition for a writ of certiorari in the Supreme Court requesting review of the *RTNDA* case, and the Court granted certiorari in the case on January 13, 1969, ordering at the same time that the *Red Lion* and *RTNDA* cases be argued together. The long battle between the broadcasters and the bureaucracy would thus reach its climax before the Supreme Court.

## THE BUREAUCRACY AND THE BROADCASTERS BEFORE THE COURT

The position of the broadcasting industry was presented to the Supreme Court in briefs filed by the Red Lion Broadcasting Company, the Radio Television News Directors Association, NBC, and CBS. The oral argument on behalf of the broadcasters was made by Archibald Cox, solicitor general during the Kennedy administration and subsequently the first special prosecutor in the Watergate investigation. The position of the FCC and the government was of course presented by Solicitor General Erwin Griswold, and the government's position was also supported by amicus curiae briefs filed by the American Civil Liberties Union, the American Federation of Labor-Congress of Industrial Organizations (AFL-CIO), and by a large group of primarily religious organizations headed by the Office of Communications of the United Church of Christ.

Administrative rules and regulations may be attacked in the courts on the ground that they are unconstitutional, that they constitute an exercise of power beyond that delegated to the agency by Congress, that the rules have not been adopted according to the procedure prescribed by Congress, or because they are arbitrary, capricious, an abuse of discretion, or otherwise not in accordance with law.

Since the FCC concededly followed the procedures required by the Administrative Procedure Act in adopting the personal attack and political editorializing rules, the broadcasters argued before the Supreme Court in the *Red Lion* and *RTNDA* cases that the commission lacked the delegated rule-making power to promulgate the rules and that, in any case, the rules were invalid invasions of the freedoms of speech and press under the First Amendment. Although the Red Lion Broadcasting Company was attacking an administrative order, rather than formal rules, the attorneys for Red Lion used essentially the same arguments that were made against the validity of the FCC's rules in the *RTNDA* case.

Arguing that the Congress had not in the Communications Act delegated the rule-making authority the FCC was purporting to exercise, the broadcasters pointed out to the Court that the commission was delegated under the act only such rule-making power "as may be necessary in the execution of its functions" or "to carry out the provisions of [the Communications Act]." "Regulating the content of public affairs programs," the broadcasters argued, "is neither a Commission function nor a purpose of the Act," especially given the provision of Section 326 of the act denying any powers of censorship to the FCC. "When personal and political liberties are at stake, only 'the most explicit authorization' will support agency action in 'an area of doubtful constitutionality,'" the broadcasters argued. "The principle is supported both by the propriety of avoiding doubtful constitutional questions and by the wisdom of requiring decisions of great constitutional import to be squarely faced by Congress rather than 'relegated by default to administrators who, under our system of government, are not endowed with authority to decide them.'"

On behalf of the FCC and the government, however, the solicitor general argued that the FCC's fairness and related doctrines had been the valid, evolutionary products of commission interpretations of the Communications Act under its congressionally delegated powers and that, contrary to the argument of the broadcasters, Congress had explicitly approved the commission's policies in this area. When Congress amended the equal time for political candidates doctrine in 1959 to exempt appearances of political candidates on newscasts, news interviews, or on-the-spot news coverage, the solicitor general argued, it also provided that nothing in the exemption should be construed as relieving broadcasters "in connec-

tion with the presentation of newscasts, news interviews, news documentaries, and on-the-spot coverage of news events, from the obligation
imposed on them under this Act to operate in the public interest and to
afford reasonable opportunity for the discussion of conflicting views on
issues of public importance." This provision, the solicitor general said, was
a clear expression by Congress of its approval of the FCC's interpretation
of the Communications Act in regard to the fairness and related doctrines,
and an indication that the commission was properly using its delegated
power in regard to those doctrines.

The broadcasters responded to this argument by pointing out that
Congress could not have expressed approval of the personal attack and
political editorializing policies in 1959, since those policies were not in
existence in 1959. And, in any case, the broadcasters argued, the personal
attack and political editorializing policies went "beyond any interpretation
of the fairness doctrine prior to 1959 both because they impose detailed
obligations based upon specific incidents without regard to the licensee's
over-all performance and because they leave no room for the honest
exercise of discretion."

Although considerable argument among the parties was thus devoted to
whether the FCC's personal attack and political editorializing rules were
within its congressionally delegated powers, the principal source of contention in the *Red Lion* and *RTNDA* cases was the freedom of speech and
freedom of the press issue. And on this point, the broadcasters made a
major effort to convince the Court that broadcasters were entitled to the
same protection under the First Amendment as the print media. The
broadcasters thus invoked in their behalf the key decisions of the Court
which protected the press from governmental regulation, and they especially relied on *New York Times* v. *Sullivan,* which the Court had decided
in 1964.

In the *New York Times* case, the Court held that a public official could
not successfully sue a newspaper for libel unless he could prove that the
newspaper had published a deliberate falsehood regarding him, or had
acted with reckless disregard of the truth or falsity of the material it
published. Public officials must meet this stringent and difficult standard
of proof in libel cases, the Court held, in light of the "profound national
commitment to the principle that debate on public issues should be
uninhibited, robust, and wide-open, and that it may well include vehe-
ment, caustic, and sometimes unpleasantly sharp attacks on government
and public officials." This "uninhibited, robust, and wide-open" debate on
public issues, the Court said, could not occur if publishers feared large
damage judgments for libel if they printed unintentional falsehoods about
public officials, since a standard of strict liability for such unintentional

falsehoods would lead to a system of self-censorship by publishers, who would avoid controversial issues and individuals for fear of the financial penalties libel judgments would involve.

Invoking the principles of *New York Times* v. *Sullivan* in the *Red Lion* and *RTNDA* cases, the broadcasters argued that debate on public issues on radio and television should also be "uninhibited, robust, and wide-open," but the FCC's personal attack and political editorializing rules inhibited such debate and indeed fostered in the broadcast industry a system of self-censorship analogous to that which the Court had held to be incompatible with the First Amendment's guarantee of freedom of the press in the *New York Times* case. "We recognize the need to face the question whether radio and television are not subject to greater governmental control over their broadcasts than the print media because of the consequences of the technology [of broadcasting]," the broadcasters told the Court. "But the examination of that question ought to begin with candid recognition of the fact that the functions performed for society by the radio and television broadcaster in the field of public affairs are the same journalistic functions performed by newspaper publishers. Broadcasting is a branch of the press." And the principles developed in such cases as *New York Times* v. *Sullivan,* the broadcasters therefore argued, were "equally applicable to radio and television."

The FCC's personal attack and political editorializing rules, like the possibility of a large damage award in a libel case, the broadcasters' argument continued, imposed financial and administrative costs on broadcasters that would lead them to avoid controversial issues and thus impose self-censorship upon themselves. The practical problems in complying with the FCC's rules, CBS thus argued, "are so burdensome that CBS and other broadcasters will as a practical matter find it necessary to regard the reply requirement like the threat of damages for libel—a risk to be avoided even at the cost of abstaining from publishing statements that engender the oppressive sanction." Whether imposed as a declaratory order, as in the *Red Lion* case, or as formal rules of the commission, as in the *RTNDA* case, the broadcasters argued, the FCC's personal attack and political editorializing policies invaded the freedom of speech and freedom of the press guaranteed by the First Amendment.

On behalf of the FCC and the government, Solicitor General Erwin Griswold responded to the broadcasters' First Amendment argument by pointing out to the Court that broadcasting was different from the print media—a fact that the Court itself had held justified differential treatment for broadcasters under the First Amendment. In *NBC* v. *United States,* decided by the Court in 1943, the solicitor general noted, the Court had rejected the proposition that broadcasters must be treated the same as the print media under the First Amendment. "Freedom of utterance is abridged to many who wish to use the limited facilities of radio," the Court had said. "Unlike other modes of expression, radio inherently is not available to all. That is its unique characteristic, and that is why, unlike other modes of expression, it is subject to governmental regulation."

Because frequencies on the airwaves were limited, governmental licensing of broadcasters was necessary, the solicitor general argued, and the system of licensing necessarily involved the denial of the right to use the airwaves to most people. Rather than allow those who obtained valuable broadcast licenses to use their monopolistic position to impose only their own views upon the public, the FCC had insisted upon fairness by broadcasters in their coverage of issues of public importance and a right of access to the airwaves under the personal attack and political editorializing rules, so that all sides of public issues would be presented to the public. "It is essentially to effectuate a right of access to the broadcasting medium to serve the public interest in having both sides of public issues that the Fairness Doctrine was evolved by the Commission," the solicitor general argued. "That doctrine, as a general principle, is plainly within the Commission's authority. Moreover, it suffers from no constitutional infirmity, but rather seeks affirmatively to foster the public interest in free and robust debate of significant issues which is central to the First Amendment."

Rather than inhibiting the freedom of speech and freedom of the press, the solicitor general continued, the FCC's fairness, personal attack, political editorializing, and related doctrines actually broadened the scope for the exercise of First Amendment rights on the airwaves by requiring broadcasters to provide access on the airwaves to divergent points of view. It was the FCC and the government that were defending true First Amendment interests in the *Red Lion* and *RTNDA* cases, Solicitor General Griswold thus told the Court. "We're fighting for the First Amendment here. I hate to yield that to the broadcasters, whose interests may not be as broad as ours." The broadcasters, Griswold added, were seeeking "to put us in opposition to the First Amendment, and we do not accept that position. I suggest on analysis it is the government and the Federal Communications Commission which are the real champions of the First Amendment here. The Commission's regulations serve to foster important First Amendment values, which our opponents would have the Court sacrifice in the guise of upholding the narrow and financially motivated claim to unfettered control of airwaves that have been licensed to their custody."

The broadcasters nonetheless challenged the government's contention that scarcity of broadcast frequencies, and thus the need for governmentally imposed diversity of views, justified greater governmental regulation of broadcasting than of the print media. As of 1969, there were 6,894 commercial broadcasting stations on the air in the United States, including 4,245 AM radio stations, 1,971 FM radio stations and 678 television stations, a number three times the approximately 1,763 daily newspapers. And, the broadcasters added, there were more than 1,000 UHF and VHF television channels and 1,000 FM radio frequencies that had been allocated but which were not being used. Not only were broadcast frequencies not as scarce as the government suggested, the broadcasters argued, but the public would have access to a diversity of broadcast views without governmental regulation, since the "number of electronic voices greatly exceed the number of newspapers in nearly all urban, suburban, and rural areas."

The solicitor general responded to this argument, however, by pointing out that no matter how many radio or television stations there might be, their sources of programming were limited to a handful of networks and that broadcasting stations, unlike newspapers and magazines, were severely limited in their service areas. And despite the contentions of the broadcasters to the contrary, the solicitor general argued, "the available frequency spectrum, which must accommodate many uses of radio in addition to broadcasting, remains inadequate to meet the existing demands, and new demands for spectrum space are constantly developing." Despite recent technological innovations, governmental regulation of broadcasting remained as essential, the solicitor general concluded, as when the Congress enacted the Radio Act of 1927 or the Federal Communications Act in 1934.

The *Red Lion* and *RTNDA* cases were argued orally before the Supreme Court on April 2 and 3, 1969, and the Court announced its decision in the cases on June 9. Despite the broadcasters determined effort to secure protection for themselves under the First Amendment equivalent to that of the print media, the Court rejected their arguments and unanimously sustained the FCC's personal attack and political editorializing rules.

*Red Lion Broadcasting Co.* v. *Federal Communications Commission*
*United States* v. *Radio Television News Directors Association*
395 U.S. 367. Argued April 2 and 3, 1969. Decided June 9, 1969.
Mr. Justice White delivered the opinion of the Court.

[Justice White first summarized the facts in the cases and traced the evolution of the FCC's personal attack and political editorializing rules.]

The statutory authority of the FCC to promulgate these regulations derives from the mandate to the "Commission from time to time, as public convenience, interest, or necessity requires" to promulgate "such rules and regulations and prescribe such restrictions and conditions. . .as may be necessary to carry out the provisions of [the Communications Act]. . . . The Commission is specifically directed to consider the demands of the public interest in the course of granting licenses. . . ; renewing them. . . ; and modifying them. Moreover, the FCC has included among the conditions of the Red Lion license itself the requirement that operation of the station be carried out in the public interest. . . . This mandate to the FCC to assure that broadcasters operate in the public interest is a broad one, a power "not niggardly but expansive". . . , whose validity we have long upheld. . . . It is broad enough to encompass these regulations.

The fairness doctrine finds specific recognition in statutory form, is in part modeled on explicit statutory provisions relating to political candidates, and is approvingly reflected in legislative history.

In 1959 the Congress amended the statutory requirement of Sec. 315 that equal time be accorded each political candidate to except certain appearances on news programs, but added that this constituted no exception *"from the obligation imposed upon them under this Act to operate in the public interest and to afford reasonable opportunity for the discussion of conflicting views on issues of public importance. . . .* This language makes it very plain that Congress, in 1959, announced that the phrase "public interest," which had been in the Act since 1927, imposed a duty on broadcasters to discuss both sides of controversial public issues. In other words, the amendment vindicated the FCC's general view that the fairness doctrine inhered in the public interest standard. Subsequent legislation declaring the intent of an earlier statute is entitled to great weight in statutory construction. And here this principle is given special force by the equally venerable principle that the construction of a statute by those charged with its execution should be followed unless there are compelling indications that it is wrong, especially when Congress has refused to alter the administrative construction. Here, the Congress has not just kept its silence by refusing to overturn the administrative construction, but has ratified it with positive legislation. Thirty years of consistent administrative construction left undisturbed by Congress until 1959, when that construction was expressly accepted, reinforce the natural conclusion that the public interest language of the Act authorized the Commission to require licensees to use their stations for discussion of public issues, and that the FCC is free to implement this requirement by reasonable rules and regulations which fall short of abridgment of the freedom of speech and press, and of the censorship proscribed by Sec. 326 of the [Communications Act]. . . .

It is true that the personal attack aspect of the fairness doctrine was not actually adjudicated until after 1959, so that Congress then did not have those rules specifically before it. However, the obligation to offer time to reply to a personal attack was presaged by the FCC's 1949 Report on Editorializing, which the FCC views as the principal summary of its ratio decidendi in this area. . . . When the Congress ratified the FCC's implication of a fairness doctrine in 1959 it did not, of course, approve every past decision or pronouncement by the Commission on this subject, or give it a completely free hand for the future. The statutory authority does not go so far. But we cannot say that when a station publishes personal attacks or endorses political candidates, it is a misconstruction of the public interest standard to require the station to offer time for a response rather than to leave the response entirely within the control of the station which has attacked either the candidacies or the men who wish to reply in their own defense. When a broadcaster grants time to a political candidate, Congress itself requires that equal time be offered to his opponents. It would exceed our competence to hold that the Commission is unauthorized by the statute to employ a similar device where personal attacks or political editorials are broadcast by a radio or television station.

In light of the fact that the "public interest" in broadcasting clearly encompasses the presentation of vigorous debate of controversial issues of importance and concern to the public; the fact that the FCC has rested upon that language from its very inception a doctrine that these issues must be discussed, and fairly; and the fact that Congress has acknowledged that the analogous provisions of Sec. 315 are not preclusive in this area, and knowingly preserved the FCC's complementary efforts, we think the fairness doctrine and its component personal attack and political editorializing regulations are a legitimate exercise of congressionally delegated authority. The Communications Act is not notable for the precision of its substantive standards and in this respect the explicit provisions of Sec. 315, and the doctrine and rules at issue here which are closely modeled upon that section, are far more explicit than the generalized "public interest" standard in which the Commission ordinarily finds its sole guidance, and which we have held a broad but adequate standard before.... We cannot say that the FCC's declaratory ruling in Red Lion, or the regulations at issue in RTNDA, are beyond the scope of the congressionally conferred power to assure that stations are operated by those whose possession of a license serves "the public interest."

The broadcasters challenge the fairness doctrine and its specific manifestations in the personal attack and political editorial rules on conventional First Amendment grounds, alleging that the rules abridge their freedom of speech and press. Their contention is that the First Amendment protects their desire to use their alloted frequencies continuously to broadcast whatever they choose, and to exclude whomever they choose from ever using that frequency. No man may be prevented from saying or publishing what he thinks, or from refusing in his speech or other utterances to give equal weight to the views of his opponents. This right, they say, applies equally to broadcasters....

Although broadcasting is clearly a medium affected by a First Amendment interest..., differences in the characteristics of news media justify differences in the First Amendment standards applied to them....

When two people converse face to face, both should not speak at once if either is to be clearly understood. But the range of the human voice is so limited that there could be meaningful communications if half the people in the United States were talking and the other half listening. Just as clearly, half the people might publish and the other half read. But the reach of radio signals is incomparably greater than the range of the human voice and the problem of interference is a massive reality. The lack of know-how and equipment may keep many from the air, but only a tiny fraction of those with resources and intelligence can hope to communicate by radio at the same time if intelligible communication is to be had, even if the entire radio spectrum is utilized in the present state of commercially acceptable technology.

It was this fact, and the chaos which ensued from permitting anyone to use any frequency at whatever power level he wished, which made necessary the enactment of the Radio Act of 1927 and the Communications Act of 1934, as the Court has noted at length before. . . . It was this reality which at the very least necessitated first the division of the radio spectrum into portions reserved respectively for public broadcasting and for other important radio uses such as amateur operation, aircraft, police, defense, and navigation; and then the subdivision of each portion, and assignment of specific frequencies to individual users or groups of users. Beyond this, however, because the frequencies reserved for public broadcasting were limited in number, it was essential for the Government to tell some applicants that they could not broadcast at all because there was room for only a few.

Where there are substantially more individuals who want to broadcast than there are frequencies to allocate, it is idle to posit an unabridgeable First Amendment right to broadcast comparable to the right of every individual to speak, write, or publish. If 100 persons want broadcast licenses but there are only 10 frequencies to allocate, all of them may have the same "right" to a license; but if there is to be any effective communication by radio, only a few can be licensed and the rest must be barred from the airwaves. It would be strange if the First Amendment, aimed at protecting and furthering communications, prevented the Government from making radio communication possible by requiring licenses to broadcast and by limiting the number of licenses so as not to overcrowd the spectrum.

This has been the consistent view of the Court. Congress unquestionably has the power to grant and deny licenses and to eliminate existing stations. . . . No one has a First Amendment right to a license or to monopolize a radio frequency; to deny a station license because "the public interest" requires it "is not a denial of free speech". . . .

By the same token, as far as the First Amendment is concerned those who are licensed stand no better than those to whom licenses are refused. A license permits broadcasting, but the licensee has no constitutional right to be the one who holds the license or to monopolize a radio frequency to the exclusion of his fellow citizens. There is nothing in the First Amendment which prevents the Government from requiring a licensee to share his frequency with others and to conduct himself as a proxy or fiduciary with obligations to present those views and voices which are representative of his community and which would otherwise, by necessity, be barred from the airwaves.

This is not to say that the First Amendment is irrelevant to public broadcasting. On the contrary, it has a major role to play as the Congress itself recognized in Sec. 326, which forbids FCC interference with "the right of free speech by means of radio communication." Because of the scarcity of radio frequencies, the Government is permitted to put restraints on licensees in favor of others whose views should be expressed on this unique medium. But the people as a whole retain their interest in free speech by radio and their collective right to have the medium function consistently with the ends and purposes of the First Amendment. It is the right of the viewers and listeners, not the right of the broadcasters, which is paramount. . . . It is the purpose of the First Amendment to preserve an uninhibited marketplace of ideas in which truth will ultimately prevail, rather than to countenance monopolization of that market, whether it be by the Government itself or a private licensee. . . . It is the right of the public to receive suitable access to social, political, esthetic, moral, and other ideas and experiences which is crucial here. That right may not constitutionally be abridged by either the Congress or the FCC. . . .

In terms of constitutional principle, and as enforced sharing of a scarce resource, the personal attack and political editorial rules are indistinguishable from the equal time provision of Sec. 315, a specific enactment of Congress requiring stations to set aside reply time under specified circumstances and to which the fairness doctrine and these constituent regulations are important complements. That provision, which has been part of the law since 1927. . . , has been held valid by this Court as an obligation of the licensee relieving him of any power in any way to prevent or censor the broadcast, and thus insulating him from liability for defamation. The constitutionality of the statute under the First Amendment was unquestioned. . . .

Nor can we say that it is inconsistent with the First Amendment goal of producing an informed public capable of conducting its own affairs to require a broadcaster to permit answers to personal attacks occurring in the course of discussing controversial issues, or to require that the political opponents of those endorsed by the station be given a chance to communicate with the public. Otherwise, station owners and a few networks would have unfettered power to make time available only to the highest bidders, to communicate only their own views on public issues, people and candidates, and to permit on the air only those with whom they agreed. There is no sanctuary in the First Amendment for unlimited private censorship operating in a medium not open to all. "Freedom of the press from governmental interference under the First Amendment does not sanction repression of that freedom by private interests". . . .

It is strenuously argued, however, that if political editorials or personal attacks will trigger an obligation in broadcasters to afford the opportunity for expression to speakers who need not pay for time and whose views are unpalatable to the licensees, then broadcasters will be irresistibly forced to self-censorship and their coverage of controversial public issues will be eliminated or at least rendered wholly ineffective. Such a result would indeed be a serious matter, for should licensees actually eliminate their coverage of controversial issues, the purposes of the doctrine would be stifled. . . .

That this will occur now seems unlikely, however, since if present licensees should suddenly prove timorous, the Commission is not powerless to insist that they give adequate and fair attention to public issues. It does not violate the First Amendment to treat licensees given the privilege of using scarce radio frequencies as proxies for the entire community...to give suitable time and attention to matters of great public concern. To condition the granting or renewal of licenses on a willingness to present representative community views on controversial issues is consistent with the ends and purposes of those constitutional provisions forbidding the abridgment of freedom of speech and freedom of the press. Congress need not stand idly by and permit those with licenses to ignore the problems which beset the people or to exclude from the airways anything but their own views of fundamental questions. The statute, long administrative practice, and cases are to this effect. . . .

The litigants embellish their First Amendment arguments with the contention that the regulations are so vague that their duties are impossible to discern. Of this point it is enough to say that, judging the validity of the regulations on their face as they are presented here, we cannot conclude that the FCC has been left a free hand to vindicate its own idiosyncratic conception of the public interest or of the requirements of free speech. Past adjudications by the FCC give added precision to the regulations; there was nothing vague about the FCC's specific ruling in Red Lion that Fred Cook should be provided an opportunity to reply. The regulations at issue in RTNDA could be employed in precisely the same way as the fairness doctrine was in Red Lion. Moreover, the FCC itself has recognized that the applicability of its regulations to situations beyond the scope of past cases may be questionable, . . . and will not impose sanctions in such cases without warning. We need not approve every aspect of the fairness doctrine to decide these cases, and we will not now pass upon the constitutionality of these regulations by envisioning the most extreme applications conceivable. . . , but will deal with those problems if and when they arise.

We need not and do not now ratify every past and future decision by the FCC with regard to programming. . . . But we do hold that the Congress and the Commission do not violate the First Amendment when they require a radio or television station to give reply time to answer personal attacks and political editorials. . . .

It is argued that even if at one time the lack of available frequencies for all who wished to use them justified the Government's choice of those who would best serve the public interest by acting as proxy for those who would present different views, or by giving the latter access directly to broadcast facilities, this condition no longer prevails so that continuing control is not justified. To this there are several answers.

Scarcity is not entirely a thing of the past. Advances in technology, such as microwave transmission, have led to more efficient utilization of the frequency spectrum, but uses for that spectrum have also grown apace. Portions of the spectrum must be reserved for vital uses unconnected with human communication, such as radio-navigational aids used by aircraft and vessels. Conflicts have even emerged between such vital functions as defense preparedness and experimentation in methods of averting midair collisions through radio warning devices. "Land mobile services" such as police, ambulance, fire department, public utility, and other communications systems have been occupying an increasingly crowded portion of the frequency spectrum and there are, apart from licensed amateur radio operators' equipment, 5,000,000 transmitters operated on the "citizens' band" which is also increasingly congested. Among the various uses for radio frequency space, including marine, aviation, amateur, military, and common carrier users, there are easily enough claimants to permit use of the whole with an even smaller allocation to broadcast radio and television than now exists.

Comparative hearings between competing applicants for broadcast spectrum space are by no means a thing of the past. The radio spectrum has become so congested that at times it has been necessary to suspend new applications. The very high frequency television spectrum is, in the country's major markets, almost entirely occupied, although space reserved for ultra high frequency television transmission, which is a relatively recent development as a commercially viable alternative, has not yet been completely filled.

The rapidity with which technological advances succeed one another to create more efficient use of spectrum space on the one hand, and to create new uses for that space by ever growing numbers of people on the other, makes it unwise to speculate on the future allocation of that space. It is enough to say that the resource is one of considerable and growing importance whose scarcity impelled its regulation by an agency authorized by Congress. Nothing in this record, or in our own researches, convinces us that the resource is no longer one for which there are more immediate and potential uses than can be accommodated, and for which wise planning is essential. This does not mean, of course, that every possible wavelength must be occupied at every hour by some vital use in order to sustain the congressional judgment. The substantial capital investment required for many uses, in addition to the potentiality for confusion and interference inherent in any scheme for continuous kaleidoscopic reallocation of all available space may make this unfeasible. The allocation need not be made at such a breakneck pace that the objectives of the allocation are themselves imperiled.

Even where there are gaps in spectrum utilization, the fact remains that existing broadcasters have often attained their present position because of their initial government selection in competition with others before new technological advances opened new opportunities for further uses. Long experience in broadcasting, confirmed habits of listeners and viewers, network affiliation, and other advantages in program procurement give existing broadcasters a substantial advantage over new entrants, even where new entry is technologically possible. These advantages are the fruit of a preferred position conferred by the Government. Some present possibility for new entry by competing stations is not enough, in itself, to render unconstitutional the Government's effort to assure that a broadcaster's programming ranges widely enough to serve the public interest.

In view of the scarcity of broadcast frequencies, the Government's role in allocating those frequencies, and the legitimate claims of those unable without governmental assistance to gain access to those frequencies for expression of their views, we hold the regulations and ruling at issue here are both authorized by statute and constitutional. The judgment of the Court of Appeals in Red Lion is affirmed and that in RTNDA reversed and the causes remanded for proceedings consistent with this opinion.

It is so ordered.
Not having heard oral argument in these cases, Mr. Justice Douglas took no part in the Court's decision.

"Broadcasters who had long opposed government intrusion into their coverage of controversial issues and who had considered themselves the electronic equivalent of print-media journalists are shaken and stunned," *Broadcasting* magazine reported regarding the reaction to the Supreme Court's decision. And some network officials denounced the Court's decision for making broadcast newsmen "second-class citizens." FCC lawyers, on the other hand, were elated by the decision. "We couldn't ask for more than this—it gives us everything we wanted," one commission lawyer said. "More," another FCC lawyer added. And one communications lawyer commented, "It will be ten years before anyone has the temerity to make those [First Amendment] arguments again."

The Supreme Court had thus not only upheld the FCC's right of reply and political editorializing rules but had also dealt a devastating blow to the hopes of the broadcasters of winning First Amendment protection equivalent to that extended the print media. Broadcasting thus remains subject to a greater degree of governmental regulation than is permitted under the First Amendment with regard to the print media.

In direct contrast to its decision in the *Red Lion* and *RTNDA* cases, the Supreme Court in *Miami Herald Publishing Co.* v. *Tornillo* thus invalidated a Florida statute requiring newspapers which editorially attacked the personal character or official record of any candidate for public office to print free of charge the candidate's reply to the charges. The Florida Supreme Court had upheld the statute, holding that freedom of speech and of the press were enhanced by its provisions which furthered the "broad societal interest in the free flow of information to the public," but the U.S. Supreme Court disagreed. "A newspaper is more than a passive receptacle or conduit for views, comment, and advertising," the Court said. "The choice of material to go into a newspaper, and the decisions made as to limitations on the size and content of the paper, and treatment of public issues and public officials—whether fair or unfair— constitute the exercise of editorial control and judgment. It has yet to be demonstrated how governmental regulation of this crucial process can be exercised consistent with First Amendment guarantees of a free press as they have evolved to this time."

The Court invalidated the Florida statute and thus reinforced the disparate treatment of the print media and the broadcast media which the *Red Lion* case had underscored. Broadcasters could be required to extend a right of reply to individuals attacked on radio or television, but the Court found a similar requirement imposed on the print media to be inconsistent with the First Amendment guarantee of freedom of the press.

More recently, in *FCC* v. *Pacifica Foundation* in 1978, the Supreme Court upheld the FCC's power to proscribe a "Filthy Words" monologue by comedian George Carlin which was broadcast during the time of the day when children would be likely to be exposed to it. Although the Court assumed that the same words used in Carlin's monologue would be protected by the First Amendment in other contexts, it continued, as in the *Red Lion* and *Tornillo* cases, to treat the broadcast media differently. The FCC possessed the power under the Federal Communications Act, the Court held, to proscribe the broadcasting of the words Carlin used during those times of the day when children would be likely to be exposed to them. As the Court held in the *Red Lion* case, the FCC thus continues to have greater power of regulation regarding the broadcast media, and the broadcast media possess less protection under the First Amendment, than other forms of communication.

Leaving aside the First Amendment implications of the FCC's right of reply and political editorializing policies, it should also be noted that the commission's formulation of its general "fairness" policy, before it resorted to rule making, appears to typify the manner in which administrative policy evolves in many federal agencies. That is, despite the grant of rule-making powers to many agencies, the agencies appear to prefer to enunciate policy on an ad hoc, case-by-case basis rather than exercising their rule-making powers and defining more precisely the policies and standards under which they are operating. The ad hoc, case-by-case approach to administrative policy making obviously allows the agencies to retain the greatest possible policy discretion, and it also allows agencies to avoid the difficult and time-consuming process of providing concrete rules that would make more definite the vague contours of their legislative mandates.

As a consequence, a major criticism of agency performance in recent years has been directed at the failure of agencies to make rules. Given the complexities of modern governmental regulation, it was perhaps inevitable that the attempts of the judiciary to limit the delegation of legislative power to administrative agencies would fail, and that legislatures would of necessity be constrained to delegate legislative powers to agencies under the vaguest and broadest of standards. That legislative power must be delegated to administrative agencies under such vague standards, however, does not mean that the agencies themselves could not define and clarify what the laws they are administering mean through the issuance of concrete and concise rules and regulations. It is doubtful, for example, that the FCC needed thirty years to begin to define what the "public interest, convenience, or necessity" meant in regard to the right of reply and political editorializing by broadcasters through the exercise of its rule-making powers.

## THE LEGISLATIVE VETO

Before concluding this discussion of administrative rule making, it should be noted that an important current issue in this field is the increasing insistence by Congress upon its having a veto over rules and regulations adopted by the bureaucracy. Although in some instances the veto power has been lodged in congressional committees, the legislative veto normally operates by allowing one or both houses of Congress to disapprove rules adopted by administrative agencies by passing a resolution of disapproval within a specified period after the rule is adopted by the agency. Since 1932, almost two hundred statutes passed by Congress and delegating rule-making powers to various agencies have embodied some form of the legislative veto, and in the early 1980s there was a proposal that the Administrative Procedure Act be amended to provide for the legislative veto with regard to all rules and regulations adopted by the agencies.

Critics of the legislative veto argue that it involves an illegitimate encroachment by Congress upon executive powers and thus violates the principle of separation of powers. In addition, critics say, the legislative veto violates the principle of bicameralism embodied in the Constitution, since disapproval of a rule by a resolution passed by one house or a committee short-circuits the normal legislative process, while disapproval of rules by resolutions passed by one or both houses also prevents the president from exercising his veto power as he may with normal legislation passed by Congress. Since recent presidents have challenged the legislative veto as being illegitimate, there is almost certain to be significant litigation on the subject, and the Supreme Court will probably be called upon ultimately to resolve the legal and constitutional issues raised by the legislative veto.

# 4

## ADMINISTRATIVE ACCESS TO INFORMATION
## AND THE CONSTITUTIONAL RIGHT TO PRIVACY

The administrative process feeds rather voraciously upon information, and access to information is a crucial need for most administrative agencies. The principal methods by which administrative agencies feed their appetites for information are (1) through the issuance of subpoenas for testimony or records and documents of individuals and businesses subject to the agencies' jurisdiction; (2) through administratively issued regulations requiring the keeping of records or the filing of reports by those subject to regulation by the agencies; and (3) through administrative inspections or searches of businesses, premises, areas, or persons subject to regulation.

All these means through which administrative agencies obtain access to information may, and sometimes do, raise serious questions regarding the right of privacy of the individuals affected. In constitutional terms, the right of privacy thus affected arises from the provisions of the Fourth Amendment and the Self-Incrimination Clause of the Fifth Amendment. The Fourth Amendment of course provides that the "right of the people to be secure in their persons, houses, papers, and effects, against unreasonable searches and seizures, shall not be violated," and that no search warrants shall issue except upon a showing of "probable cause, supported by Oath or affirmation, and particularly describing the place to be searched, and the person or things to be seized." And the Self-Incrimination Clause of the Fifth Amendment provides that no person "shall be compelled in any criminal case to be a witness against himself. . . ." Demands by administrative agencies for information, testimony, reports or records from individuals or businesses subject to administrative regulation are thus sometimes met by strenuous objections that the agencies' information requirements violate either the Fourth Amendment or the right against self-incrimination guaranteed by the Fifth Amendment.

## HURDLING THE SELF-INCRIMINATION CLAUSE

The Supreme Court has interpreted the Self-Incrimination Clause to apply not only in criminal trials but also in any governmental proceeding in which an individual is compelled to produce either testimony or other information which would tend to furnish evidence to support a criminal prosecution against the individual. The Self-Incrimination Clause therefore may be validly invoked in an administrative proceeding, even though noncriminal in nature, if the testimony or information sought by an administrative agency might tend to incriminate the individual involved. As the Supreme Court has said, the Self-Incrimination Clause "can be asserted in any proceeding, civil or criminal, administrative or judicial, investigatory or adjudicatory; and protects against any disclosures that the witness reasonably believes could be used in a criminal prosecution or could lead to other evidence that might be so used." The Self-Incrimination Clause has nonetheless proven to be a relatively easily overcome barrier to administrative access to information because of the availability of statutory grants of immunity from prosecution and judicially created doctrines limiting the scope of the clause in the administrative process.

## IMMUNITY STATUTES

Historically, immunity statutes were the earliest devices available to administrative agencies allowing them to overcome invocations of the right against self-incrimination by individuals from whom agencies desired to obtain either testimony or other information. Under immunity statutes, administrative agencies are granted the power to confer immunity from prosecution upon individuals who invoke their right against self-incrimination against the production of testimony or other information. Under a grant of immunity, the individual is assured that the testimony or information he produces will not form the basis of any subsequent criminal prosecution against him.

The central constitutional problem regarding grants of immunity from prosecution has been what the scope a grant of immunity must be in order to supplant the individual's right against self-incrimination. Rejecting an argument that the Self-Incrimination Clause protected an absolute right to silence in the face of official inquiries, the Supreme Court ruled in *Brown* v. *Walker* in 1896 that an immunity statute that conferred transactional immunity (also known as bath immunity) upon an individual was a constitutionally valid grant of immunity. Under a grant of transactional immunity, an individual is given total immunity from prosecution with regard to the criminal transaction about which he is compelled to testify or furnish personal records or documents.

More recently, however, the Court ruled in *Kastigar* v. *United States* in 1972 that the immunity provisions of the Organized Crime Control Act of 1970 were constitutionally valid. Those provisions authorize the granting of use and derivative use immunity, not transactional immunity. Under a grant of use and derivative use immunity, an individual is promised that none of the testimony or documents he is required to produce, or any evidence to which his testimony or documents may lead, will be used against him in a subsequent criminal prosecution. Unlike transactional immunity, which totally removes the possibility of a subsequent prosecution, use and derivative use immunity allows the government to prosecute an individual who has been given such immunity if the government discovers evidence unconnected to any testimony or documents that have been produced under a grant of use or derivative use immunity.

Although the form of immunity granted by administrative agencies was traditionally transactional immunity, under the *Kastigar* decision, grants of use and derivative use immunity are now deemed sufficient to overcome self-incrimination claims. It should be noted, however, that if a person is granted use and derivative use immunity and subsequently prosecuted, the Court held in the *Kastigar* case that the prosecution would have "the affirmative duty to prove the evidence it proposes to use is derived from a legitimate source wholly independent of the compelled testimony."

Grants of immunity to witnesses who are summoned before administrative agencies and who invoke their right against self-incrimination is therefore a well-established and effective means by which agencies are able to obtain testimony or other information they desire without running afoul of the Self-Incrimination Clause. A grant of immunity to an individual, however, is only necessary when that individual has validly invoked the Self-Incrimination Clause against furnishing testimony or other information. And the Self-Incrimination Clause has been construed by the courts not to apply to many types of information that administrative agencies frequently seek—as the corporate records doctrine illustrates.

## THE CORPORATE RECORDS DOCTRINE AND ITS PROGENY

The corporate records doctrine is traceable to the decisions of the Supreme Court in *Hale* v. *Henkel* in 1906 and *Wilson* v. *United States* in 1911, in which the Court ruled that the Self-Incrimination Clause did not apply to governmental demands for the production of the records of corporations. The corporate records doctrine is based upon two premises. First, corporations are presumed to be created by the states for the benefit of the public, and therefore their records are to be regarded as "public" rather than private in nature. Secondly, the records of corporations belong to the corporation as a legal entity, and are not therefore the personal records of the corporate official in whose custody they happen to be. While a corporate official may invoke the protection of the Self-Incrimination Clause against the compulsory production of his own personal records, he may not claim a right under the Self-Incrimination Clause against the production of corporate records in his custody, since the corporate records are not his "personal" records but rather belong to the corporation as a legal entity. And since the right against self-incrimination is a personal right, it may not validly be invoked against the production of corporate records that do not belong to the corporate official having custody of them.

Although the corporate records doctrine thus originally was based upon the premise that corporate records were public in nature and not the personal records of corporate officials having custody of them, it is the latter premise that has served as the principal rationale for the more recent extensions of the doctrine to cover records belonging to unincorporated organizations or entities. In *United States* v. *White,* decided in 1944, the Supreme Court held that a union official who possessed the books of an unincorporated labor union could not invoke the Self-Incrimination Clause against the production of the union books, since the books were not the personal records of the union official but rather belonged to the union as a separate entity. And in *Bellis* v. *United States* in 1974, the Court similarly held that a member of a three-person partnership could not claim self-incrimination against the production of the records of the partnership in his possession, since the records belonged to the partnership as an entity and were not the personal records of any of the members of the partnership.

The result of the *Hale-Wilson-White-Bellis* line of cases is that governmental access to the records of artificial entities such as corporations, labor unions, and associations even as small as a three-person partnership meets no real obstacle insofar as the Self-Incrimination Clause is concerned. Construing the Self-Incrimination Clause to cover only personal records, the courts have made the invocation of the clause ineffective against the compulsory production of the books and papers of organizations. And since these are precisely the kinds of records that are the frequent objects of administrative investigations or inquiries, the corporate records doctrine and its progeny have made the Self-Incrimination Clause a largely ineffective barrier to the conduct of administrative investigations.

## THE REQUIRED RECORDS DOCTRINE

Another judicially created doctrine under the Self-Incrimination Clause holds that records that are required to be kept by those subject to a valid congressional regulation are also not covered by the right against self-incrimination and must be produced at the request of the appropriate regulatory agency. This required records doctrine was applied by the Supreme Court in *Shapiro* v. *United States,* decided in 1948, to records required to be kept by businesses subject to the Emergency Price Control Act, which imposed price controls during World War II. Even though Shapiro's records revealed information that subjected him to a criminal prosecution for violating price controls, the Court held, he could not invoke the Self-Incrimination Clause against the production of those records. Records required to be kept by a valid congressional statute, the Court said, were public in nature and could not be considered to be the personal records of those required by law to keep them, and since the Self-Incrimination Clause applied only to personal testimony or records, records required to be kept by a regulatory statute were not covered by the clause.

Probably because the required records doctrine, if pushed to its logical conclusion, would result in the almost complete repeal of the Self-Incrimination Clause, the Supreme Court subsequently limited the circumstances in which the doctrine applies. In *Marchetti* v. *United States,* decided in 1968, the Court thus held that the required records doctrine applied only to records of a kind customarily kept by individuals or businesses being regulated, records that have public rather than personal aspects, and records that are required to be kept under an essentially noncriminal regulatory statute applicable to individuals who do not belong to a criminally suspect class of persons. If, on the other hand, records are required to be produced by the government of a kind not customarily kept by an individual, the records are essentially personal rather than public in nature, and the regulation the government is enforcing is essentially criminal in nature and is being applied to an individual belonging to a criminally suspect class, then, the Court held in the *Marchetti* case, the required records doctrine does not apply and the right against self-incrimination may be asserted against a demand for such records.

The required records doctrine thus remains as a way around the Self-Incrimination Clause in the administrative process, although after the *Marchetti* case it exists in a rather uneasy juxtaposition to the more stringent self-incrimination standards applicable in the criminal law field. Indeed, the Court's decision in the *Marchetti* case illustrates the fact that constitutional limitations that are strictly enforced when the government is regulating criminal behavior are frequently relaxed by the courts as they apply to the essentially noncriminal administrative process.

The corporate records and required records doctrines have been in large part based upon the concept that the Self-Incrimination Clause prohibits the compulsory production of potentially incriminating private, personal papers and records but not papers and records which lack those characteristics. The Supreme Court thus indicated in *Boyd* v. *United States* in 1886 that the Self-Incrimination Clause not only prohibited governmental compulsion of a person's testimony against himself but also the compulsory production of a person's private papers and records. The Court has nonetheless also recently begun to restrict the scope of protection afforded personal, private papers and records under the Self-Incrimination Clause.

In *Andresen* v. *Maryland,* decided in 1976, the Court thus held that the seizure of an individual's private papers during a valid search, and the subsequent use of those private papers as evidence in a criminal prosecution, are not prohibited by the Self-Incrimination Clause. The seizure of a person's private papers in a valid search does not, the Court held, "compel" the production of the papers by the individual affected. A subpoena for the same papers, requiring the individual to produce them himself, the Court held on the other hand, might violate the Self-Incrimination Clause.

"Thus, although the Fifth Amendment may protect an individual from complying with a subpoena for the production of his personal records in his possession because the very act of production may constitute a compulsory authentication of incriminating information. . . ," the Court said in the *Andresen* case, "a seizure of the same materials by law enforcement officers differs in a crucial respect—the individual against whom the search is directed is not required to aid in the discovery, production, or authentication of incriminating information." In so holding, the Court repudiated the earlier statement in *Boyd* v. *United States* that "we have been unable to perceive that the seizure of a man's private books and papers to be used in evidence against him is substantially different from compelling him to be a witness against himself."

## THE FOURTH AMENDMENT AND THE ADMINISTRATIVE PROCESS

In addition to problems under the Self-Incrimination Clause raised by administrative requirements for information, questions also arise in this regard under the Fourth Amendment's prohibition of unreasonable searches and seizures. The Fourth Amendment was a direct response to the American colonists' experience with the attempts of British officials to enforce acts of Parliament imposing taxes upon goods imported into the colonies. In response to the smuggling of goods into the colonies and the consequent evasion of taxes on the smuggled goods, British officials resorted to writs of assistance, or general search warrants, which allowed those searching for smuggled goods virtually unlimited powers to conduct general searches. The colonial resistance to the use of the writs of assistance by Crown officers thus became an important part of the resistance to British rule in America.

When the validity of the writs of assistance was attacked in proceedings in Boston in 1761, James Otis denounced their use in eloquent terms and declared that the writs placed "the liberty of every man in the hands of every petty official." And John Adams felt that the attack on the writs of assistance by Otis marked the beginning of the Revolution. "Then and there, was the first scene of the first act of opposition, to the arbitrary claims of Great Britain," Adams said. "Then and there, the child Independence was born. In fifteen years, i.e., in 1776, he grew up to manhood and declared himself free."

In response to the colonial experience with writs of assistance, the framers of the Bill of Rights thus provided in the Fourth Amendment that the "right of the people to be secure in their persons, houses, papers, and effects, against unreasonable searches and seizures, shall not be violated" and that "no Warrants shall issue, but upon probable cause, supported by Oath or affirmation, and particularly describing the place to be searched, and the persons or things to be seized." The Warrant Clause, therefore, requires that before a warrant of arrest or search is issued, officers seeking the warrant must make a factual justification (probable cause) for the issuance of the warrant to a judge or magistrate. The Fourth Amendment also requires that a supposedly neutral magistrate must be convinced of the need for the issuance of a warrant before the warrant will be issued. And by requiring that warrants specify the place to be searched or the person or things to be seized, the Fourth Amendment prohibits general search warrants, like the writs of assistance, which place no limits upon the scope or objects of the searches they authorize.

## ADMINISTRATIVE SUBPOENAS AND THE FOURTH AMENDMENT

In seeking information required for administrative purposes, it is not unusual for administrative agencies to issue subpoenas to individuals or businesses requiring either testimony or the production of books, records, or papers. While such administrative subpoenas may be resisted by those affected under the Self-Incrimination Clause, subpoenas for books, papers, records, etc. are also sometimes resisted on the ground that they constitute unreasonable searches and seizures under the Fourth Amendment. By refusing to comply, and forcing the agency to seek court enforcement of its subpoena, those subject to administrative subpoenas may obtain judicial review of the lawfulness of the subpoenas.

Under principles enunciated in the leading Supreme Court decision in *Oklahoma Press Publishing Co.* v. *Walling,* decided in 1946, the courts will uphold an administrative subpoena under the Fourth Amendment if (1) the investigation being conducted by the agency is authorized by law and Congress has validly authorized the agency to conduct the investigation; (2) if the books, papers, etc. subject to the subpoena are relevant to the administrative investigation being conducted; (3) and if the subpoena is not overly broad or insufficiently specifies the papers, books, or documents required by the agency. These elements meet the Fourth Amendment's requirement of probable cause and the specification of the things to be seized, and unlike a criminal search warrant, an agency need not allege a violation of the law or regulations before issuing a subpoena in pursuance of an administrative investigation.

## ADMINISTRATIVE SEARCHES AND INSPECTIONS

Although the Fourth Amendment was a response to what were perceived as abuses of the power to search warehouses and business premises, as well as homes, for smuggled goods, until very recently the law governing the relationship between the Fourth Amendment and rather similar administrative searches and inspections was simple: the Fourth Amendment, the courts held, did not apply to administrative searches and inspections. The restrictions upon searches and seizures imposed by the Fourth Amendment were held by the courts to apply to searches involved in the enforcement of the criminal law, but the Fourth Amendment restrictions did not apply to noncriminal, administrative searches and inspections. In *Frank* v. *Maryland,* decided in 1959, the Supreme Court thus held that city health inspectors did not need a warrant in order lawfully to inspect a home suspected of rat infestation.

The view reflected in the *Frank* case was nonetheless subjected to mounting criticism. The Fourth Amendment was intended to protect the privacy of individuals, it was argued, and unreasonable administrative searches often invaded that privacy just as much as searches conducted as aspects of criminal investigations. Also, it was pointed out, under the

*Frank* decision a person suspected of a crime was afforded greater protection under the Fourth Amendment than persons not suspected of criminal activity.

Recognizing the cogency of such criticism, the Supreme Court in 1967 repudiated the traditional rule that the Fourth Amendment did not apply to administrative searches in its decisions in *Camara* v. *Municipal Court* and *See* v. *Seattle.* In the *Camara* case, the Court held that the Fourth Amendment required warrants to authorize building code inspections, absent consent by the occupant of the building to be inspected. "It is surely anomalous to say that the individual and his private property are fully protected by the Fourth Amendment only when the individual is suspected of criminal behavior," the Court said. In its decisions interpreting the Fourth Amendment, the Court continued, "one governing principle, justified by history and by current experience, has consistently been followed: except in certain carefully defined classes of cases, a search of private property without proper consent is 'unreasonable' unless it has been authorized by a valid search warrant." The Court therefore concluded that administrative inspections or searches to enforce building codes, fire codes, and health codes involved "significant intrusions upon the interests protected by the Fourth Amendment, that such searches when authorized and conducted without a warrant procedure lack the traditional safeguards which the Fourth Amendment guarantees to the individual, and that the reasons put forth in *Frank* v. *Maryland* and in other cases for upholding these warrantless searches are insufficient to justify so substantial a weakening of the Fourth Amendment's protections."

In *See* v. *Seattle,* decided as a companion case to the *Camara* case, the Court similarly held that an inspection of a commercial warehouse to enforce a fire code required a warrant, lacking consent to the search by the owner. "The businessman, like the occupant of a residence, has a constitutional right to go about his business free from unreasonable official entries upon his private commercial property," the Court held in *See.* "The businessman, too, has that right placed in jeopardy if the decision to enter and inspect for violation of regulatory laws can be made and enforced by the inspector in the field without official authority evidenced by a warrant."

Requiring a warrant to authorize administrative searches, the Court pointed out, would serve the purpose of informing the person whose premises were to be searched that the search was authorized by law, that the search was limited by the terms of the warrant, and that the person conducting the search was acting under proper authorization. But while the Court abandoned the traditional rule governing the relationship between the Fourth Amendment and administrative searches, it also made it clear in the *Camara* and *See* cases that the requirement of probable cause (that is, the factual justification) for the issuance of a warrant to conduct an administrative search would not be as stringent as the probable cause requirement for warrants to conduct criminal searches.

In the *Camara* case, the Court thus indicated that the probable cause necessary to justify the issuance of a warrant to conduct a building code inspection would not "necessarily depend upon specific knowledge of the condition of the particular dwelling." And, indeed, the Court indicated that warrants could be issued for the purpose of building code inspections of areas of a city and which could be justified on the basis of such factors as the passage of time since previous inspections, the nature of the building to be inspected, and the condition of the entire area. "In determining whether a particular inspection is reasonable—and thus in determining whether there is probable cause to issue a warrant for that inspection—the need for the inspection must be weighed in terms of. . .reasonable goals of code enforcement," the Court held. "The warrant procedure is designed to guarantee that a decision to search private property is justified by a reasonable governmental interest. But reasonableness is still the ultimate standard. If a valid public interest justifies the intrusion contemplated, then there is probable cause to issue a suitably restricted search warrant."

In the *Camara* and *See* cases, the Court therefore created a category of "administrative search warrants" that could be much more easily obtained than warrants authorizing searches for the fruits, instruments, or evidence of a crime. In conducting a criminal investigation, the police may not secure a search warrant without a demonstration of probable cause to believe that the fruits, instruments or evidence of a crime are at a specific place, and a warrant authorizing a criminal search of a whole area would clearly be invalid under the Fourth Amendment. Yet the Court indicated in the *Camara* and *See* cases that the more stringent probable cause requirement for the issuance of criminal search warrants would not apply to administrative searches and inspections. While the Fourth Amendment would henceforth be applicable to many administrative searches and inspections, it was also clear that the standards governing the issuance of warrants for administrative searches would be much more flexible and relaxed than those governing the issuance of criminal search warrants.

Since the Court applied the Fourth Amendment to administrative searches for the first time in the *Camara* and *See* cases, the result of those decisions was to produce further litigation testing the relationship between the Fourth Amendment and a variety of administrative searches that had previously not been considered to raise constitutional problems. And in subsequent decisions the Court indicated that not all administrative searches must be authorized by warrants and that, indeed, some administrative searches were not subject to the restrictions of the Fourth Amendment at all.

The Court has, for example, traditionally recognized the validity of emergency searches and seizures when the need for swift governmental action is obvious and when, because of exigent circumstances, there is no time to secure a warrant. The validity of these kinds of emergency searches and seizures was clearly not affected by the Court's decisions in the *Camara* and *See* cases. Emergency seizures by administrative officers of unwholesome food, or requirements of compulsory vaccinations or the imposition of health quarantines, although not authorized by warrants, remained valid administrative actions even after the *Camara* and *See* cases.

## BORDER AND IMMIGRATION SEARCHES

The Supreme Court has always held that the Fourth Amendment also does not apply to border searches of persons and property of individuals seeking entry into the United States. The Border Patrol, however, customarily stopped and searched vehicles for illegal aliens, without probable cause or warrants to do so, up to one hundred miles from the border. Such searches, it was argued, were equivalent to searches at the borders and therefore were not covered by the Fourth Amendment. In *Almeida-Sanchez* v. *United States,* decided in 1973, however, the Supreme Court held that the stopping and searching of vehicles by roving patrols of Border Patrol officers, well beyond the border and without probable cause to believe the vehicles were being used in illegal activities, violated the Fourth Amendment. Although the Court reaffirmed its 1925 decision in *Carroll* v. *United States* that warrants are not required to stop and search moving vehicles, it also held that probable cause to believe that such vehicles were engaged in illegal activities was required in order for them to be stopped and searched.

In a later case, *United States* v. *Brignoni-Ponce,* decided in 1975, the Court further held that roving patrols of the Border Patrol could not stop vehicles and question the occupants regarding their citizenship without a minimal probable cause to do so. Since stopping vehicles is a "seizure" within the meaning of the Fourth Amendment, the Court held that, except "at the border and its functional equivalents, officers on roving patrol may stop vehicles only if they are aware of specific articulable facts, that reasonably warrant suspicion that the vehicles contain aliens who may be illegally in the country."

The Court subsequently distinguished between the stopping of vehicles by roving patrols and the stopping of vehicles by the Border Patrol at permanent checkpoints established at some distance from the border. Although the Court held that private vehicles could not be searched at fixed checkpoints without consent or probable cause, it also held in *United States* v. *Ortiz* in 1975 and *United States* v. *Martinez-Fuerte* in 1976 that "stops for brief questioning routinely conducted at permanent checkpoints are consistent with the Fourth Amendment and need not be authorized by warrant." A stop for brief questioning at a permanent checkpoint was a very limited intrusion into the privacy of individuals, the Court held, and, unlike stops by roving patrols, the permanent check-point was clearly recognizable by motorists as a law enforcement device, stops at such checkpoints were less likely to frighten motorists, and the discretion of the officers at the checkpoints was more under the control of their superiors.

## WELFARE "VISITATIONS"

As a part of the administration of various welfare programs, welfare caseworkers have traditionally engaged in visits to the homes of welfare recipients. In *Wyman* v. *James,* decided in 1971, Mrs. James was the mother of a young child who applied for and was granted benefits under the Aid to Families with Dependent Children (AFDC) program in New York City. Subsequently, a caseworker informed Mrs. James by letter that the caseworker would visit Mrs. James's home on a certain date. Mrs. James argued that the "visit" by the caseworker was in essence a search within the meaning of the Fourth Amendment and that it therefore should be justified by a warrant. Since she refused to allow the caseworker to visit her home without a warrant, Mrs. James's welfare benefits were terminated, and the Supreme Court sustained that action on the ground that a welfare visit upon written notice and during daylight hours was not a search within the meaning of the Fourth Amendment. Even assuming such visits were searches, the Court held, they were reasonable searches and justified by the government's interest in seeing to it that public funds were being lawfully spent and in checking on the well-being of the child who was supposed to be the primary beneficiary of AFDC benefits.

## THE "OPEN FIELDS" EXCEPTION

The Supreme Court recognized another exception to the requirement of a warrant for administrative searches in *Air Pollution Variance Board* v. *Western Alfalfa Corp.*, decided in 1974. In the *Western Alfalfa* case, a health inspector entered the outdoor premises of the Western Alfalfa Corporation's property to conduct a test for air pollution with respect to plumes of smokes being emitted from the corporation's chimneys. Upon being cited for violation of air quality standards, the corporation challenged the citation on the ground that the inspector had engaged in unreasonable search and seizure. The Supreme Court, however, held that the inspector had merely "sighted what anyone in the city who was near the plant could see in the sky—plumes of smoke" and that the Fourth Amendment did not apply to "sights seen in 'the open fields.'" The test administered by the health inspector was therefore held not to have violated the Fourth Amendment, since the Court held that the inspector was "well within the 'open fields' exception to the Fourth Amendment. . . ."

## THE PERVASIVELY REGULATED BUSINESSES EXCEPTION

In *Colonnade Catering Corp.* v. *United States,* decided in 1970, and *United States* v. *Biswell* in 1972, the Supreme Court also held that businesses that are "pervasively regulated" or "closely regulated" or "long subject to close supervision and inspection" under acts of Congress may be subjected to warrantless searches or inspections by governmental officials without offending the Fourth Amendment. In the *Colonnade Catering Corp.* case, the Court thus upheld a warrantless search of the business premises of a federally licensed liquor dealer, and in the *Biswell* case the Court similarly sustained the validity of a warrantless search of the business premises of a federally licensed firearms dealer.

Persons entering into such "pervasively regulated" businesses, the Court said, must know that their business premises are subject to warrantless inspections and in effect waive their Fourth Amendment rights by entering into such businesses. "We have little difficulty in concluding," the Court thus said in the *Biswell* case, "that where, as here, regulatory inspections further urgent federal interests, and the possibilities of abuse and the threat to privacy are not of impressive dimensions, the inspection may proceed without a warrant when specifically authorized by statute."

Although the Court had held that the Fourth Amendment applied to some administrative searches and inspections in the *Camara* and *See* cases, its subsequent decisions scrutinizing various administrative searches had resulted in holdings that certain of those searches could be conducted without warrants, as in the *Biswell* and *Colonnade Catering Corp.* cases, and that indeed some administrative inspections, such as welfare visits, were not searches at all within the meaning of the Fourth Amendment, as *Wyman* v. *James* indicated. And in the *Biswell* and *Colonnade Catering Corp.* cases, the Court appeared to have endorsed the concept that one's right to privacy under the Fourth Amendment could be substantially eroded or abolished altogether, depending upon whether Congress chose to subject particular businesses and industries to "pervasive regulation."

The result was that some observers began to question whether the Court was not slowly repudiating the holdings in the *Camara* and *See* cases that the Fourth Amendment applied to administrative searches and inspections. The Court, however, rejected an opportunity to further undermine the *Camara* and *See* cases with its 1978 decision in *Marshall* v. *Barlow's, Inc.,* a case involving the massive administrative inspection powers of the Occupational Safety and Health Act of 1970. We shall now examine the litigation in *Marshall* v. *Barlow's, Inc.,* in detail.

### CASE STUDY
### BILL BARLOW CAN'T WE PLEASE COME IN?
OSHA Searches and the Fourth Amendment

Injuries to workers have long been a subject of governmental concern and action in the United States. Until the 1970s, however, the subject of job-related injuries to American workers was largely regulated at the state level. A traditional remedy for workers who are injured in the course of their employment is the suit for damages against employers, afforded by the common law as enforced by the law courts. Around the turn of the century, most states also adopted systems of workmen's compensation requiring employers to carry insurance against industrial accidents and providing payments to workers or their heirs for job-related injuries or deaths.

Despite the availability of suits for damages and workmen's compensation systems, however, Congress decided in 1970 that the existing incentives to employers to provide safe working conditions for their employees were insufficient. By the late 1960s, 14,500 persons were being killed annually in industrial accidents, more persons than were being killed in the Vietnam war. An additional 2.2 million persons were being disabled annually, resulting in the loss of 250 million man days of work and a loss of $1.5 billion in lost wages as well as an $8 billion loss to the Gross National Product. And the hazards of the workplace appeared to be increasing for workers, since the number of disabling injuries per million man hours worked increased by 20 percent between 1958 and 1970.

## THE OCCUPATIONAL SAFETY AND HEALTH ACT OF 1970

In response to these conditions, Congress enacted the Occupational Safety and Health Act of 1970. The act applied to all businesses having employees whose activities affected commerce and provided that each employer subject to the act "shall furnish to each of his employees employment and a place of employment which are free from recognized hazards that are causing or are likely to cause death or serious physical harm to his employees." The act authorized the secretary of Labor to issue rules and regulations governing worker safety and directed employers to "comply with occupational safety and health standards promulgated under this Act."

To enforce the occupational safety and health standards imposed under the act, an Occupational Safety and Health Administration (OSHA) was created in the Department of Labor. If, upon inspection of a workplace, a violation of safety or health standards was discovered, the secretary of Labor was authorized under the act to issue a citation against the employer, and the secretary was also authorized to impose a monetary penalty for the violation. If the employer did not challenge the citation within fifteen days, the secretary's citation became final and unreviewable by "any court or agency." If, however, the employer contested the citation, a hearing would be held by an administrative law judge, whose decision was in turn appealable to the Occupational Safety and Health Review Commission. The decisions of the commission in turn were appealable to the U.S. courts of appeals.

The monetary penalties the secretary of Labor was authorized to impose under the act could range up to $1,000 for serious violations or to a maximum of $10,000 for willful or repeated violations. The secretary was also authorized to seek injunctions from the federal district courts prohibiting violations of the act which were willful violations resulting in imminent dangers to employees. And the secretary could impose penalties of up to $1,000 per day on employers refusing to comply with administrative directives to correct dangerous conditions or refusing to comply with federal court injunctions. Finally, the secretary was authorized to refer to the Justice Department for criminal prosecution those cases in which employers committed willful violations of the act that could result in death to employees. A conviction for criminal violation of the act was punishable by a maximum fine of $10,000 and six months imprisonment.

The administrative machinery for the enforcement of the Occupational Safety and Health Act was soon challenged on constitutional grounds. The act's authorization of the secretary of Labor to impose monetary penalties upon employers for violations of health and safety standards promulgated under the act, it was argued, in essence involved a delegation of power to the secretary to impose money damages upon employers. The imposition of monetary penalties by the secretary of Labor, and the adjudication of the validity of such penalties by administrative law judges and the Occupational Safety and Health Review Commission, it was argued, violated the Seventh Amendment to the Constitution, which provides that the trial of all cases at common law involving more than twenty dollars must be by jury. Since the act in effect authorized the secretary of Labor to impose damages upon employers who violated the act, and the imposition of money damages was a traditional remedy in a suit at common law, it was further argued, the act was unconstitutional. According to the Seventh Amendment, Congress instead should have provided that monetary penalties could be levied against employers who violated the act only after a trial of the issue in a federal court before a jury.

In *Atlas Roofing Company* v. *Occupational Safety & Health Review Commission,* decided in 1977, however, the Supreme Court rejected these arguments and upheld the validity of the Occupational Safety and Health Act. The act, the Court held, did not involve the enforcement of common law rights requiring trials in the federal courts before juries for their enforcement, but rather the act created new, statutory "public rights" which were unknown to the common law. And "when Congress creates new statutory 'public rights,'" the Court said, "it may assign their adjudication to an administrative agency with which a jury trial would be incompatible, without violating the Seventh Amendment's injunction that jury trial is to be 'preserved' in 'suits at common law.'" "Congress is not required by the Seventh Amendment to choke the already crowded federal courts with new types of litigation or prevented from committing some new types of litigation to administrative agencies with special competence in the relevant field," the Court concluded. "This is the case even if the Seventh Amendment would have required a jury when the adjudication of those rights is assigned to a federal court of law instead of an administrative agency."

## OSHA INSPECTIONS

Although the machinery for the administrative enforcement of the Occupational Safety and Health Act was thus upheld, other provisions of the act raised still more constitutional questions. The heart of the act, as far as its enforcement was concerned, was its provision for inspections by the Occupational Safety and Health Administration (OSHA) of the workplaces of employers. The provisions of the act authorizing OSHA inspections were contained in Section 8(a) and read as follows:

Section 8(a): In order to carry out the purposes of this Chapter, the Secretary [of Labor], upon presenting appropriate credentials to the owner, operator, or agent in charge, is authorized—
(1) to enter without delay and at reasonable times any factory, plant, establishment, construction site, or other area, workplace or environment where work is performed by an employee of an employer; and
(2) to inspect and investigate during regular working hours and at other reasonable times, and within reasonable limits and in a reasonable manner, any such place of employment and all pertinent conditions, structures, machines, apparatus, devices, equipment, and materials therein, and to question privately any such employer, owner, operator, agent, or employee.

Since the Occupational Safety and Health Act applied to any business with employees which affected commerce, the inspection provisions of the act thus authorized OSHA inspectors to inspect virtually every workplace in the United States. It was estimated that sixty-five million persons, or 80 percent of the entire work force, and five million workplaces, were covered by the act, since the act, as one federal court said, "embraces indiscriminately steel mills, automobile plants, fishing boats, farms and private schools, commercial art studios, accounting offices, and barber shops—indeed, the whole spectrum of unrelated and disparate activities which compose private enterprise in the United States."

Under the terms of the act, three types of inspections were most commonly carried out by OSHA. Emergency inspections held the highest priority, since these inspections were performed to discover safety violations posing "imminent danger" to workers. Inspections upon demand held the second priority, and were conducted pursuant to complaints by employees that safety violations were occurring. The lowest priority inspections were "spot checks" (also called by OSHA "general schedule" or "regional programmed" inspections), which were random inspections of businesses when there was no reason to believe safety violations existed.

The secretary of Labor and OSHA took the position that none of these varieties of inspections were subject to the Fourth Amendment's prohibition of unreasonable searches and seizures, and therefore no warrants were required to authorize the OSHA inspections provided for by the act. Beginning with the effective date of the act in 1971, OSHA inspectors thus began conducting eighty thousand inspections of business premises annually without the benefit of search warrants. The OSHA inspections were intended to enforce the health and safety standards promulgated by the secretary of Labor under the act, standards that filled 250 pages of the *Federal Register*.

Given the fact that the Occupational Safety and Health Act applied to many businesses that had previously been subject to little or no federal regulation, it was not surprising that there was a rising tide of complaints by businessmen against the health and safety standards promulgated under the act as well as against the warrantless searches being used by OSHA to enforce the standards. Rather than advising businessmen on how to comply with the act, it was charged, OSHA inspectors were exclusively concerned with citing and imposing monetary penalties on employers for violations that were often technical if not picayune. One employer, for example, complied with OSHA standards by installing the required number of fire extinguishers on the walls of his plant. The employer in fact had one fire extinguisher more than was required by OSHA regulations, so he placed that extinguisher on the floor below another extinguisher installed on a wall. An OSHA inspector, however, cited and fined the employer because under OSHA regulations all fire extinguishers had to be installed on the walls of workplaces. It was incidents like this one, perhaps, that led even an OSHA administrator to admit that the agency had elevated "getting off on the wrong foot to a near art form."

The warrantless searches through which the act was being enforced were also the focus of complaints, and OSHA inspections were soon being compared to the searches by British agents under the infamous writs of assistance which had in part led to the inclusion of the Fourth Amendment in the Constitution. OSHA was thus soon being charged with engaging in "Tory" and "Gestapo" tactics, and one congressional critic of the act charged that "OSHA is the kind of [program] the Bill of Rights was designed to protect Americans against."

The American Conservative Union organized a STOP OSHA project, headed by conservative Republican Congressman George Hansen of Idaho. Hansen introduced legislation in Congress to amend the act to require search warrants for OSHA inspections as well as legislation to repeal the act entirely. "Americans have suffered long enough," he said, "under the inequities, absurdities, and bureaucratic dictatorship of OSHA. The need for relief, particularly in preserving constitutional rights, is more than evident." Organized labor, on the other hand, argued that OSHA was not being effective in reducing the risks to workers. More effective enforcement of health and safety standards, it was argued, would occur only if Congress increased OSHA's appropriations as well as the number of inspectors.

## OSHA ENCOUNTERS FERROL G. "BILL" BARLOW

As the debate of the merits of the Occupational Safety and Health Act thus proceeded, an OSHA inspector arrived on September 11, 1975, at Barlow's, Inc., an electric, plumbing, and air conditioning firm, located at 225 West Pine Street in Pocatello, Idaho. Under OSHA guidelines, inspectors were required to display their credentials when seeking to inspect a workplace, and if doubt still existed as to an inspector's identity on the part of an employer, the employer could call toll free to OSHA to confirm the authenticity of the inspector's credentials. At Barlow's, Inc., OSHA inspector T. Daniel Sanger produced his credentials for Ferrol G. "Bill" Barlow, who was president and owner of Barlow's, Inc. The place of business of Barlow's, Inc., was divided between a customer service area open to the public and a workplace where approximately thirty employees performed their various tasks, and Sanger informed Bill Barlow that he desired to inspect the employees' workplace as authorized by the Occupational Safety and Health Act.

Bill Barlow, however, was a member of the archconservative John Birch Society and firmly attached to his views of the Constitution, a copy of which was displayed on the wall of his office. Barlow inquired of Sanger the reason for the inspection, and if any complaints had been received by OSHA regarding health or safety violations at Barlow's, Inc. Sanger explained that there had been no complaints and that he was merely conducting a "spot check" inspection of the premises. As Sanger reported later, however, Barlow informed him "that my entry was denied because I did not possess a warrant and that it was his right as a citizen to due process and that a warrant was necessary before he would permit me to make the inspection." Sanger telephoned a report of Barlow's refusal to permit an inspection to his OSHA superiors, and, after informing Barlow that they would meet again, left the premises.

OSHA subsequently instituted a proceeding in the U.S. District Court for the District of Idaho in Boise seeking a judicial order requiring Bill Barlow to permit an inspection of Barlow's, Inc. And on December 30, 1975, the district court issued an order authorizing OSHA to conduct an "inspection and investigation" of Barlow's, Inc., and enjoining any interference with such an inspection by any agent or employee of Barlow's. Armed with this judicial order, T. Daniel Sanger returned to Barlow's, Inc., on January 5, 1976, and served the court's order on Bill Barlow, demanding that the order be obeyed and that Barlow permit an inspection of the premises. As Barlow said later, however, he "respectfully declined to allow such inspection upon the grounds of the rights guaranteed by the Fourth Amendment."

The following day, attorneys for Bill Barlow filed a complaint in the U.S. District Court for the District of Idaho seeking a declaratory judgment that Section 8(a) of the Occupational Safety and Health Act was unconstitutional, because it authorized warrantless inspections by OSHA in violation of the Fourth Amendment, and also seeking an injunction against the secretary of Labor prohibiting him and OSHA from subjecting

Barlow's, Inc., to unconstitutional searches. After a hearing on the complaint on January 16, 1976, U.S. District Judge J. Blaine Anders determined that the complaint raised a serious question as to the constitutional validity of Section 8(a), and he thus requested that the chief judge of the U.S. Court of Appeals for the Ninth Circuit convene a three-judge district court to hear the case.

A three-judge court was duly convened to hear the *Barlow's, Inc.* case, and on December 15, 1976, the court held Section 8(a) of the Occupational Safety and Health Act unconstitutional. The court rejected the government's argument that the case should be dismissed because Barlow's, Inc., had failed to exhaust administrative remedies. The case raised the sole issue of the constitutionality of Section 8(a) of the act, the court said, and the administrative remedies within OSHA were not competent to finally determine that constitutional issue. The court also rejected the government's argument that the Fourth Amendment should not be held to apply to OSHA inspections under the Supreme Court's decisions in *Colonnade Catering Corp.* v. *United States* and *United States* v. *Biswell,* in which the Court had exempted inspections of "pervasively regulated" businesses from the warrant requirement of the Fourth Amendment. The three-judge court concluded, on the contrary, "that the warrantless inspection scheme pursuant to OSHA is more properly aligned with and must be controlled by the holdings in *Camara* and *See,*" in which the Supreme Court had subjected administrative searches to Fourth Amendment requirements.

The government had additionally argued that, even if the three-judge court found the Fourth Amendment to require warrants before OSHA inspections could be carried out, Section 8(a) should be construed by the court to require warrants rather than being invalidated by the court as unconstitutional. The court ruled, however, that it could not "accept the proposition that the language of the OSHA inspection provisions envision the requirement that a warrant be obtained before any inspection is undertaken. Certainly, Congress was able, had it wished to do so, to employ language declaring that a warrant must first be obtained, the procedures under which it is to be obtained, and other necessary regulations. Congress did not do so and we refuse to accept that duty." "We therefore hold," the court concluded, "that the inspection provisions of OSHA which have attempted to authorize warrantless inspections of those business establishments covered by the Act, are unconstitutional as being violative of the Fourth Amendment."

Bill Barlow's refusal to allow a warrantless OSHA inspection of his business on Fourth Amendment grounds was thus vindicated by the three-judge court, which issued an injunction prohibiting warrantless OSHA inspections in Idaho. Although some federal courts had upheld the warrantless inspection provisions of the Occupational Safety and Health Act, the decision of the three-judge court in the *Barlow's, Inc.* case conformed to the views of a majority of the federal courts that the act could not validly authorize warrantless inspections of businesses. The other federal courts which had disapproved warrantless inspections under the act, however, had not declared Section 8(a) unconstitutional, but had rather construed Section 8(a) to require search warrants in those instances where businessmen refused to consent to warrantless inspections. The court in the *Barlow's, Inc.* case had nonetheless refused to so construe Section 8(a), and thus avoid the question of the section's constitutionality, and it became the first federal court to invalidate Section 8(a) under the Fourth Amendment. As a consequence, the government on January 4, 1977, filed a notice of appeal of the *Barlow's, Inc.* case to the U.S. Supreme Court, and the Court indicated it would hear the case on the merits on April 18.

## THE APPEAL TO THE SUPREME COURT

Bill Barlow's legal confrontation with OSHA proved to be a godsend for Republican Congressman George Vernon Hansen, who as representative of Idaho's second congressional district found himself in deep political trouble in the mid-1970s. Hansen had won his first term in Congress in 1964 and was easily reelected in 1966. Despite opposition from Idaho's Republican leaders, however, Hansen contested Democratic Senator Frank Church for his Senate seat in 1968 and was soundly defeated. After losing yet another bid for the Senate in 1972, Hansen ran again for Congress and was reelected in 1974.

In his 1974 campaign for Congress, Hansen violated the new federal campaign financing laws and pleaded guilty to two misdemeanor charges of filing late and incomplete financial reports. He thus became the first sitting Congressman to be sentenced to prison in nineteen years. Subsequently, however, U.S. District Court Judge George Hart suspended Hansen's prison sentence and instead fined him $2,000. Hansen, Judge Hart said in explanation of this action, was "stupid, but not evil." The Congressman was nevertheless again in trouble in 1976, when it was charged that he had been late in filing some of his personal income tax returns from 1962 to 1975.

As a consequence of these difficulties, Hansen was barely reelected to Congress in 1976, winning with only a 1.2 percent majority over his opponent. But Bill Barlow's defiance of OSHA was quickly perceived by Hansen as a means of rehabilitating his political fortunes, and the Congressman transformed Barlow's case into a crusade against OSHA and a symbol of opposition to bureaucratic overreaching. Hansen made his office in Washington a clearing-house for complaints against OSHA, and he organized the Committee for Constitutional Challenge to OSHA, which solicited contributions—most of which were reportedly supplied by the American Conservative Union—to defray Barlow's legal expenses. Bill Barlow thus became a nationally known hero in conservative circles. As the John Birch Society's publication, *American Opinion,* noted, Barlow was "something of a folk hero of businessmen everywhere—large and small. . . ." "Every federal agency with inspection powers," *American Opinion* continued, "could be adversely affected if the high court decision goes against OSHA. Naturally we are all *very* alarmed that the sleep of the bureaucratic brownshirts may be disturbed by all of this!"

In urging the Supreme Court to reverse the three-judge court's decision and to uphold warrantless inspections under the Occupational Safety and Health Act, the U.S. solicitor general conceded on behalf of the government that the Court had held in *Camara* v. *Municipal Court* that, except "in certain carefully defined classes of cases, a search of private property without proper consent is 'unreasonable' unless it has been authorized by a valid search warrant." The solicitor general nonetheless argued that the Court had recognized that warrantless searches were reasonable under the Fourth Amendment in some circumstances, and he sought to convince the Court that warrantless OSHA inspections fell within the "carefully defined classes" of cases in which warrantless searches were considered to be reasonable. "Contrary to the district court's conclusion, this case is not controlled by *Camara* v. *Municipal Court. . .*and *See* v. *Seattle,*" the solicitor general thus argued. "As we shall show, this case is governed by the analysis in the Court's subsequent decisions in *Colonnade Catering Corp.* v. *United States. . .*and *United States* v. *Biswell. . .*which. . .upheld the constitutionality of properly limited warrantless inspections under closely similar federal regulatory statutes."

In determining whether or not a particular search was reasonable, the solicitor general continued, the Court should weigh the importance of the privacy interest involved, and the extent to which that privacy interest was invaded by a warrantless search, against the societal or governmental interest in conducting a warrantless search. Whether "a search or an inspection without a warrant is *per se* unreasonable. . . ," he said, "depends upon a determination whether the privacy interest at stake is of such magnitude that the interposition of a neutral and detached magistrate should be required to authorize the search or the inspection."

Under such an analysis, the solicitor general contended, it would appear that an employer's privacy interest, and thus his right not to be subjected to warrantless searches, was relatively slight as far as the area of his business where his employees performed their tasks was concerned. "While the work areas of a conventional factory housing a legitimate business enterprise may be closed to the general public...," he pointed out, "their routine occupation by the owner's employees and the frequent visits by those outside parties who deliver materials for the conduct of the enterprise effectively diminish any claim of privacy by the factory owner with respect to such areas—especially *vis-a-vis* inspectors whose mission is to insure the health and safety of the very employees whom the owner has assigned for his profit to the areas at issue." Since the owner's employees could freely observe and report any violations of safety and health standards at their workplaces, the solicitor general argued, OSHA inspections of those same workplaces without warrants "during 'regular working hours' when the employees are present can hardly be said to intrude upon the employer's right of privacy in the same degree as would a search of his home, office or person." "Thus, in important respects, in a routine OSHA inspection of an employer's workplace, the invasion of privacy 'if it can be said to exist, is abstract and theoretical.'"

In contrast to the minimal privacy interests of employers that were affected by OSHA inspections, the solicitor general argued that important governmental interests were served by warrantless inspections. Congress had determined that unannounced inspections were essential to the enforcement of the health and safety standards promulgated under the act, it was noted. And for the Court to require warrants for OSHA inspections would result in placing "an unwarranted burden on limited judicial and enforcement resources, creating needless delays in implementing inspections, to the detriment of the Act's basic purpose of assuring the swiftest possible abatement of occupational hazards."

Finally, the solicitor general pointed out that the Court had recognized in the *Colonnade Catering Corp.* and *Biswell* cases that those who engaged in closely regulated businesses forfeited some of their rights to privacy. Businesses affecting interstate commerce had been subject to a variety of federal regulations for two generations, he argued, and thus the warrant requirement of the Fourth Amendment should not be applicable to such businesses. The Court's decision in the *Biswell* case, he concluded, "reflects the Court's recognition that the gun inspection powers there at issue were necessary to implement a regulatory system of great importance to society. Here, Congress has similarly determined that the safety of the Nation's workers is of great social importance. As we have pointed out..., if the Occupational Safety and Health Act is to be an effective means of assuring 'so far as possible every working man and woman in the Nation safe and healthful working conditions...,' unannounced inspections are essential to the statutory scheme."

In direct contrast with the solicitor general's argument supporting warrantless OSHA inspections, counsel for Barlow's, Inc., contended that their case was clearly governed by the Court's decisions in *Camara* v. *Municipal Court* and *See* v. *Seattle*. And they particularly relied upon the Court's language in *See* that the "businessman, like the occupant of a residence, has a constitutional right to go about his business free from unreasonable official entries upon his private commercial property. The businessman, too, has that right placed in jeopardy if the decision to enter and inspect for violation of regulatory laws can be made and enforced by the inspector in the field without official authority evidenced by a warrant." The three-judge court had therefore properly ruled, counsel for Barlow's argued, that "taken together, *Camara* and *See* stand for the proposition that where non-consensual administrative inspections of commercial premises are authorized, such inspections may only be accomplished upon presentation of a warrant based upon satisfaction of a flexible probable cause standard."

It was clearly incorrect, as the government's argument implied, that the Fourth Amendment somehow applied with less vigor to businessmen and business enterprises than to other persons and other areas, counsel for Barlow's contended. The Fourth Amendment had been added to the Constitution in partial reaction to the use of writs of assistance by the British, it was noted, and the writs of assistance had primarily been directed at authorizing the search of business premises. "It is precisely because of the threat of recurrence on a massive scale of such high-handed, judicially unsupervised search measures in the present day," counsel for Barlow's said, "that the history of the Fourth Amendment as the national remedy to, and safeguard against, unwarranted governmental intrusion must be carefully reviewed." And a "proper historical interpretation of the Fourth Amendment inescapably leads to the conclusion that privacy interests in the context of private enterprises, private property, private domain, business and commerce, as well as privacies of the home, are protected by its provisions." "Barlow's submits that the constitutional protections forged on the anvil of American history include privacy interests associated with private property and domain and are not limited to the 'core interests' of home or office."

Contrary to the government's position, counsel for Barlow's contended that the fact that "employees are present in the enclosed work areas of the business premises is irrelevant." While conceding that the privacy interests of the businessman in such areas were diminished by the fact that employees were present, counsel for Barlow's nonetheless argued that the businessman retained a right to privacy free from warrantless governmental intrusion in such work areas under the Fourth Amendment. "Significantly. . .Barlow's work area is non-public," counsel noted, "and, as such, Barlow's has a legitimate privacy interest to be protected against warrantless, governmental intrusion in those enclosed work areas."

Finally, counsel for Barlow's argued, the Court's decisions in the *Colonnade Catering Corp.* and *Biswell* cases were, contrary to the government's contentions, inapplicable to an enterprise such as Barlow's. Those cases had upheld warrantless inspections of businesses engaged in the liquor trade and in firearms, businesses traditionally subject to pervasive governmental regulation, and clearly distinguishable from an enterprise such as Barlow's. "As is the case with the great majority of approximately five million businesses with their sixty million employees," counsel concluded, "Barlow's is not licensed by the federal government, nor does it do any business in any pervasively regulated industry or enterprise."

In addition to the arguments on behalf of the government and Barlow's, Inc., several amicus curiae briefs were filed in the *Barlow's, Inc.* case by various organizations seeking to influence the outcome of the case in the Supreme Court [See Table 1]. The Court thus received dire warnings regarding the consequences of a decision either upholding or invalidating warrantless OSHA inspections. Speaking on behalf of organized labor, the AFL-CIO as amicus curiae therefore warned the Court that if the decision of the three-judge court invalidating warrantless inspections were upheld, such a decision would "render it impossible for the Secretary of Labor effectively to enforce OSHA, and thereby endanger the health and safety of millions of American workers." The Chamber of Commerce, on the other hand, warned that if the decision of the three-judge court were reversed by the Court, the effect would be to "signal a broad repeal of the Fourth Amendment protections traditionally applicable to businesses."

Division over the validity of warrantless OSHA searches was also present among the states, since the attorneys general of Idaho and Utah as amici curiae opposed warrantless inspections, while eleven other states supported such inspections. The eleven states pointed out that Congress had authorized the states which developed nationally approved programs to take over the responsibility of enforcing OSHA standards within their jurisdictions. Effective state enforcement of health and safety standards, the eleven states warned, would be undermined if warrantless inspections were disapproved. The attorneys general of Idaho and Utah argued, on the other hand, that "the Fourth Amendment to the United States Constitution cannot be subjected to such severe erosion" as had occurred under the Occupational Safety and Health Act.

In addition to the effect the Court's decision would have upon OSHA inspections, other amici pointed out the broader implications the Court's decision would have. The solicitor general had pointed out to the Court that its decision in the *Barlow's, Inc.* case would also affect a host of other federal programs which were dependent upon effective inspections for their enforcement, and the Sierra Club, Oil, Chemical, and Atomic Workers Union, and Friends of the Earth reemphasized that point to the Court. The Clean Air Act of 1970, the Federal Water Pollution Control Act of 1972, the Federal Environmental Pesticide Control Act of 1972, the Safe Drinking Water Act of 1974, the Resource Conservation and Recovery Act of 1976, the Toxic Substances Control Act of 1976, and many other federal environmental, health, and safety measures, the Sierra Club and its allies warned, were in part dependent upon warrantless inspections for their enforcement. And thus a decision by the Court invalidating warrantless OSHA inspections would have a far-reaching and detrimental impact upon other federal programs designed to protect a healthy environment.

## TABLE 1
### AMICUS CURIAE PARTICIPANTS IN MARSHALL v. BARLOW'S, INC.

| Pro Warrantless Inspections | Anti Warrantless Inspections |
|---|---|
| Eleven States[1] | American Farm Bureau Federation |
| Sierra Club[2] | American Conservative Union |
| Oil, Chemical, and Atomic Workers Union[2] | Pacific Legal Foundation |
| | Mountain States Legal Foundation |
| Friends of the Earth[2] | National Federation of Independent Business |
| AFL-CIO | States of Idaho and Utah |
| | Chamber of Commerce of the U.S. |
| | Roger Baldwin Foundation of the American Civil Liberties Union, Illinois Division |

1. The eleven states were: Kentucky, Michigan, Minnesota, New Jersey, New Mexico, North Carolina, Pennsylvania, South Carolina, Vermont, Virginia, and Wyoming.
2. The Sierra Club, Oil, Chemical, and Atomic Workers, and Friends of the Earth filed a joint brief amici curiae .

While the Sierra Club and its allies perceived the *Barlow's, Inc.* case as posing a potential threat to a whole spectrum of federal environmental programs, organized conservatives perceived the case as a means of attacking governmental regulation generally. Representative George Hansen, head of the American Conservative Union's STOP OSHA project, and organizer of the Committee for Constitutional Challenge to OSHA which financed Bill Barlow's case, thus pointed out that the *Barlow's, Inc.* case "is merely a vehicle" and predicted that "a victory for Barlow would cripple most regulatory agencies."

It was not surprising, therefore, that the American Conservative Union in its amicus brief denounced OSHA and all its works. "OSHA's arrogant and gestapo-like actions," the Conservative Union told the Court, "have aroused the concern of legislators, courts and businessmen nationwide. Agency representatives have told employers, 'We don't give a damn about your constitutional rights. As far as we are concerned, you don't have any because you are in business.'" The "protections of liberty that have been deemed fundamental in this country since before the Revolution," the Conservative Union declared, "are not 'the beat of an antique drum,' but remain both vital and viable shields against every new experiment on our liberties."

Although the closely balanced values involved in the *Barlow's, Inc.* case were thus reflected in the arguments of the solicitor general, counsel for Barlow's, and the amici curiae, they were perhaps epitomized by the position of the American Civil Liberties Union in the case. The ACLU has of course traditionally been vigorously opposed to any threat to the rights in the Bill of Rights, such as those guaranteed in the Fourth Amendment, but as the *Barlow's, Inc.* case was pending before the Supreme Court, attorneys in the ACLU's national office evenly divided over whether the union should file an amicus curiae brief attacking warrantless inspections in the case. The ACLU's national board of directors, however, voted 30 to 20 in June of 1977 to file an amicus brief opposing warrantless inspections, but the following September the board of directors reversed itself by narrowly voting by a margin of only six or seven votes not to participate as amicus in the *Barlow's, Inc.* case. The result was that there was no amicus curiae brief in the case on behalf of the national ACLU, although the Illinois Division of the ACLU's Roger Baldwin Foundation did participate as amicus in opposition to the warrantless OSHA inspections.

The issues in the *Barlow's, Inc.* case proved to be as divisive for the members of the Supreme Court as they had been for the ACLU. The case was argued on January 9, 1978, and when the Court's decision was announced on May 23, 1978, warrantless OSHA inspections were invalidated by the narrowest of margins. Justice White wrote the majority opinion, which was joined by Chief Justice Burger and Justices Marshall, Stewart, and Powell, while Justices Stevens, Blackmun, and Rehnquist dissented. Having been ill, Justice Brennan did not participate in the decision of the Court.

## Marshall v. Barlow's, Inc.
### 436 U.S. 307. Argued January 9, 1978. Decided May 23, 1978.
### Mr. Justice White delivered the opinion of the Court.

Section 8(a) of the Occupational Safety and Health Act of 1970 (OSHA or Act) empowers agents of the Secretary of Labor (Secretary) to search the work area of any employment facility within the Act's jurisdiction. The purpose of the search is to inspect for safety hazards and violations of OSHA regulations. No search warrant or other process is expressly required under the Act.

On the morning of September 11, 1975, an OSHA inspector entered the customer service area of Barlow's, Inc., an electrical and plumbing installation business located in Pocatello, Idaho. The president and general manager, Ferrol G. "Bill" Barlow, was on hand; and the OSHA inspector, after showing his credentials, informed Mr. Barlow that he wished to conduct a search of the working areas of the business. Mr. Barlow inquired whether any complaint had been received about his company. The inspector answered no, but that Barlow's, Inc., had simply turned up in the agency's selection process. The inspector again asked to enter the nonpublic area of the business; Mr. Barlow's response was to inquire whether the inspector had a search warrant. The inspector had none. Thereupon, Mr. Barlow refused the inspector admission to the employee area of his business. He said he was relying on his rights as guaranteed by the Fourth Amendment of the United States Constitution.

Three months later, the Secretary petitioned the United States District Court for the District of Idaho to issue an order compelling Mr. Barlow to admit the inspector. The requested order was issued on December 30, 1975, and was presented to Mr. Barlow on January 5, 1976. Mr. Barlow again refused admission, and he sought his own injunctive relief against the warrantless searches assertedly permitted by OSHA. A three-judge court was convened. On December 30, 1976, it ruled in Mr. Barlow's favor.... Concluding that Camara v. Municipal Court...and See v. Seattle...controlled this case, the court held that the Fourth Amendment required a warrant for the type of search involved here and that the statutory authorization for warrantless inspections was unconstitutional. An injunction against searches or inspections pursuant to Sec. 8(a) was entered. The Secretary appealed, challenging the judgment, and we noted probable jurisdiction....

The Secretary urges that warrantless inspections to enforce OSHA are reasonable within the meaning of the Fourth Amendment. Among other things, he relies on Sec. 8(a) of the Act...which authorizes inspection of business premises without a warrant and which the Secretary urges represents a congressional construction of the Fourth Amendment that the courts should not reject. Regrettably, we are unable to agree.

The Warrant Clause of the Fourth Amendment protects commercial buildings as well as private homes. To hold otherwise would belie the origin of that Amendment, and the American colonial experience. An important forerunner of the first 10 Amendments to the United States

Constitution, the Virginia Bill of Rights, specifically opposed "general warrants, whereby an officer or messenger may be commanded to search suspected places without evidence of [a crime being] committed." The general warrant was a recurring point of contention in the Colonies immediately preceding the Revolution. The particular offensiveness it engendered was acutely felt by the merchants and businessmen whose premises and products were inspected for compliance with the several parliamentary revenue measures that most irritated the colonists. "[T]he Fourth Amendment's commands grew in large measure out of the colonists' experience with the writs of assistance...[that] granted sweeping power to customs officials and other agents of the King to search at large for smuggled goods".... Against this background, it is untenable that the ban on warrantless searches was not intended to shield places of business as well as of residence.

This Court has already held that warrantless searches are generally unreasonable, and that this rule applies to commercial premises as well as homes. In Camara v. Municipal Court...we held: "[E]xcept in certain carefully defined classes of cases, a search of private property without proper consent is 'unreasonable' unless it has been authorized by a valid search warrant."

On the same day, we also ruled: "As we explained in Camara, a search of private houses is presumptively unreasonable if conducted without a warrant. The businessman, like the occupant of a residence, has a constitutional right to go about his business free from unreasonable official entries upon his private commercial property. The businessman, too, has that right placed in jeopardy if the decision to enter and inspect for violation of regulatory laws can be made and enforced by the inspector in the field without official authority evidenced by a warrant." See v. Seattle....

These same cases also held that the Fourth Amendment prohibition against unreasonable searches protects against warrantless intrusions during civil as well as criminal investigations.... The reason is found in the "basic purpose of this Amendment...[which] is to safeguard the privacy and security of individuals against arbitrary invasions by governmental officials".... If the government intrudes on a person's property, the privacy interest suffers whether the government's motivation is to investigate violations of criminal laws or breaches of other statutory or regulatory standards. It therefore appears that unless some recognized exception to the warrant requirement applies, See v. Seattle would require a warrant to conduct the inspection sought in this case.

The Secretary urges that an exception from the search warrant requirement has been recognized for "pervasively regulated business[es]," United States v. Biswell...and for "closely regulated" industries "long subject to close supervision and inspection." Colonnade Catering Corp. v. United States.... These cases are indeed exceptions, but they represent responses to relatively unique circumstances. Certain industries have such a history of government oversight that no reasonable expectation of privacy... could exist for a proprietor over the stock of such an enterprise. Liquor (Colonnade) and firearms (Biswell) are industries of this type; when an entrepreneur embarks upon such a business, he has voluntarily chosen to subject himself to a full arsenal of governmental regulation.

Industries such as these fall within the "certain carefully defined classes of cases," referenced in Camara. . . . The element that distinguishes these enterprises from ordinary businesses is a long tradition of close government supervision, of which any person who chooses to enter such a business must already be aware. "A central difference between those cases [Colonnade and Biswell] and this one is that businessmen engaged in such federally licensed and regulated enterprises accept the burdens as well as the benefits of their trade, whereas the petitioner here was not engaged in any regulated or licensed business. The businessman in a regulated industry in effect consents to the restrictions placed upon him". . . .

The clear import of our cases is that the closely regulated industry of the type involved in Colonnade and Biswell is the exception. The Secretary would make it the rule. . . . [T]he Secretary attempts to support a conclusion that all businesses involved in interstate commerce have long been subjected to close supervision of employee safety and health conditions. But the degree of federal involvement in employee working circumstances has never been of the order of specificity and pervasiveness that OSHA mandates. It is quite unconvincing to argue that the imposition of minimum wages and maximum hours on employers. . .prepared the entirety of American interstate commerce for regulation of working conditions to the minutest detail. Nor can any but the most fictional sense of voluntary consent to later searches be found in the single fact that one conducts a business affecting interstate commerce; under current practice and law, few businesses can be conducted without having some effect on interstate commerce. . . .

The critical fact in this case is that entry over Mr. Barlow's objection is being sought by a Government agent. Employees are not being prohibited from reporting OSHA violations. What they observe in their daily functions is undoubtedly beyond the employer's reasonable expectation of privacy. The Government inspector, however, is not an employee. Without a warrant he stands in no better position than a member of the public. What is observable by the public is observable, without a warrant, by the Government inspection as well. The owner of a business has not, by the necessary utilization of employees in his operation, thrown open the areas where employees alone are permitted to the warrantless scrutiny of Government agents. That an employee is free to report, and the Government is free to use, any evidence of noncompliance with OSHA that the employee observes furnishes no justification for federal agents to enter a place of business from which the public is restricted and to conduct their own warrantless search. . . .

The Secretary nevertheless stoutly argues that the enforcement scheme of the Act requires warrantless searches, and that the restrictions on search discretion contained in the Act and its regulations already protect as much privacy as a warrant would. The Secretary thereby asserts the actual reasonableness of OSHA searches, whatever the general rule against warrantless searches might be. Because "reasonableness is still the ultimate standard". . .the Secretary suggests that the Court decide whether a warrant is needed by arriving at a sensible balance between the administrative necessities of OSHA inspections and the incremental protection of privacy of business owners a warrant would afford. He suggests that only a decision exempting OSHA inspections from the Warrant Clause would give "full recognition to the competing public and private interests here at stake". . . .

The Secretary submits that warrantless inspections are essential to the proper enforcement of OSHA because they afford the opportunity to inspect without prior notice and hence to preserve the advantages of surprise. While the dangerous conditions outlawed by the Act include structural defects that cannot be quickly hidden or remedied, the Act also regulates a myriad of safety details that may be amenable to speedy alteration or disguise. The risk is that during the interval between an inspector's initial request to search a plant and his procuring a warrant following the owner's refusal of permission, violations of this latter type could be corrected and thus escape the inspector's notice. To the suggestion that warrants may be issued ex parte and executed without delay and without prior notice, thereby preserving the element of surprise, the Secretary expresses concern for the administrative strain that would be experienced by the inspection system, and by the courts, should ex parte warrants issued in advance become standard practice.

We are unconvinced, however, that requiring warrants to inspect will impose serious burdens on the inspection system or the courts, will prevent inspections necessary to enforce the statute, or will make them less effective. In the first place, the great majority of businessmen can be expected in the normal course to consent to inspection without warrant; the Secretary has not brought to this Court's attention any widespread pattern of refusal. In those cases where an owner does insist on a warrant, the Secretary argues that inspection efficiency will be impeded by the advance notice and delay. The Act's penalty provisions for giving advance notice of a search. . .and the Secretary's own regulations. . .indicate that surprise searches are indeed contemplated. However, the Secretary has also promulgated a regulation providing that upon refusal to permit an inspector to enter the property or to complete his inspection, the inspector shall attempt to ascertain the reasons for the refusal and report to his superior, who shall "promptly take appropriate action, including compulsory process, if necessary". . . . The regulation represents a choice to proceed by process where entry is refused; and on the basis of evidence available from present practice, the Act's effectiveness has not been crippled by providing those owners who wish to refuse an initial requested entry with a time lapse while the inspector obtains the necessary process. Indeed, the kind of process sought in this case and apparently anticipated by the regulation provides notice to the business operator. If this endangers the efficient administration of OSHA, the Secretary should never have adopted it, particularly when the Act does not require it. Nor is it immediately apparent why the advantages of surprise would be lost if, after being refused entry, procedures were available for the Secretary to seek an ex parte warrant and to reappear at the premises without further notice to the establishment being inspected.

Whether the Secretary proceeds to secure a warrant or other process, with or without prior notice, his entitlement to inspect will not depend on his demonstrating probable cause to believe that conditions in violation of OSHA exist on the premises. Probable cause in the criminal law sense is not required. For purposes of an administrative search such as this, probable cause justifying the issuance of a warrant may be based not only on specific evidence of an existing violation but also on a showing that "reasonable legislative or administrative standards for conducting an. . .inspection are satisfied with respect to a particular [establishment]".... A warrant showing that a specific business has been chosen for an OSHA search on the basis of a general administrative plan for the enforcement of the Act derived from neutral sources such as, for example, dispersion of employees in various types of industries across a given area, and the desired frequency of searches in any of the lesser divisions of the area, would protect an employer's Fourth Amendment rights. We doubt that the consumption of enforcement energies in the obtaining of such warrants will exceed manageable proportions.

Finally, the Secretary urges that requiring a warrant for OSHA inspectors will mean that, as a practical matter, warrantless-search provisions in other regulatory statutes are also constitutionally infirm. The reasonableness of a warrantless search, however, will depend upon the specific enforcement needs and privacy guarantees of each statute. Some of the statutes cited apply only to a single industry, where regulations might already be so pervasive that a Colonnade-Biswell exception to the warrant requirement could apply. Some statutes already envision resort to federal court enforcement when entry is refused, employing specific language in some cases and general language in others. In short, we base today's opinion on the facts and law concerned with OSHA and do not retreat from a holding appropriate to that statute because of its real or imagined effect on other, different administrative schemes.

Nor do we agree that the incremental protections afforded the employer's privacy by a warrant are so marginal that they fail to justify the administrative burdens that may be entailed. The authority to make warrantless searches devolves almost unbridled discretion upon executive and administrative officers, particularly those in the field, as to when to search and whom to search. A warrant, by contrast, would provide assurances from a neutral officer that the inspection is reasonable under the Constitution, is authorized by statute, and is pursuant to an administrative plan containing specific neutral criteria. Also, a warrant would then and there advise the owner of the scope and objects of the search, beyond which limits the inspector is not expected to proceed. These are important functions for a warrant to perform, functions which underlie the Court's prior decisions that the Warrant Clause applies to inspections for compliance with regulatory statutes. . . . We conclude that the concerns expressed by the Secretary do not suffice to justify warrantless inspections under OSHA or vitiate the general constitutional requirement that for a search to be reasonable a warrant must be obtained.

We hold that Barlow's was entitled to a declaratory judgment that the Act is unconstitutional insofar as it purports to authorize inspections without warrant or its equivalent and to an injunction enjoining the Act's enforcement to that extent. The judgment of the District Court is therefore affirmed.

So ordered.

Mr. Justice Brennan took no part in the consideration or decision of this case.

[Justice Stevens, joined by Justices Blackmun and Rehnquist, filed a dissenting opinion. Warrantless administrative inspections of commercial premises, for the purpose of enforcing congressionally mandated health and safety standards, Justice Stevens argued, were "reasonable" searches within the meaning of the Fourth Amendment. In addition, Justice Stevens argued, the Court's requirement of an administrative search warrant absent consent to such searches would not significantly increase the protection of the right of privacy secured by the Fourth Amendment.]

Reactions to the Court's decision followed rather predictable lines. A spokesman for the AFL-CIO deplored the decision and asserted that it would "delay and complicate" the enforcement of the Occupational Safety and Health Act, while the National Association of Manufacturers hailed the decision as "good news," and the National Federation of Independent Business foresaw a "dramatic" beneficial effect on small businesses as a result of the Court's action. The U.S. Chamber of Commerce similarly characterized the decision as a "blow for freedom," and the American Conservative Union said the decision was a "great victory."

The Court's decision was of course a personal victory for sixty-one-year-old Bill Barlow. "The businessmen were afraid of [OSHA inspectors]," Barlow said. "It's frightening when you think that a bureaucracy can come in and close down a business." Barlow was lionized by Idaho Congressman George Hansen, who declared that Barlow had brought about an "historic landmark decision upholding the constitutional rights of businessmen against harassment and warrantless inspections." "It took the courage and determination of one small businessman to stand up to a runaway bureaucracy indulging wholesale in the unreasonable searches and seizures prohibited by the Constitution," Hansen said. "Bill Barlow, a Pocatello, Idaho, businessman, in the face of possible jail and costs of well over $100,000 proved his point in the gallant fashion of American patriots, and all who value liberty owe him a great debt for this effort in basic citizens' rights." His support of Barlow's cause also had political benefits for Congressman Hansen, since in contrast to his narrow victory in the election of 1976, he was reelected by the voters of Idaho's second congressional district in 1978 by a margin of 57 percent of the votes over his opponent's 40 percent.

While the *Barlow's, Inc.* case had been pending in the courts, OSHA administrators had conceded that some of the agency's health and safety standards were petty, and the agency had begun concentrating on abating major health and safety hazards rather than cracking down on minor violators of OSHA standards. The response of OSHA to the Court's decision was consequently rather low key. "We will, of course, conform our policies and procedures to the Court's ruling," Assistant Secretary of

Labor Eula Bingham said. "We are studying this decision carefully and will quickly issue appropriate instructions to our field staff on the procedures they should follow." And a Department of Labor lawyer indicated that to the "maximum extent possible" OSHA inspectors would seek search warrants in advance of inspections.

Assistant Secretary Bingham also noted that OSHA hoped the great majority of businessmen would continue to consent to inspections, and she pointed out to businessmen that it remained their responsibility "to provide safe and healthful workplaces and this decision in no way alters that responsibility." "So, even though the decision may ultimately require us to alter our inspection procedures somewhat, workers need have no fear that their safety and health will go unprotected," Bingham concluded. "It is OSHA's intention to continue to carry out its mandate of assuring that employers carry out their responsibilities under the Occupational Safety and Health Act."

In the *Barlow's, Inc.* case, the Court declined the government's invitation to expand the "pervasively regulated businesses" exception to the warrant requirement of the Fourth Amendment which it had created in the *Biswell* and *Colonnade Catering Corp.* cases. A holding by the Court in the *Barlow's, Inc.* case, that the application of the Occupational Safety and Health Act to the businesses subject to its provisions had transformed those businesses into "pervasively regulated" businesses subject to warrantless inspections, would have obviously created a major loophole in the Fourth Amendment. The Court nonetheless reaffirmed the "pervasively regulated businesses" exception to the warrant requirement of the Fourth Amendment in the *Barlow's, Inc.* case, but it has remained rather uninformative as to the point at which governmental regulation of a business or industry becomes "pervasive."

The Court's indication in the *Barlow's, Inc.* case, that it would evaluate the inspection process involved in many other governmental regulatory programs on a case-by-case basis, may perhaps in the future throw more light upon the question of when a business is or is not "pervasively regulated." Some reasoned limitation upon the "pervasively regulated businesses" exception is in any case sorely needed, since the exception appears to suggest that Fourth Amendment rights may be swept aside any time Congress decides to "pervasively" regulate a particular subject matter. The "pervasively regulated businesses" exception to the Fourth Amendment is thus rather similar to the required records doctrine in the Self-Incrimination Clause field, since both suggest that constitutional rights may be forfeited if Congress decides to legislate.

Although the Court held that, absent consent, OSHA inspections must be justified by warrants in the *Barlow's, Inc.* case, it continued its adherence to the concept that administrative search warrants need not be based upon the probable cause requirements that criminal search warrants must meet. An OSHA inspection would not "depend on[the Secretary of Labor's] demonstrating probable cause to believe that conditions in violation of OSHA exist on the premises," the Court said. "Probable cause in the criminal law sense is not required." Rather, the Court held, probable cause for the issuance of a warrant for an OSHA inspection could be established on a showing that "reasonable legislative or administrative standards for conducting an. . .inspection are satisfied with respect to a particular [establishment] ," and that a "warrant showing that a specific business has been chosen for an OSHA search on the basis of a general administrative plan for the enforcement of the Act derived from neutral sources such as, for example, dispersion of employees in various types of industries across a given area, and the desired frequency of searches in any of the lesser divisions of the area, would protect an employer's Fourth Amendment rights."

The *Barlow's, Inc.* case thus joined the *Camara* and *See* cases in recognizing a category of administrative search warrants which may be obtained without the traditional probable cause requirement for criminal search warrants having been met. The creation of a category of administrative search warrants, which are rather easily obtained under relaxed probable cause standards, of course raises the problem that such warrants might be used as a pretext to skirt the more stringent probable cause requirements for criminal search warrants. That is, easily obtained administrative search warrants might be obtained by governmental officials and entry into premises protected by the Fourth Amendment gained, when the actual purpose of the officials was to search for evidence of crime. Or, even absent bad faith on the part of officials, entry to premises might be obtained upon the basis of an administrative search warrant and a good faith administrative inspection conducted, but evidence of criminal activities might be discovered during the inspection. In either case, the Fourth Amendment's traditional probable cause requirements for criminal searches would be skirted.

That such problems are not the products of mere idle speculation is evidenced by the Supreme Court's decision in *Michigan* v. *Tyler,* decided approximately a week after the *Barlow's, Inc.* case. In the *Tyler* case, a furniture store caught fire, and after the fire was extinguished, fire investigators entered the store to determine the origin and cause of the fire. The first entry into the burned-out building occurred immediately after the fire had been extinguished and while firemen were still dousing the smoldering embers. On this occasion the fire investigators found plastic containers of flammable liquid, which they seized. Further investigation was postponed because of darkness and smoke and steam at the scene. The following morning the investigators returned to the building and found burn marks which indicated a fuse had been used to start the fire, and pieces of carpet and a section of stairs containing the burn marks were removed. Subsequent entries into the building were made by investigators four days, seven days, and twenty-five days after the fire, and more evidence of arson was seized during these entries. All the evidence seized during the investigation of the fire was subsequently used in a criminal prosecution for arson against Tyler, who had leased the burned building. But after his conviction, he appealed to the Supreme Court, alleging that the evidence against him had been obtained by unreasonable searches and seizures in violation of the Fourth Amendment.

The Supreme Court held in the *Tyler* case that obviously firemen did not require search warrants in order to enter property to fight fires. The Court applied the long-recognized rule that search warrants are unnecessary in circumstances in which there is "compelling need for official action and no time to secure a warrant," such as when police are in hot pursuit of an armed robber. "A burning building clearly presents an exigency of sufficient proportions to render a warrantless entry 'reasonable,'" the Court said. "Indeed, it would defy reason to suppose that firemen must secure a warrant or consent before entering a burning structure to put out a blaze. And once in a building for this purpose, firefighters may seize evidence of arson that is in plain view." The Court additionally held that "officials need no warrant to remain in a building for a reasonable time to investigate the cause of a blaze after it has been extinguished. And if the warrantless entry to put out the fire and determine its cause is constitutional, the warrantless seizure of evidence while inspecting the premises for these purposes also is constitutional."

Under this reasoning, the Court held that the entry of the fire investigators into the burned furniture store immediately after the fire was extinguished and the morning after the fire did not require a search warrant, and the warrantless seizure of the containers of flammable liquid and evidence of a fuse on those occasions was valid. The entries occurring subsequently, the Court held, however, had been unreasonable searches because they were not authorized by search warrants. After a fire has been extinguished, and a reasonable time for investigations of its cause has expired, entries into a burned building to determine the cause of the fire may be effected by an administrative search warrant, the Court held. If, during investigation of the cause of a fire pursuant to an administrative search warrant, evidence of arson is discovered, that evidence may be validly seized. But if further entry into the building is desired by officials after there is probable cause to believe that arson has been committed, then a criminal search warrant must be secured.

"In summation," the Court said, "we hold that an entry to fight a fire requires no warrant, and that once in the building, officials may remain there for a reasonable time to investigate the cause of the blaze. Thereafter, additional entries to investigate the cause of the fire must be made pursuant to the warrant procedures governing administrative searches [citing *Camara* v. *Municipal Court, See* v. *Seattle* and *Marshall* v. *Barlow's, Inc.*] ." "Evidence of arson discovered in the course of such investigations is admissible at trial," the Court continued, "but if investigating officials find probable cause to believe that arson has occurred and require further access to gather evidence for a possible prosecution, they may obtain a warrant only upon a traditional showing of probable cause applicable to searches for evidence of crime."

Under the Court's decision in the *Tyler* case, therefore, it appears that officers seeking to conduct an administrative inspection, such as an inspection to determine the cause of a fire, may secure an administrative search warrant under the relaxed probable cause standards sanctioned in the *Camara, See,* and *Barlow's, Inc.* cases. If, in the course of such an administrative inspection, evidence of crime is discovered, it may be seized and used as evidence in a criminal prosecution. And, finally, if further entry into the premises is desired, the officials must secure a criminal search warrant meeting traditional probable cause standards, but presumably evidence discovered or viewed during the administrative search may be used for that purpose.

In creating a category of administrative search warrants under the Fourth Amendment, the Court has therefore created a situation rather similar to that which arose with its relaxation of the Self-Incrimination Clause as it applies to the administrative process. In both instances, the Court has construed constitutional limitations upon exercises of governmental power more flexibly as they apply to the administrative process than when they apply to the criminal process. In doing so, however, the Court has created dual sets of precedent—one more stringent set applicable to the criminal process and the other more flexible set applicable to the administrative process—which are rather uneasily juxtaposed in the Court's jurisprudence. And the danger in the field of searches and seizures is the same as that encountered in the self-incrimination field—that the more flexible precedents applicable in the administrative process may ultimately provide the rationale for across-the-board dilutions of constitutional protections.

# TABLE OF CASES

# INDEX